THE Studio Musician's HANDBOOK

THE Studio Musician's HANDBOOK

BY BOBBY OWSINSKI
AND PAUL ILL

Hal Leonard Books
An Imprint of Hal Leonard Corporation
New York

Published in 2009 by Hal Leonard Books
An Imprint of Hal Leonard Corporation
7777 West Bluemound Road
Milwaukee, WI 53213

Trade Book Division Editorial Offices
19 West 21st Street, New York, NY 10010
www.halleonard.com

Book design by Stephen Ramirez
Cover photo: Edward Colver

Library of Congress Cataloging-in-Publication Data

Owsinski, Bobby.
The studio musician's handbook / Bobby Owsinski; Paul Ill.
p. cm.
Includes index.
ISBN 978-1-4234-6341-2
1. Sound recording industry—Vocational guidance. 2. Music trade—Vocational guidance.
3. Musicians—Interviews. I. Ill, Paul. II. Title.
ML3790.O97 2009
781.4'38—dc22
2009025834

Printed in the United States of America

CONTENTS

Foreword . . . xi
Introduction . . . xiii
Meet the Contributors . . . xv
Acknowledgments . . . xix

Part One The Making of a Session Musician . . . 1

Chapter 1 The History of the Studio Musician . . . 3
The Studio Bands . . . 3
The Rise of the Independents . . . 9

Chapter 2 Why Playing in the Studio Is Different from Playing Live . . . 13
Sixteen Ways That Playing in the Studio Differs from Playing Live . . . 13

Chapter 3 Who Hires Session Musicians? . . . 21
Contractors . . . 22
Producers . . . 22
Musicians . . . 23
Artists . . . 25
Composers . . . 26
Recording Studio Staff . . . 27
Artist Managers . . . 28

Chapter 4 Types of Sessions . . . 31
Demos . . . 32
Jingles . . . 33
Film and Television . . . 36
Library Music Sessions . . . 37
Episodic Television . . . 37
Film Dates . . . 37

Record Dates. 38
Home Studio Dates. 40

Chapter 5 How Do I Become a Studio Musician?. 43
Ways to Become a Session Musician. 43
Your Band. 43
By Referral. 44
By a Contractor. 44
By a Recording. 45
By Association. 45
Now That You're There. 47
Has Great Chops. 47
Has Great Gear. 48
Is Easy to Work With. 48
Has No Ego. 49
Takes Criticism Well. 50
Has Proper Studio Etiquette. 50

Chapter 6 How Much Money Can I Make?. 53
Union Gigs. 54
Types of Union Pay Scales. 54
Additional Fees. 57
Nonunion Gigs. 58
Set Your Rates. 59
Your Invoice. 59
Getting Paid. 60

Chapter 7 What Equipment Do I Bring to a Session?. 63
Different Gear for Different Jobs. 64
Well-Maintained Equipment Required. 64
The Comfort Factor. 65
Tailor What You Bring. 66
Is Vintage Gear Necessary?. 68
Guitars. 70
Guitar Amplifiers. 71
Basses. 72
Bass Amps. 72
Pedals. 72
Keyboards. 73
Drums. 73

Chapter 8 Before the Session Begins . . . 75
What Kind of Session Is It? . . . 76
Who's the Artist (if it's a record date)? . . . 76
What Type of Music Will Be Recorded? . . . 76
What Direction Will the Music Go In? . . . 77
Who's the Producer? . . . 77
Which Studio Is Being Used? . . . 78
What Time Does the Session Begin? . . . 78
How Long Do You Expect the Session to Last? . . . 79
How Many Songs or Cues Will Be Recorded? . . . 79
Who Are the Other Musicians on the Session? . . . 79
What Is Expected of Me? . . . 80
Is There Any Particular Sound That's Desired? . . . 80
Are There Any Particular Instruments, Amps, or Effects to Be Used? . . . 81
How Much Are You Being Paid? . . . 81
Take Care of Your Individual Needs . . . 82

Chapter 9 Session Musician101 . . . 83
Your Roots . . . 84
Your Mind-Set . . . 84
Your Musicality: Ears, Chops, and Feel . . . 85
Your Chops . . . 85
Your Technique: Purity, Not Perfection . . . 86
Your Reading . . . 86
Your Ears . . . 87
Your Feel . . . 88
Styles . . . 89
Preparation . . . 90
Serving the Muse: Playing the Music, Not the Instrument . . . 93

Chapter 10 Session Etiquette . . . 95
Before the Session Begins . . . 96
While Recording . . . 97
When the Session Ends . . . 100

Chapter 11 The Session . . . 103
Your Studio Comfort . . . 103
The Signal Chain . . . 104
The Headphone Mix . . . 105
Working with the Engineer . . . 106

Working with the Producer. 107
Working with the Artist. 108
A Session Example: A Typical Record Date. 110

Part Two: Player's Guides. 115

Chapter 12 Guide for Guitar Players. 117
Before the Session Begins. 117
Your Sound. 118
Less Is More. 120
That's What Tone Controls Are For. 120
Different Instruments and Amplifiers. 122
Clash of the Guitar Tracks. 122
Laying In with the Rhythm Section. 124
What to Bring. 125
Standard Session Procedure. 127
The Guitar Player's Utility Kit. 130

Chapter 13 Guide for Bass Players. 133
Before the Session Begins. 133
Your Sound. 134
Locking In. 136
What to Bring. 136
Standard Session Procedure. 137
The Bass Player's Utility Kit. 141

Chapter 14 Guide for Drummers. 143
Simple Is Best. 143
The Concepts of Feel and Internal Time. 145
Rushed or Lazy Fills. 146
Are You Playing Too Loudly?. 147
What Makes a Drum Kit Sound Great?. 147
Tuning the Drums. 148
Tuning Tips from the Drum Doctor. 148
How Long Does It Take to Tune a Drum Kit?. 149
Prepping the Drums for New Heads. 149
New Heads. 149
The Tuning Technique. 150

Tuning the Snare. 151
Snare-Drum-Tuning Tips. 152
Tuning the Kick Drum. 153
Tuning the Toms. 153
Cymbals. 155
Standard Session Procedure. 155
The Drummer's Utility Kit. 160

Chapter 15 Guide for Keyboard Players. 163
Your Sound. 164
Hauling Your Gear. 166
The Quick Setup. 167
Standard Session Procedure. 169
The Keyboard Player's Utility Kit. 172

Chapter 16 Guide for Vocalists. 175
The Three Ps: Pitch, Pocket, Passion. 175
Pitch. 176
Pocket. 177
Passion. 178
Take Care of Yourself. 179
Take Some Lessons. 181
Mic Technique. 183
Phrasing Is Everything. 184
Attacks and, Especially, Releases. 184
Standard Session Procedure. 184
The Singer's Utility Kit. 187

Chapter 17 Guide for Horn Players. 189
Mic Technique. 190
You've Got to Hear Yourself. 190
Standard Session Procedure. 191
The Horn Player's Utility Kit. 194

Chapter 18 Guide for String Players. 197
During the Session. 198
Headphones. 199
Standard Session Procedure. 201
The String Player's Utility Kit. 203

Chapter 19 Guide for Percussionists . . . 205
Motion, Dynamics, and Texture . . . 205
Standard Percussion Items . . . 207
Just Owning the Instrument Isn't Enough . . . 208
Standard Session Procedure . . . 208
The Percussionist's Utility Kit . . . 211

Part Three: The Interviews . . . 213

Chapter 20 The Interviews . . . 215
Ronnie Ciago—Drummer and Percussionist . . . 215
Charlie Drayton—Bassist and Drummer . . . 222
Bernie Dresel—Drummer and Percussionist . . . 226
Frank Fitzpatrick—Composer and Producer . . . 236
Onree Gill—Keyboard Player and Drummer . . . 240
Eric Gorfain—Violinist and String Arranger . . . 244
Jerry Hey—Trumpet Player . . . 247
Rami Jaffee—Keyboard Player . . . 250
Ricky Lawson—Drummer . . . 254
Brian MacLeod—Drummer . . . 260
Denny Seiwell—Drummer . . . 274
Leland Sklar—Bass Player . . . 279
Gary Solt—Guitar Player . . . 284
Peter Thorn—Guitar Player and Vocalist . . . 399

Glossary . . . 305
Index . . . 309

FOREWORD

My sister and I were both born music obsessed to parents supportive of our wonderful state of mind and body. Not only was Paula (I know, "Paul and Paula...") six years older than me and far more talented, she also was gifted with excellent taste in music and a real knack for "figuring things out."

Like so many mid-20th century American kids, we loved the Beatles, the Rolling Stones, Bob Dylan, James Brown, Led Zeppelin, Sly, Elton, and Bowie. We slipped willingly into love with Motown, Stax/Volt, and the Black music coming out of the Deep South. And we fell under the spell cast by the sonic wands wielded from Southern California by Brian Wilson and Phil Spector.

Thanks to my sister's enhanced musical perception, sometime very early in our lives she came to the realization that although this treasure trove of amazing music was seemingly endless, there were records made by self-contained bands and there were records made by *other people*.

I remember it like it was yesterday—LPs in two groups loosely scattered across our shag-carpeted basement floor. Arms folded across her chest, Paula pointed at the first pile. "Those are made by the bands. The guys on the covers play all the parts." Lifting her chin and shifting her gaze to the left she spoke like a detective, "But these are made by *other people* ... "

This book is about those other people—the session musicians. Anonymous, except to other musicians, and highly revered by their peers and "those in the know," session musicians have created and continue to create a huge chunk of the soundtrack of our lives. Most of the music we listen to—radio hit singles, underground classics in all genres, and just about all the music you hear on television and in film—is created by session musicians. Our hope is that this book offers insight into our wonderful world—a sonic reality where the Muse is truly the Master. I want to dedicate my contributions to this book to my sister, my parents, and my dear friend, co-author, and facilitator, Bobby Owsinski. Their lifelong support and encouragement are responsible for my contributions to this book and everything else I do.

Paul Ill, May 2009

INTRODUCTION

In my time in Los Angeles, I've been around a lot of people who've made their living by playing in the studio. I've done it a little myself, but certainly not on the scale of some of the giants of the business, the guys whose performances you hear on the radio, television, and movies every day. As a producer I've had the pleasant opportunity to hire these guys (I use that term generically—there are a lot of female studio musicians on the orchestral side of things) frequently, and many have become close friends (Paul Ill, my co-writer, has been one of my best friends since way before he became one of the top studio guys in town).

There are two things that come to mind whenever I think of my experiences with most studio musicians. The first is how creative they are. They bring more to the table than their chops (which usually are amazing). They bring ideas on how to make a piece of music sound better than you imagined. If you listen to them, you'll frequently end up with a far better track than you envisioned in the first place. But if you have your own vision, they're ever so accommodating in helping you reach it, with zero ego along the way.

The second is how much fun they usually are. Most of them have outgoing, sunny personalities that make them a joy to be around. They're not exactly extroverts, but they're not shrinking violets, either. They like being around people and, let's face it, you can't get much closer than when you're couped up in a studio working for 12 hours. This personality trait is perhaps the untold secret of being a studio musician.

So this book is part tribute and part instruction. It will illustrate how high a level these guys operate at, and it will show you how to get there if that's what you aspire to.

When we connected on the concept of this book, Paul and I thought that we each brought something unique to share, because he looks at things from one side of the glass while I see it from the other. Between us, we'll give you a total picture of just what it takes to be a studio musician, from the chops and gear that's required to the way you're expected to act before, during, and after a session.

And I think you'll find the DVD interesting, too. It's a look inside a real session in Studio B of a state-of-the-art Hollywood studio. (Can't reveal the name, unfortunately, as it belongs to a publicity-shy producer.) It's a candid look at just how it all goes down, complete with a player on her first big-time session, just as you might be someday.

Even if you don't have aspirations to be a studio musician, you'll find this a good and informative read, and the DVD will be a fun watch, too. Enjoy.

Bobby Owsinski, May 2009

MEET THE CONTRIBUTORS

We interviewed a host of studio musicians—players of all different genres and instruments, because we knew the more viewpoints we received, the more valuable you'd find it. The interviews were so good that we decided to include them in a separate section at the end. Here are the players you'll find there.

Ronnie Ciago is the very image of a modern percussionist in that he's as proficient on drums as he is as on percussion. With credits on projects by Ricki Lee Jones, Bill Ward (of Black Sabbath fame), Brand-X, Randy Stonehill, Mick Taylor (ex-Rolling Stone), Patrick Moraz, The Riverdogs, Jaco Pastorius, Robert Downey Jr., and high-profile producers like Jack Douglas and Linda Perry, as well as movies, television, and jingle sessions under his belt, there are few more qualified to speak about the role of the percussionist in the studio.

Charlie Drayton is a unique and special player who's equally adept and in demand as a drummer and bass player, so his perspective is that of the total rhythm section. Charlie's long and eclectic list of credits includes such names as Herbie Hancock, Keith Richards, Johnny Cash, Chaka Khan, Mariah Carey, Michelle Branch, Seal, Iggy Pop, Neil Young, Janet Jackson, and Courtney Love, among many others.

Bernie Dresel is noted for his ability not only to play any musical style, but also to step in to play orchestral percussion or groove hand percussion as well. Widely recognized for his 15 years with The Brian Setzer Orchestra, Bernie now does a variety of studio work that goes anywhere from television shows like *The Simpsons* and *Family Guy* to movies like *Speed Racer* to the blues-rock of Carl Verheyen to the big band sound of Gordon Goodwin

Big Phat Band to R&B icons like Chaka Khan and Patti LaBelle.

Being in the middle of the Detroit music scene as he grew up helped shape the background that eventually made **Frank Fitzpatrick** one of Hollywood's most sought-after composers and music supervisors. Frank's credits are many, having created the soundtracks for over two dozen feature films (including *Scary Movie 3, Queen of the Damned, Friday,* and *In Too Deep*) and scores and themes for several television shows, including the renowned *Larry Sanders Show*. Frank also has written and produced songs for Gold and Platinum artists including Jill Scott, Fat Joe, Dave Hollister, K-Ci & JoJo, Brownstone, Lina, Carl Anderson, Ice Cube, Akil (of Jurassic 5), Jazz (of Dru Hill), and The London Symphony, and contributed the opening song for *High School Musical.* As a successful producer in multiple genres, Frank's perspective is invaluable."

Currently the musical director for superstar Alicia Keys, keyboardist and drummer **Onree Gill** has worked with a diverse list of artists that includes Missy Elliott, Kelly Price, DMX, Sean "P. Diddy" Combs, Stevie Wonder, Gwen Stefani, Lenny Kravitz, Carlos Santana, Eric B, Anthony Hamilton, Angie Stone, John Mayer, Eve, Big Daddy Kane, Naughty by Nature, Bono, Arturo Sandoval, Paul Simon, Usher, and many more.

Eric Gorfain combined classical training with rock 'n' roll sensibilities to become one of the most in-demand violinists and string arrangers on the scene today. Eric's list of credits are indeed impressive, having played violin with rock gods Jimmy Page, Robert Plant, Eric Clapton, and Rod Stewart; pop divas Christina Aguilera, Kelly Clarkson, and Pink; mainstream artists Bryan Adams, Vanessa Carlton, and Fiona Apple; soul giants Ray Charles and James Brown; and alternative bands Wilco, Live, and A Perfect Circle, to name just a few.

One of the most widely recorded and most respected studio musicians of all time, trumpet player and arranger **Jerry Hey** has been a "first call" session player for more than 25 years. Jerry has played on thousands of recordings with just about every major artist, as well as commercials and movie soundtracks too numerous to mention.

Rami Jaffee is one of L.A.'s most prolific session figures, receiving his break in the business playing keyboards for the Platinum-selling band the Wallflowers. Rapidly expanding into session work, Rami has played on recordings by diverse acts like Fall Out Boy, LeAnn Rimes, Pearl Jam, Melissa Etheridge, Keith Urban, and Ziggy Marley, among many others. He's also now an unofficial member of the Foo Fighters.

Ricky Lawson has performed with the likes of Quincy Jones, the Brothers Johnson, Phil Collins, Steely Dan, Eric Clapton, Babyface, Lionel Ritchie, Anita Baker (*The Rapture*), and Whitney Houston ("I Will Always Love You"), and has worked as musical director for Michael Jackson. Ricky was also the original drummer for the Yellowjackets, with whom he won a Grammy for best R&B Instrumental ("And You Know That") in 1986. There's obviously a reason why these musical superstars have Ricky on a first-call basis, and that's because he is not only massively talented and guaranteed to give a record a giant groove, but also exceedingly humble and helpful to others as well.

Brian McLeod has been one of the most in-demand session drummers in L.A. ever since his stint as a member of *The Tuesday Night Music Club*, which shot Sheryl Crow to fame. If you're a fan of the television shows *The Office* or *Dirty Sexy Money*, you've heard him—he's playing on the theme song. Add to this credits like Christina Aguilera, Madonna, Chris Isaac, John Hiatt, Tears for Fears, Jewel and many more, and you get the picture of just why the Brian McLeod touch is so sought after.

Denny Seiwell established himself as one of the premier session drummers in New York and then took a side trip into rock 'n' roll beginning with an invitation from Paul McCartney to move to London and become a founding member of his post-Beatles group Wings. Adept at any musical style, Denny's signature drumming can be heard on records by Art Garfunkel, James Brown, Astrud Gilberto, Deniece Williams, Janis Joplin, Billy Joel, and, of course, Paul McCartney.

Leland Sklar is one of the most respected and in-demand bass players on the scene today, having contributed his skills to literally thousands of albums, soundtracks, films, and television shows with such diverse artists as Clint Black, Jackson Browne, Jimmy Buffet, Crosby, Stills, and Nash, The Doors, Vince Gill, Ricky Martin, Diana Ross, and of course, James Taylor, with whom Lee has played for over two decades.

Gary Solt is one of the few guitar players versatile enough to play orchestral dates for television shows, such as all the recent *Star Trek* series (*Next Generation, Deep Space Nine, Voyager,* and *Enterprise*), *Knots Landing,* and *Becker,* as well as numerous shows for National Geographic and Showtime.

Peter Thorn left his native Canada for Hollywood, soaked up as much information as he could, worked constantly on his chops and sound, and eventually became a much-in-demand session and touring guitarist and artist in his own right. Peter's credits include Chris Cornell, Alicia Keys, Daniel Powter, Jewel, and many more.

ACKNOWLEDGMENTS

I want to thank Linda Perry, Guy Chambers, Jack Douglas, Joe Beck, Doug D'Angelis, and every other producer, singer, songwriter, musician, DJ, programmer, and engineer I have ever created music with for helping to make me who I am and allowing for me to share in the healing power of music. And finally, I want to thank Natalia Jovovich for her love and support. Natalia, you make it all worthwhile.

Paul Ill

Thanks to the great Edward Colver for the cover photos, Larry Gerbrandt for many of the interior photos and the great photo of the authors on the rear cover, Don DiPietro for directing the video and being a great friend, everyone at "the studio that shall remain nameless" for their help and support, all the contributors for their excellent and informative interviews, and everyone at Hal Leonard for making the creation of this book as painless as possible.

Bobby Owsinski

Part One

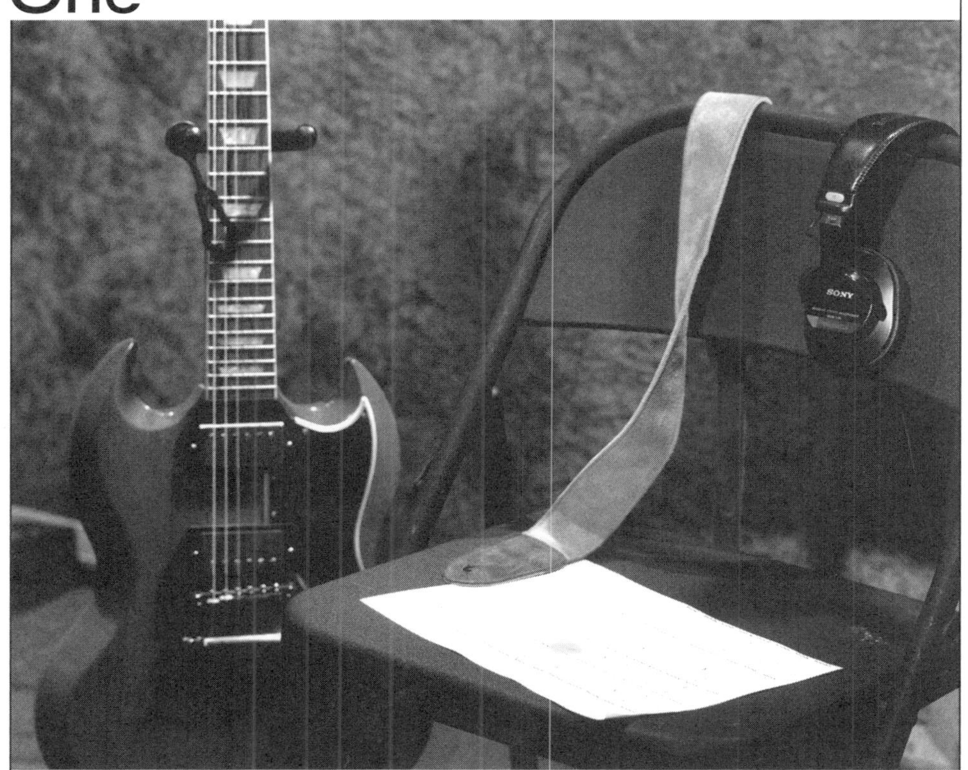

The Making of a Session Musician

CHAPTER 1

The History of the Studio Musician

The studio musician's role as we know it today is a somewhat recent phenomenon. The profession started in the 1920s and '30s when fledgling record labels, film studios, and radio broadcast networks employed studio bands that were made up of some of the era's best jazz players, such as Tommy and Jimmy Dorsey, Benny Goodman, and Jack Teagarden. The musicians during this period played in the studio bands during the day and in their own bands at night (there were strictly held schedules). This was the birth of the studio musician.

The Studio Bands

As recording gear became less expensive and more accessible, more and more record labels opened their own studios in the 1950s and, as a consequence, began hiring permanent groups of musicians to play on their records. The more the same musicians played with each other, the better they sounded together, and the more often they were hired as a package. The first of these groups was the Blue Moon Boys, which consisted of Bill Black on bass, DJ Fontana on drums, and Scotty Moore on guitar (the three players who eventually became Elvis Presley's backup band). The **Blue Moon Boys** played on many of the early releases from the legendary Sun Records in Memphis and made such an indelible musical impact that they were elected to the Musicians Hall of Fame in 2007.

With the '60s came more studio bands as more record labels continued the trend of installing their own studios. Perhaps the most famous of these bands was Motown's **Funk Brothers**, a group of about 20 local Detroit jazz and R&B musicians who played interchangeably on Motown hits. The Funk Brothers played on such as songs as The Temptations' "My Girl," Marvin Gay's and Gladys Night and the Pips' versions of "I Heard It Through the Grapevine," The Supremes' "Baby Love," Stevie Wonder's "Signed, Sealed, Delivered I'm Yours," The Four Tops' "I Can't Help Myself," Smokey Robinson and the Miracles' "The Tears of a Clown," and literally hundreds more. The Funk Brothers played like such a well-oiled machine that legend has it that they once cut three No. 1 hits in a single three-hour session. Musicians included bass players James Jamerson (considered by many to be the most influential bass player ever) and Bob Babbitt, keyboardists Earl Van Dyke and Johnny Griffith, vibes and tambourine player Jack Ashford, drummers Uriel Jones and William "Benny" Benjamin, and guitarists Joe Messina, Robert White, and Eddie Willis. They were also inducted into the Musicians Hall of Fame in 2007. The *Standing in the Shadows of Motown* DVD about the Funk Brothers is a must-have for every musician's collection.

At about the same time, farther south down in Memphis, Stax Records had its own house band called the **Mar-Keys**. The group consisted of keyboardist Booker T. Jones, guitar player Steve Cropper, bassist Donald "Duck" Dunn, drummer Al Jackson, trumpet player Wayne Jackson, and sax player Andrew Love. The Mar-Keys played on all the

Southern soul hits from that label, including "Dock of the Bay" by Otis Redding, "Midnight Hour" by Wilson Pickett, and "Hold On, I'm Comin" by Sam and Dave. Jones, Cropper, Dunn, and Al Jackson went on to record several hits of their own as the influential Booker T. and the MGs, while Wayne Jackson and Love went on to enjoy long session and touring careers as the Memphis Horns.

Over the years a number of legendary artists enlisted members of **The Memphis Boys** to perform on their recordings. The band included Bobby Wood (keyboards), Reggie Young (guitar), Mike Leech (bass), Bobby Emmons (organ), and Gene Chrisman (drums). Although the group wasn't a studio band connected to a record label, this group of outstanding musicians contributed to famous recordings such as Elvis's "Suspicious Minds," "In the Ghetto," and "Kentucky Rain"; Neil Diamond's "Sweet Caroline"; Willie Nelson's "Always on My Mind"; Billy Swan's "I Can Help"; Dusty Springfield's "Son of a Preacher Man"; and B. J. Thomas's "Hooked on a Feeling."

On the West Coast, another similar group of studio musicians called the **Wrecking Crew** played on virtually every hit record, television show, and movie made in L.A. during that era. While almost inventing the Southern California pop sound of the '60s and '70s, the Wrecking Crew played on such legendary recordings as "You've Lost That Loving Feeling" by the Righteous Brothers, "Bridge over Troubled Water" by Simon & Garfunkel, "Close to You" by The Carpenters, "Good Vibrations" by the Beach Boys, "I Got You Babe" by Sonny & Cher, and "Mr. Tambourine Man" by The Byrds, as well as on countless movie and television soundtracks for such shows as *Hawaii Five-O*, *Twilight Zone*, *Green Acres*, and *MASH* to name just a few. Players from the Wrecking Crew included Hal Blaine (drums), Carol Kay (bass), Glen Campbell (guitar), Mike Deasy (guitar), Larry Knechtel (keyboards), Don Randi (keyboards), Leon Russell (piano), Tommy Tedesco (guitar), and Plas Johnson (sax). An enjoyable new movie outlining the history and exploits of this amazing group of musicians is now available (another must-see, must-have).

In the '50s, '60s, and '70s, one thing the studios in Nashville had in common with all other recording centers was that they had a relatively small number of select musicians who played on 80 to 90 percent of the recordings made in that city. During that time, when a producer in Nashville needed to book a session, rather than naming each musician individually, he would just say, "Book the **A-Team**." The A-Team's roots took hold in what is now known as Music Row, beginning in the Quonset Hut Studio and RCA Studio B. The core members of the A-Team consisted of Harold Bradley (guitar), Floyd Cramer (piano), Pete Drake (steel guitar), Ray Edenton (guitar), Hank Garland (guitar), Buddy Harmon (drums), Tommy Jackson (fiddle), Grady Martin (guitar), Charlie McCoy (harmonica/guitar/bass), Bob Moore (bass), Boots Randolph (sax), Hargus "Pig" Robbins (piano), and later, Jerry Kennedy (guitar). These musicians played on a combined 130,000 recording sessions that occurred from the '50 s through the '70s.

Over in London during the Swinging '60s, many of the hits that came along with the British Invasion originated with of a band made up of Jimmy Page (guitar) and John Paul Jones (bass and keyboards), both later of Led Zeppelin; Big Jim Sullivan (guitar); Nicky Hopkins (piano); and Clem Cattini (drums). This group played on hits by Donovan, Herman's Hermits, Tom Jones, Petula Clark, Engelbert Humperdinck, and even the Rolling Stones.

While Muscle Shoals, Alabama, isn't a giant media center (it's not a media center at all, in fact), the **Muscle Shoals Rhythm Section** had a huge influence on the sound of the '70s as they crafted what became known as the "Muscle Shoals Sound"—a sound that was coveted by many hit artists of the day. Based around the town's FAME Recording Studios, the section consisted of David Briggs (keyboards), Norbert Putnam (bass), Earl "Peanut" Montgomery (guitar), Terry Thompson (guitar), Spooner Oldham (keyboards), and Jerry Carrigan (drums). They played on hits by artists such as The Tams, Tommy Roe, and Joe Tex. Some of these players returned in the '80s to play on hits by Jerry Reed,

Mac Davis, and the Gatlin Brothers before leaving for more lucrative session work in Nashville.

A second-generation FAME rhythm section that was commonly known as **The Swampers** (known affectionately as "The Swamp Rats" and referred to in Lynyrd Skynyrd's "Sweet Home Alabama"), became the more famous of the two rhythm sections that worked at the studio. The Swampers consisted of Jimmy Johnson (guitar), David Hood (bass), Roger Hawkins (drums), Junior Lowe (guitar and bass), and Barry Beckett (piano). The legendary Duane Allman (guitar) and Spooner Oldham (keyboards) also played with this band. This section cut hits with FAME artists such as Wilson Pickett, Etta James, Aretha Franklin, Arthur Conley, Clarence Carter, Candi Staton, and James and Bobby Purify. After later opening the competing Muscle Shoals Sound Studio, Johnson, Hawkins, Hood, and Beckett ran off a string of hits of their own for Paul Simon, Rod Stewart, The Staple Singers, The Rolling Stones, R. B. Greaves, Bob Seger, and many more.

In another non-major-media center, the **Atlanta Rhythm Section** originally came together as the house band at Studio One recording studios. The band consisted of guitarist J. R. Cobb, keyboardist Dean Daughtry, drummer Robert Nix, guitarist Barry Bailey and bassist Paul Goddard. Over the years, the band recorded with Joe South, Bonnie Bramlett, Dickey Betts, B. J. Thomas, and Billy Joe Royal, and later went on to make 16 albums and have a number of hit singles themselves.

In Jamaica, another famous and influential rhythm section consisting of drummer Lowell Dunbar (nicknamed "Sly" after Sly Stone, one of his favorite musicians) and bass guitarist Robbie Shakespeare became one of reggae's most prolific and long-lasting teams after they started working together in the mid-1970s. Sly and Robbie may well be the most prolific recording artists ever. One estimate is that they have played on or produced some 200,000 songs, considering that some of their *riddims* (instrumental versions of a song, such as "Revolution," used in reggae, dub, and dancehall genres) have been used on more than 100 songs.

In 1970's Los Angeles, **The Section** was the de facto house band of Asylum Records, and the music they played came to define that decade's easy-listening singer-songwriter sound. Danny Kortchmar (guitar), Craig Doerge (keyboards), Leland Sklar (bass), and Russ Kunkel (drums) appeared together and individually on albums by Crosby & Nash, James Taylor, Carole King, and Jackson Browne. The Section often did double- and triple-duty as band members, rotating from tour to tour for many of these esteemed artists.

An extension of that same sound also developed in New York during the '70s, as a group based loosely around the rhythm section of drummer Steve Gadd, bass player Will Lee, keyboardist Richard Tee, and guitarist Eric Gale played on more than 400 albums with such music luminaries as Barbra Streisand, Paul Simon, Eric Clapton, Grover Washington Jr., and Peter Gabriel. Other magnificent talents that were part of this unnamed session group include Mike Manieri (marimba and vibraphone); Chris Parker, Alan Schwartzberg, Rick and Jerry Marrotta (drums); Joe Beck, Dave Spinozza, Hiram Bullock, Steve Kahn, and Bob Mann (guitar); Randy and Michael Brecker (trumpet and tenor saxophone); Dave Sanborn (alto sax); Ralph MacDonald and Rafael Cruz (percussion); Don Grolnick (piano); and Tony Levin (bass). Many of these session monsters went on to solo success as jazz-fusion artists, others toured with pop greats, and still others (like Sanborn and the late Michael Brecker) managed to do both!

New York also gave us the infamous but unnamed Atlantic Records soul rhythm section that played on so many of that label's R&B hits of the '60s and '70s, and later became most famous as the core of Aretha Franklin's recording and touring band from 1970 to 1975. Built upon the leadership of tenor saxophonist King Curtis and the ferocious backbeat of drummer Bernard Purdie, the group was most frequently joined by bassists Jerry Jemmott or Chuck Rainy, guitarist Cornell Dupree, pianists Truman Thomas, and conga player Pancho Morales. This marvelous band created hits recorded primarily at Atlantic's Midtown Manhattan studio. Although Curtis was senselessly murdered just as the band's own fame crested, it continued on under Purdie's leadership. The group's stellar discography includes classics recorded for Aretha Franklin, Ray Charles, B. B. King, Freddie King, Nina Simone, Wilson Pickett, and The (Young) Rascals.

Also in the early '70s, Pennsylvania's Philadelphia International Records had an impressive string of hits built around a studio band composed of Earl Young (drums); Ronnie Baker (bass); Roland Chambers, Norman Harris, and Bobby Eli (guitar); Larry Washington (percussion); Vincent Montana Jr. (vibes); Leon Huff, Ron Kersey, and Leonard Pakula (keyboards); and Don Renaldo (strings and horns). Virtually the same musicians played on a long list of well-known "Philly Soul" records that included "If You Don't Know Me By Now" by Harold Melvin and the Blue Notes, "Me and Mrs. Jones" by Billy Paul, and the ever-popular "Love Train" by The O'Jays.

The Rise of the Independents

In the '80s and '90s, studio musicians came into their own as independent players thanks to the widespread proliferation of independent studios that seemed to be springing up everywhere. In New York, players such as Will Lee (bass), Steve Gadd (drums), and Elliot Randall (guitar) played as many as four three-hour sessions a day. In Los Angeles Larry Carlton, Steve Lukather, Lee Ritenour, and Jay Graydon (all on guitar), Neil Stubenhouse (bass), Jeff Pocaro (drums), and David Foster and Michael Boddicker (keyboards) were limited in work only by the number of hours in the day as they sped between sessions for commercials, movie scores, and records. Session work became increasingly lucrative as the work increased thanks to the growing number of studios and paying opportunities.

Unfortunately, as the '90s came to a close, the days of never-ending session work ended as sample libraries and home studios came within financial reach of most working musicians. Horn and string players were the first to feel the decreased number of gigs, as composers for film and television began using samplers like GigaStudio to record their scores instead of using real players. Record producers who previously needed simple horn and string parts found they could get by with a synthesizer playing the parts. Producers of commercials (which are done mostly on spec) found it a lot cheaper to program as much of the music as they could instead of using real players.

Soon the rhythm-section musicians also began to feel the pinch. An inexpensive programmer with FXpansion's BFD drums could sometimes be a viable option to using a high-priced session drummer (providing the programmer was good), even if the playing wasn't as nuanced. Cut-and-paste functions on a DAW meant that if a guitar- or bass player recorded the part correctly once, you could just repeat it again in other places in the song. And MIDI meant that you could program keyboard parts instead of having someone actually play them. As a result, session work for studio musicians on commercials, low-budget films and television shows, and music-demo work was severely and adversely affected.

These new abilities also caused a contraction of budgets for music production, since the actual hard costs for a score came way down. Composers began to underbid each other, and once the film and television studios and the publishing and record companies saw how inexpensively a reasonably good product could be produced with the help of machines, their budgets went down accordingly. Not good if you depended on session work, since there was now a lot less money around to hire you.

If that wasn't enough, the file-sharing era arrived and CD sales tanked, and budgets shrank even further. Therefore, the typical studio musician who might've had as many as four sessions a day in LA or New York during the early '90s might be down to four or six sessions a month in the early 2000s.

But does that mean there isn't any studio work out there? Absolutely not. While the cream-of-the-crop gigs might not be as plentiful as they used to be, there are still lots of gigs around for a professional player, and you don't have to be in a major media center to have them available, either.

People will always need to record, and despite what the musical technoids would have you think, experienced producers know that the fastest, best-sounding, and ultimately, cheapest way to get things done is to use a pro. This book is going to prepare you to be the go-to person in your area when someone wants to record, because they'll know that you'll get the job done in a professional manner and therefore make their project sound a lot better. But remember, as a studio musician, you'll be standing on the shoulders of the giants; so work hard, have fun, and do your best to serve them well!

CHAPTER 2

Why Playing in the Studio Is Different from Playing Live

All musical performances are really about "the moment." Live music happens in the moment *for* that moment. Recorded music captures that moment so that it can last forever. The former is like a live TV news feed of an event, while the latter is like a carved statue of the same subject material.

You've probably had a lot of experience playing live, but playing in the studio is a distinctively different experience. The thought process is different, the mind-set is different, the approach is different, and the chain of command is different.

Sixteen Ways That Playing in the Studio Differs from Playing Live

In an effort to contrast these two different experiences, let's move from the most obvious differences to those that are, shall we say, a bit more subtle.

1. **Repertoire.** Most live gigs rarely change repertoire without rehearsal. Only on the fringes of the jazz community do musicians show up at a live gig prepared to wing it at every show. A session musician has to be ready to change material on the fly. If it's a one-tune record date for a singer-songwriter, the song may take on a completely new character within moments. The session may start with the artist playing the tune by himself or herself. As the rhythm section falls in, they are expected not only to learn it "on the fly," but also to come up with the appropriate parts that will help make the song as memorable as possible and as accessible and pleasing to the artist, the producer, and the listeners who may make the song part of their lifetime's musical soundtrack. No pressure!

2. **Scrutiny.** On stage, whatever you play is gone as soon as you play it. In the studio, what you play is under a microscope and will likely be analyzed, dissected, and reorganized all in the name of making the performance stronger.

3. **Equipment.** The gear you use on a gig won't always translate to the studio. You choose the gear for a live gig based upon its versatility, durability, and general ruggedness. But in the studio, the only thing that counts is the sound. While one size might fit all on a gig, the same equipment usually makes for a boring recording, especially if you're recording multiple tracks or more than one song. The studio requires a wide range of sonic possibilities, so you'll need to bring different instruments and accessories to get there (more on gear in chapter 7).

4. **Leadership.** On a gig, you have a bandleader that calls the songs and counts them off, may possibly direct the solos, and ends the songs. In the studio, you're answering to a hierarchy consisting of the producer, artist, and engineer (in cases of sonics). The producer is the ultimate decision maker, with ultimate authority over everything you play.

5. **Nuance.** The little things count in the studio. Everything you play can be critical, so nuances are just as

important as the body of what you're playing. When you play live, the nuances are usually gone in the wind, overcome by the stage volume, acoustics, and attention of the players and audience. In the studio, everything you play is scrutinized, and that's too much pressure for some players. On stage, your bandmates may be listening hard (if they're good they will be), but the audience will be grooving to the music as a whole. No pressure, just play. In the studio, you've got to be great every time, every take.

6. **Live feel versus studio feel.** Rest assured that watching drum god Steve Gadd play live with Eric Clapton is a whole different experience than listening to his studio work with ol' Slowhand. There is definitely a different feel required when playing in the studio. Players well versed in both idioms tend to exhibit more finesse and restraint in the studio, and they cut loose in a different way. Remember, music in a studio terminates with some kind of recording or broadcast. Live music just disperses into the ether. Recording in the studio requires that the musician play to a set of variables (created by the signal chain) that differ significantly from the ones you deal with on stage.

7. **Etiquette.** You can get away with being a jerk on a live gig since the other players will usually put up with you (up to a point) as long as you perform well and the audience loves you. Not so in the studio. In order to take the music to the level it needs to go to, a constant give and take is required with everyone in the studio. If you make someone feel even slightly uncomfortable for any reason, chances are you probably won't be asked back. There are too many great players with accommodating personalities waiting in line for the chance.

8. **Hard work.** That's not to say that playing or singing on a four- or five-hour gig isn't difficult, but you are able to play a lot of different songs every set and get the glory of audience feedback. In the studio, the only feedback you get is from the producer, the artist, and maybe the engineer, and 99 percent of the time they're analyzing how you can play

a part better, rather than singing your praises. And the level of concentration definitely goes up a few notches. On a gig you can breeze through the music, almost losing yourself in your playing. In the studio, every note counts and requires your utmost attention. It's not unusual to spend hours on the same song (or even the same phrase), playing or singing it over and over until it fits perfectly. On the other hand, some sessions require that you play it perfectly the first time (or in a few takes), which brings a pressure all its own.

9. **Preparation.** Live gigs almost always require sufficient rehearsal. Most recording sessions, however, happen with little or no preparation. As a result, a session musician has to be highly adaptable and able to learn music "on the fly."

10. **Approach.** Studio musicians can be asked to change their approach in the middle of a take. Imagine you're on a session where you're recording a TV score. The producer and music supervisor are sitting with the show's director listening to you do a Hammond organ overdub on a chase scene that starts in a ghetto bar on foot and ends with the bad guy and the cop hopping into their respective cars, with the bad guy stepping just ahead of our hero. As the cars speed away into an industrial neighborhood, the scene crossfades into a close-up of the cop's mom in church, lost in prayer. You're cranking on the Hammond to a prerecorded backing track, playing your best Jimmy McGriff– or Jimmy Smith–inspired growly blues runs. Upon completion, you think to yourself, "That take was great." But after a brief pause during which you watch your audience of three in intense conversation through the control-room glass, the music supervisor leans on the talkback and says, "Pretty good. Now at bar 17 on your chord chart, can you make it sound more "rock," say like Deep Purple? Then for the last 6 or 7 bars, can you switch up to more of a gospel feel? And by the way, we're going to kill the track around bar 32, but we'll leave in the click so that you can make a solo transition from the "rockier" stuff to the gospel on your own, okay? And remember there's 11 more bars after bar 32, so don't forget to count!" And you thought that your take was seamless!

11. Pace. Early in a session, studio musicians often hear, "We really like what you're doing, but we don't like the sound. We're going to change a few things in here." Now think of those countless gigs you've played. Rarely, if ever, do you stop during a live performance to tweak, but it's very common in any recording context for those people on the production/engineering side of the glass to stop midtake and say, "You're doing great, but we have to fix a few things." Often, after a series of takes, everyone in the studio band will hear over their headphones, "You guys are definitely in the zone, but we need to change out the snare drum," or, "That was a great solo, but can you do it again on your Strat this time?" A session player needs to always be ready to move at the pace determined by the environment. Things may change on the fly from breakneck speed to time-crawling meticulousness. If you get booked with a producer like Roy Thomas Baker, you may be slaving over the same basic track for days at a time, but if Comedy Central calls you in for a series of cues for a cartoon series, you may be expected to complete 30 to 50 short pieces of music in less than three hours—so you must be ready for both and everything in between!

12. Creation versus interpretation. Live musicians are usually expected to re-create a preexisting repertoire, whereas the studio cats *create* the repertoire. Motown's famously influential Funk Brothers helped create the soundtracks for several generations of music consumers, and you can bet that popular-music culture—from bar bands to recording artists—are going to be duplicating their licks and parts for decades and maybe even centuries to come.

13. Required skill set. This will be looked at in greater detail in chapter 9, but let's look briefly at the differences. For rhythm players, there's a whole different level of musical literacy required when playing live. Top session musicians not only read music well, but also can access a variety of styles and feels on a moment's notice. You must also have a really good set of ears and musical taste buds to make it to the top of the session-musician hierarchy. If you often wonder why Led Zeppelin was so good, consider the thousands of sessions logged by Jimmy Page and John Paul Jones in London studios between 1962 and 1968. Together and separately they played on everything from Tom Jones's "Its Not Unusual" to Donovan's "Hurdy Gurdy Man" to the Kinks' "You Really Got Me" to the Stones' *Their Satanic Majesties Request*. All that studio work not only honed their already formidable chops, but it informed their taste buds and fine-tuned their ears as well.

14. Artist versus entertainer. Live musicians are entertainers, while studio musicians help create, shape, and put entertainment in a tangible form. It's like the difference between going to see actors in a play and actors on the silver screen. Both achieve the same end, but theater changes from performance to performance, while film is a one-time document meant to stand the test of time and weather repeated exposures. Are you up to the task? Chances are you are—you just need to be willing to do the work.

15. Venue variables. Live performance almost always presents the musician with similar circumstances. His or her instrument(s), collaborators, and set lists usually won't change much, or without fair warning. Not so in the studio. Except for the great studio bands of the '60s and '70s, studio musicians are used to seeing new faces frequently and almost always play new material, and although the venues change, it's not in the ways that live venues do. Granted, the acoustics and the crowd may change on a live gig from night to night, but most everything else remains the same. Not so in the studio. The session musician learns to expect change at any moment, since the tune can morph and he may be asked to play a different part or instrument.

16. Live wolf pack versus studio lone wolf. Unless you're a DJ or a solo singer-songwriter, most live performances require a group and a sizable supporting cast. Recording musicians usually convene at a studio, arriving on their own, so a camaraderie exists that's different from the "We're all together on this bus!" mentality of live work. Recording musicians are independent and can work with different people every time they play music. Not usually so for live players.

As you can see, there are a lot of differences between playing live and in the studio, but you can't say that one is better or more exciting than the other, because they both have their high and low points. But it's not about which is better; it's about knowing the differences so that you can be better prepared for what you might face.

CHAPTER 3

Who Hires Session Musicians?

You can have the greatest chops and the best gear, and play fluently in every style on the planet, but if you're sitting at home and the phone doesn't ring, you'll never get a chance to show the world your talent. Before that phone rings, you've got to know exactly who'll be calling, so let's take a look at who's who in what may be considered the session musician's Holy Grail: the people who hire musicians for studio work.

Since music today is recorded professionally everywhere—from bedrooms onto laptop programs like GarageBand to 2,500-square-foot near-perfect acoustical environments attached to control rooms loaded with recording gear worth millions of dollars—it's safe to say that almost anyone making music will be able to hire you for a professional recording session. If you're in demand, you'll probably get all sorts of playing opportunities from sources that you wouldn't suspect. That being said, the top three sources for session work are contractors, producers, and highly respected session musicians.

Contractors

The contractor usually acts as a go-between for musicians and producers, and is required to be present at all times during the session when his contracted musicians are recording. Contractors come in two varieties: union and independent. Both types are usually musicians themselves who supervise and provide additional services for a session. A contractor can help musicians and singers prepare by supplying them with the necessary information for the session and making sure that they and their specified instruments and equipment arrive at the event or session on time. He or she coordinates the event, coaches, conducts, computes session fees, and submits the proper union forms (if it's a union date) to the employer and the union office.

Contractors often specialize in a specific area of the business such as jingles, orchestral dates, or film/television sessions. For a contractor, it's all about relationships. His or her reputation is founded on the level of experience and quality of the musicians he or she makes available, so it really makes sense to cultivate relationships with the local contractors.

Producers

It is the career goal of every session musician to become the " first-call" player for as many successful producers as possible. In the vast majority of recording situations, the producer decides who plays what, when they play it, how the music should sound, and most importantly, who plays it.

All successful producers have a cadre of players that, as a result of previous excellent session experiences, they've grown comfortable using because of previous excellent session experiences. Sometimes the musicians have played on a project that has met with some success, so these players act as sort of a good-luck charm and, as a result, keep getting calls from the producer. Sometimes the players are a big part of the producer's "sound," and he wants to make sure to maintain that sound by hiring the same players.

If the producer is producing a band, sometimes he calls in a musician to play a part that the band member just can't execute. Sometimes this is with full knowledge of the band, but other times a session player could also be asked to "ghost" a part secretly without the band's knowledge. Sometimes the band has to leave for the road with the record still unfinished, and the producer will call in his favorite players in an effort to get the project quickly out the door. And sometimes he calls in a player to perform on an instrument that no band member plays.

If a producer is working with a solo artist, the chances for work grow exponentially, because a studio band is needed for all the tracking and for individual work on the overdubs. This could be for the artist's album, a song for a movie or television, an event like the Olympics or the Super Bowl, or simply a demo of the artist's new song.

Most producers specialize. Some are involved in only television or radio commercials (referred to as "jingles"), which are usually pressure packed three-hour dates just like the old days: tracking for the first hour, overdubbing in the second, fixing and mixing during the third (more on jingle dates later in chapter 4). Others produce only record dates, with some producers working with bands and others just with solo artists. Regardless of whom you start with, producers are the main source for work for a studio musician, and it sure helps the career and the pocketbook to be on call with more than one.

Musicians

Most everyone in the music business likes to create work for friends. Artists, composers, studio staffers, producers, contractors, and managers all trust the musicians they respect to make appropriate referrals for sessions.

Musicians create session work for other musicians through the process of recommendation to artists and producers. Top session musicians like to refer other musicians they know and do so frequently. Believe it or not, during the '60s and early '70s, session musicians gauged their success by how much work they turned down for themselves and passed on to other players. Just think how much work these men and women created for their friends and protégés! True, the producer makes the final call, but a referral from a musician that the producer likes to use is usually golden.

> *My big break in session work was mainly from Benmont Tench passing my number along to the biggest producers around. Being a player after Benmont's style, being a Grammy winner, and selling millions of albums didn't hurt either.*
>
> Rami Jaffee

Here's an example of how it can work. Imagine being in New York City in the hot summer. You're new in town, fresh off a two-year stint fronting a show band. Your vocal chops are in great shape, you've got your finger on the pulse of current popular music, and you've relocated to the Big Apple looking for work as a session singer. Unfortunately, all you've managed to conjure up in your first six weeks in town is a three-song feature at the Monday night jam session at Kenny's Castaways in the Village. It's too hot and humid for 10 p.m., but you stroll downtown anyway, looking forward to the opportunity to wail on some blues even if you're not getting paid. As you turn the corner on Bleeker Street, you spot a guy from behind with long blond hair squatting in a murky puddle trying not to muddy his clothes. He's wrenching a tire iron struggling to fix a flat. As you approach you offer, "Hey man, need some help?" and lo and behold, staring up at you just like on the cover of your favorite Brecker Brothers record, you immediately recognize Will Lee, studio bassist extraordinaire looking up at you as he sighs, "Oh, yeah! Thanks, man! I'm on my way to meet my wife for a dinner date, and I had a flat! Don't wanna get my clothes wet!" So you help out, get some stains on your jeans, and compliment him on his great playing.

As you finish up, Will billows over with profuse thanks and asks about you. You give him the CliffsNotes version of your musical life, to which he replies, "Well, not many people know this, but I make more money singing on commercials than I do playing bass. Maybe the lovely lady and I will stop down tonight after dinner."

Two and a half hours later, half way through your rendition of Otis Redding's "Try a Little Tenderness," you open your eyes and see Will with a willowy blonde on his arm beaming at you. After your show-stopping Wilson Pickett "Midnight Hour" finale, you step offstage dripping in sweat to be greeted by Will with this: "Man, that was killing! You're more than good, man." Looking fondly at his wife, Will continues, "We've decided to take a few days off later this week and hit the Hamptons. I've got a Budweiser commercial on Thursday. You want to sub for me?" Casting a conspiratorial glance at his wife, he continues, "That way we can split a day early." And the rest, as they say, is history.

Sometimes musicians hire other musicians for their own sessions if they are trying to make the jump and establish themselves as producers or if they have songs or music for a film or television show that they wish to record. That session guy who you're competing with now for gigs could someday be a producer who's your main source for work, so be sure to treat everyone nicely (but you knew that already, didn't you).

Artists

Artists often insist on recording with specific musicians, either because of reputation, previous affiliation, or just hearing something they really liked along the way. If a budding new rock star who grew up in the '90s gets a record deal, and she happened to see the infamous Bowie/ Nine Inch Nails tour of 1996, she may insist to everyone involved, "Get me that guy who used to make all those weird guitar noises for David Bowie!" Seemingly out of nowhere, Reeves Gabrels gets the call!

Sometimes an artist wants the feel or the sound that a certain musician or group of musicians brings. Bob Seger recorded some his best albums with the Muscle Shoals rhythm section after hearing them on Arthur Conley's "Sweet Soul Music," and just about everyone in Nashville wanted the A-Team during the long period when they were hot.

Composers

Composers are sort of a hybrid in the work category. They are both artist and producer, but they're still a great source for work. A successful television composer can usually provide steady session employment (unusual for a session musician), since cues are required for each episode. While the nature of the cues change and the players with it, the same group of musicians generally stays with the show for comfort and continuity's sake.

Film composers are a little different in that hiring for a large orchestral session is usually done by a contractor, although the composer will request certain players as he requires them. Smaller nonorchestral sessions may use a contractor or be hired directly by the composer. Usually, the smaller the session, the more likely it is that the composer will hire you directly.

The best way to create opportunities to record film and television music is to cultivate relationships with composers, contractors, and music supervisors. Many players transition to composers. Session musicians are perhaps the biggest contributors to film and television libraries, and the vast majority of composers were players first.

Recording Studio Staff

Occasionally, studio staff will hire you. Imagine this: over the Christmas holiday season in a small college town, a string quartet has been assembled to record a last-minute advertising jingle for a radio and television ad campaign for the local New Year's Parade. But they're in a jam. On her way to the session, the cellist (who teaches at the local college and knows every string player for miles) slid on some ice while driving and totaled her brand-new Prius! She's okay and her instrument's undamaged (by far her greatest concern), and even though she's a little shaken, she calls the studio to try to help get a sub. Too bad she can't think of anyone, because her best students are out of town and the other cello instructor is skiing. In the studio foyer, the receptionist Katie overhears the engineer, producer, and first violinist trying to work things out, and she remembers meeting *you* just yesterday, when you were in town to pick up your high school sweetheart and drive home for the holidays. You just happened to be walking up the stairs to your girlfriend's apartment *with your cello* as Katie was coming home from work. Voila! Katie calls your girl, and you get the gig.

In similar fashion, in June of 2008 this author (Paul Ill) received a call from Richard Flack, an engineer friend based in London whom I'd worked with on frequent sessions for esteemed producer Guy Chambers. Renowned session drummer Brian MacLeod, Richard, Guy, and I had been on sessions together for world-class artists such as Tina Turner, Asyln, and Annie Lennox, to name a few. Early in the summer of that year, Richard found himself on hush-hush sessions with Jimmy Page and Leona Lewis. A team was being assembled to record a backing track for the UK's contribution to the opening ceremony for the 2008 Olympics in China. Page and Lewis were slated to perform Led Zeppelin's classic "Whole Lotta Love" over a backing track. Being more than familiar with Brian's and my work, and having seen us play Led Zeppelin's music live with Linda Perry and the Section String Quartet, Richard was more than confident when he recommended us to Jimmy Page. MP3 files were sent via email and we got the gig, only to lose it later on that day because we weren't British citizens. The only saving grace was that for the rest of our lives, Brian and I could say that we were Page's rhythm section for all of five minutes, but this story illustrates how a referral from an engineer can turn into very illustrious work.

Artist Managers

Artist managers or someone in their office are occasionally charged with the responsibility of putting together players for a session, and their first call is to someone they trust for a referral. While this is usually a musician or producer they've worked with before, the referral can come from sources outside the norm.

Here's a good example. A very prominent singer-songwriter with a worldwide hit behind him secretly wanted to stretch out a little in the studio and come up with a new direction. Instead of sticking to his typical pop rhythm-section format, he wanted to continue to play piano but also to work with a neojazz rhythm section composed of upright bass and drums. On top of that, he wanted to play with a DJ who was capable of matching his breakbeats to the jazz drummer and tuning his scratches to the key of the song. This has been a challenge for all DJ-based ensembles for years, and very few DJs have the skills to make themselves musically subordinate to an ensemble's key and tempo choices. The artist and rhythm section had tried out a few well-known DJs but no one had really jelled yet, so the word went out to the artist's management to find a DJ that would fit.

Now here's where it gets interesting. A friend of his manager's assistant works FOH (front-of-house—a fancy acronym for "soundperson") at a renowned venue in a major market mixing everything from hip-hop to punk to jazz to India rock, and everything in between. His reputation around his home city is golden, and he seems to know everybody in the biz. Soon he got the call from a managerial assistant in the artist's office who was a regular at the concert club and knew that he knew everything and everyone that was musically happening in town. She expressed that they were at a loss for the right DJ, but not to worry—our soundman to the rescue! He frequently mixed shows for DJ Peyote Coyote, a veteran of numerous live bands and just the right man for this job. DJ PC got the call, got the gig, and wound up working on some sessions that were highly interesting and experimental (but, unfortunately, yet to be released). Lesson learned: regardless of who hires you, anyone may recommend you for session work.

Types of Sessions

When musicians think of playing a session, they usually conjure up a vision of playing in the studio with a high-profile artist and top-flight producer. But there are numerous other kinds of dates that can and are offered to session musicians.

Historically, sessions are broken down into five basic groups: demos, jingles, television- and movie-score dates, record dates, and live broadcasts. With the emergence of the Internet and DAW-based recording, Web sessions and owner-operated studio sessions now figure more and more into the studio musician's day-to-day life. Let's take a look at the most basic of sessions, the demo.

Demos

The word *demo* is the abbreviated version of the term *demonstration recording,* and it represents an example of what the final version can sound like. These recordings are then played for record execs, producers, managers, and sometimes even the artists themselves in hopes that they'll produce a master version of the song.

The amount of time spent on perfecting the recording is what usually separates a demo from a master take. Demos are recorded as quickly as reasonably possible, and while they are performed capably, less time is spent on specific sounds or parts as long as the song has the right feel and vocal performance. A master track for a record release may have no time limit, with perfection in sound, playing precision, and feel being the ultimate goal.

In the old analog days, demos rarely became the final product that made it to record or radio, but with the advent of inexpensive DAWs having the ability to cut-and-paste, the need for session musicians to perform on demo recordings has decreased. That being said, studio musicians are still called to record demos in recording environments that range from home studios to the greatest facilities in the world.

Producers and songwriters often have their own recording studios and frequently call musicians in to demo a song for a specific artist, TV show, or movie. Sometimes the demo is a mix of prerecorded tracks and/or MIDI tracks and new live tracks that a player or group of players are called in to perform on to help "sweeten" the track. Sweetening is the process of overdubbing an additional part or parts so that a recording becomes more musical.

Quite often a demo of a song is written, recorded, and produced to be "pitched" (presented) to a particular artist. Here's an example of how that might work. Leticia, an up-and-coming singer-songwriter from west Tennessee who just signed a lucrative publishing deal, wakes up in the morning, grabs her guitar, and, before she's finished her second cup of coffee, feels she's written Carrie

Underwood's next big hit. Before lunch she bangs out a very listenable demo through her Mbox onto her laptop that consists of two guitar tracks, a lead vocal, two stereo pairs of background vocals, and a never-changing drum loop. By 2 p.m. she's in the office of her publisher, who gets so excited about the song's hooky chorus that he musters the troops, and by dinnertime (well, studio people tend to eat late!) their favorite bassist, drummer, and pedal-steel player have cut their tracks. Leticia and her publisher decide to keep her background vocals and rhythm guitar and even make use of her original drum loop in the bridge, but they decide to recut her lead vocal because her voice sounds "smokier" at night. By 10 p.m. they've cut a smokin' vocal, and just before midnight they pass Carrie's personal email address to their engineer who immediately sends the superstar an MP3. This is the stuff dreams are made of!

Although the demo session is far more infrequent in today's digital recording world than back in the analog years, demos still get made, so you need to know what to expect when you get called to do this kind of session. Be prepared to learn fast and work fast. Usually the song is charted or there's a very simple recorded version for you to transcribe or listen to. You may be expected to come up with your own part in a specific style, and occasionally whoever is running the session (could be the songwriter, the producer, or a representative from the music publisher) may want to record the song in more than one style or key.

Most music publishers have demo studios in their main offices, so if you're working in New York, London, Nashville, or L.A., hopefully you'll be working on your own or with a small ensemble in one of these studios soon. Regardless of where you record, do your best work as quickly as you can.

Jingles

A jingle is any form of music used for an advertising spot on radio, television, or online. Often a jingle is just an instrumental track, but most likely there's ad copy sung in a pop format, like Miller's sweetly sung "If you've got the time, we've got the beer . . ." Most frequently formatted to last 30 or 60 seconds, jingles are primarily the domain of advertising agencies, which contract the work out to composers and producers on behalf of their clients, the companies whose products the commercial will be featuring.

Like demos, jingles are usually recorded very quickly. In advertising, time is money, so the schedule's pretty tight (usually a three-hour session, with the first hour to track, the second hour for overdubbing, and the third for mixing). So get ready to work quickly. Since the dawn of commercial music advertising, it's been a widely held belief that a jingle's vocal track is what really sells that product; for that reason the jingle's instrumental track is done as quickly as possible so that the most time can be devoted to recording the vocals. In their '60s to '80s heyday, jingles done in New York and Los Angeles were usually booked for one hour with a "possible 20," which meant that regardless of the recording ensemble's size or the jingle's musical complexity, the entire session for the instrumental backing track might run only 80 minutes tops!

Each jingle has a definite musical direction based on the demographic that the ad agency is trying to reach. For example, if a DJ is called in to scratch on a hip-hop-styled national TV spot for a fast-food company, he or she will be told exactly what type of scratching sounds the ad agency is looking for. Or, if the jingle is for a commercial advertising the newest line of hybrid SUVs coming out of Detroit and is meant to appeal to fans of mainstream country music, then the session guitarist may be told to bring his best acoustic and a Telecaster. Each jingle will try to simulate a different style of music that best fits the feel of the commercial, so the more styles you can play well, the more likely you'll get the call for this kind of session.

As with just about every session, the session musician is expected to show up ahead of schedule, be ready to play at the appointed time (the session's "downbeat"), and play in the style required. But perhaps more than any other type of date, being on time is most important since everything is under such a tight schedule. Having reading skills is a huge plus for jingle work, as one frequently sees charts on jingle dates. Slight changes in sound, content, and style may be asked for, so there is some room for creativity. But usually a jingle is precomposed, so the recording date is about an accurate rendering of a score, not about your classiest licks or newest bold ideas. Regardless, the session is expected to be over as quickly and as efficiently as possible, yielding the most desirable musical results.

Often session musicians make the jump to become jingle composers. Anyone capable of creating a master recording on his or her own, and who has the right combination of additional skills, can become a self-contained producer or jingle composer. Multi-instrumentalists and highly skilled MIDI programmers all fare well in the jingle world and often transition from session musician to composer-producer.

Jingle singing is some of the most lucrative work available to studio musicians. Session fees for in-demand singers are on the higher end of the pay scale, and jingle vocal dates are some of the few that pay residuals to recording musicians. Jingle singers are some of the best sight-readers in the business and are expected to be able to switch from their own unique vocal sound and to emulate other vocal styles on the fly.

The days of the session musician running all over town from jingle session to jingle session five days a week are for the most part long gone. Nowadays many jingles are composed, recorded, and produced by an individual composer or a small production team that is solely responsible for delivering the finished product to the ad agency or someone acting in the role of music supervisor. To make these jingle recordings more competitive, composers and producers often bring a few live instrumentalists to add a distinctive flavor by replacing prerecorded MIDI tracks and/or loops so that the music has a more live sound and feel, and is therefore more pleasing to the ear. Similar to the "sweetening" sessions mentioned in the previous section on demos, overdubbing on a jingle has to happen as quickly and efficiently as possible.

Many jingles are done on "spec," or speculation, meaning that there is no money paid up-front, with the promise to get paid later if the track is subsequently used. An ad agency or music supervisor pitches the spot to numerous composer-producers who all are expected to deliver a master in the allotted time while covering their own production expenses. Only the winner gets paid! If a musician or singer is called in to play on these "spec dates," sometimes they are paid a nominal fee in the form of an advance on an agreed amount to be paid if the work is selected for use. Sometimes spec dates are no-pay situations in which everyone gambles with their time. In today's extremely competitive climate, most musicians are willing to do some spec work, and since jingles require so little time, doing a spec jingle is not that difficult a proposition to embrace. All that's required is a little time and maybe some gas.

Over time, most composer-producers who manage to continue to work in this high-stakes spec game eventually hit the jackpot in one form or another. Not only do they appreciate excellent musicianship and a positive attitude but, like all other successful leaders, they also value commitment and loyalty. So if you're invited to a spec date with a working producer or composer, it's a good idea to take them up on it, especially if it's a jingle date. Just don't sacrifice paying work for it. If a spec offer creates a conflict with a paid booking, ask the spec's producer to bend the schedule a few hours or move the session to another day to accommodate your paying work conflict. Things usually work out so that you can do both gigs and keep yourself and everyone else happy, too.

Film and Television

Like the entire recording industry, the universe of film and television music is constantly evolving and, as a result, film and TV dates span a broad gamut. Today, some extremely successful film and television composers are creating everything from soundtracks to first-run features in garage- or bedroom studios. There are still some full-fledged orchestral scoring dates that utilize a full rhythm section, a choir, and a 72-piece orchestra, but sadly, they're not the norm anymore because of the costs involved. Let's look at the basic strata of film and television recording sessions that you might be called to participate in.

LIBRARY MUSIC SESSIONS

The simplest TV and film dates are those that yield cues for library music. Typically, a library cue is two to two-and-a-half minutes long, and consists of an A section, a B section, and maybe a few alternate endings. Cues are usually compiled stylistically, and then delivered in groups of 12 to 15 to a library house or directly to a music supervisor.

EPISODIC TELEVISION

Some composers have the good fortune of creating music for a successful series of episodic shows. Episodic television music is the next rung up the ladder from library cues in the world of music composition. Recording musicians like this kind of work because it's not only lucrative but also style specific, and they're usually hired because they have the right sound and feel to meet the composer's needs. Sometimes these are union dates paid for by a parent production company, but more often than not the composer pays the musicians directly. Rates vary with the budgets involved.

FILM DATES

Film work has always been top dog in the various ways that a musician can make money playing sessions. Films make more money than TV shows, and TV shows make more money than CD and download sales, so nowadays film music is tops.

On a large TV- or film-scoring date, musicians are expected to be in their seats and ready to play at the scheduled start time (commonly known as the "downbeat"). Most often everyone is expected to be able to sight-read the music that is on his or her stand, regardless of its complexity. Therefore, film and television sessions demand the highest level of sight-reading skills, which is why only a select set of musicians play these dates. They are a very small, elite group, and one usually sees the same faces at these sessions. If you aspire to play top-level film and TV dates, practice your sight-reading daily. The day you find yourself seated on a soundstage about to play on the next Spielberg blockbuster, you don't want your folding chair to turn into a hot seat because your sight-reading abilities are limited!

Musicians who come from an orchestral background tend to fare best in the world of film and television music. Since string and horn players tend to be the best sight-readers, rhythm section players should aspire to achieve the music-reading ability levels demonstrated by their orchestral brothers and sisters. It's safe to say that on most high-end film and TV dates, it's really all about the reading.

Record Dates

Now we come to the granddaddy of all recording sessions, the record date. A *record*, these days a somewhat antiquated term, now refers to any recording by an artist or a band that will be released for distribution to the public. This distribution can be either on a physical piece, such as a CD or vinyl record (the real "record"), or in the digital domain, like an MP3 or iTunes file.

Studio musicians can be booked to record either a single song (sometimes called a track) or an entire CD of 10 to 15 songs. With all the changes at hand in the music business, studio musicians see more and more of the focus switch from bookings for an entire album to bookings for single songs or songs in groups of three and four. Since the market for music now closely resembles the American music business's pre–British Invasion years of the late '50s and early '60s, studio players find themselves working more and more in a "singles" market than an "album" market. It's a re-inventive climate that is exciting to be sure. Whether you're called for one song or for 20, this is the most prestigious and lucrative work available for studio musicians, especially if it's with a best-selling artist.

Time is the primary and most prevailing influence on any record date, and most decisions made on a date are based on "time spent." Successful studio musicians know how to make best use of time spent in the studio, and they develop a sixth sense about how to pace themselves while working. Studio musicians know they will vacillate between pressure-cooker dates, where the work has to happen fast, and introspective, "take your time" sessions, where the goal is to explore the music and "find" the track. Flexibility and adaptability are the keys to smooth sailing on ever-changing waters in the ocean of record dates.

Regardless of where you work, how long you work, or how much you get paid, as a session musician your goal is to do your best to help paint a permanent masterpiece in the time allotted, regardless of circumstance. What that artist or producer wants from you is to best serve a musical vision that is an audio snapshot into that artist's condition in that moment, but that is also meant to endure forever.

On a record date, your drum track, background vocal, or tambourine overdub may seem a bit inconsequential in your moment—but that's not the case! A record date deals with songs, and songs contain our culture's most memorable musical moments. Case in point: Maria Muldaur is fondly remembered for her song "Midnight at the Oasis," which was cut entirely by session musicians. They, too, are remembered, if not in name, as being a part of the result of a magic moment in time.

Similarly, producer-songwriter Linda Perry wrote and recorded "Beautiful" for Christina Aguilera, providing that pop diva with perhaps her most memorable career high and brightest musical moment. Perry played everything on this contemporary classic except drums (which was handled by Brian MacLeod) and some vintage keyboards (handled by Damon Fox). Alongside the far more visible Christina Aguilera and the widely respected Linda Perry, Brian and Damon too have made their indelible contribution to people's lives through their somewhat anonymous but highly musical contributions to this modern masterpiece. This is why the record dates are the granddaddy of all recording sessions. On a record date, you really have the ability to affect people's lives with your playing.

Home Studio Dates

There is currently a move away from world-famous independent studios with names like the Record Plant and the Hit Factory and label-owned studios like the magical Capitol Records Studios (located in its fabled circular Hollywood skyscraper) to producer, artist, and even session-musician-owned home studios. With the advent of Internet sessions, musicians are providing recorded music via these digital pathways from studios around the world to other locations continents away!

The digital audio workstation tidal wave of the past 20 years allows musical artists to produce professional recordings in their home environments. Everyone from Thom Yorke of Radiohead to Peter DiStefano (ex-Porno for Pyros) to kids at your local junior high are recording, mixing, and mastering music at home on their laptops or towers. If you're pursuing a career as a session musician, prepare yourself to be hired by anyone with a home studio for whatever service they require at a pay scale dictated by their budget. That's the current take on the professional home-recording boom, and for all of us the news is favorable. And if you, the local session musician, have a home-recording environment compatible with that singer-songwriter down the street who you thought was just a pleasant housewife, sometimes that artist will give you a hard drive containing the session(s) and let you work at home unsupervised. Wherever they happen, these home-studio recording sessions, once considered entry level and not particularly lucrative, have in recent years become important sources of income for the session musician.

Even though some professional recording opportunities are in decline, talent and tenacity are always rewarded, so don't become discouraged by changing climates and business conditions. Music will always be needed, and there will always be sessions that are sources of income.

CHAPTER 5

How Do I Become a Studio Musician?

On the journey to becoming a successful studio musician, a lot of roads lead to the same place. But the way it usually works is that someone hears and likes your playing and either hires you or refers you as a result. Here are some of the many ways it could happen.

Ways to Become a Session Musician

YOUR BAND

Your band is recording with a producer. The producer notices that you play really well and have a great feel, and he calls you to play on other records. Sometimes it might be the engineer on the session that remembers you (remember, many in-demand engineers become producers at some point). Either way, in the course of doing your own record, you show up on the radar of someone who can hire you later.

> *If you're in a band and working with a producer, really pay attention and work with him to help him make that record sound better. You're more likely to be called for another project afterwards. He might have had so much fun working with you in your band that he'll think of you for a solo artist he's working with. That's how I developed myself. I worked with Tim Palmer in London with my own band, and that's how I got the job playing with Tears for Fears. So I've developed relationships with all the producers I've worked with over the years in my own band.*
>
> Brian MacLeod

BY REFERRAL

If you have a friend who does a lot of session work who likes how you play, chances are that you'll get a referral at some point. If a player can't make a date or doesn't get on with the client, a referral from someone established will get you in the door.

> *If you're looking to get into session work as a drummer, you can't do it* [by yourself]. *You just have to play a lot of gigs and wait for the time where you get that opportunity.*
>
> Bernie Dresel

BY A CONTRACTOR

A contractor is a person that hires musicians for a gig. Most times he or she is also a musician on the session, but that doesn't always have to be. Many contractors hire musicians for a variety of gigs, not just for recording sessions. If you become a trusted insider for everyday live gigs, chances are that soon you'll be hired on a studio date as well.

BY A RECORDING

Many times an artist or a producer will hear you on a recording and want your style or sound. It's more likely you'll be called if the recording you played on was a hit, since everyone likes to use the same team or sound of something already successful. If that happens, be happy that you've been lucky twice.

> [Producer] *Patrick* [Leonard] *said, "Hey Brian, if you lived in L.A., I would use you on the records I work on." Ironically, the engineer/coproducer on that record was Bill Bottrell* [who eventually went on to produce Sheryl Crow, Michael Jackson, and Shelby Lynn], *and he said the same thing to me. So I had two top-of-the-line producers tell me that if I lived in L.A., they'd use me on their records. It became a no-brainer for me to run up to the Bay Area, pack my things in a U-Haul, and get my butt to L.A. Then it kind of expanded from there.*
>
> Brian MacLeod

BY ASSOCIATION

The old adage "All boats rise and fall with the tide" is really true. If someone within your circle of players makes it "big," they'll most likely take you with them, at least on some level. Maybe you have something unique in your sound or your feel that your player friend will remember. Maybe he just wants to help you out because you're such a cool person. Maybe it's some payback for a good deed long in the past. Doesn't matter as long as you're remembered and get the call. Once you're called for one session and do well, chances are you'll be called for another as word gets around and your résumé builds.

> *I was playing on a little "jazzual"* [a jazz casual] *with a piano player who was wired in to the TV show* Knots Landing *because he was the piano player for one of the main actors on the show, who was a singer. The piano player got us on a*

couple of episodes to be the backup band for the singer. The production people loved it, and that developed into the piano player being able to score a bunch of sessions. After that I met a few other guys and got called to play on their stuff, and finally, Jay [Chattaway] *left New York and moved out here* [Los Angeles]. *I knew him on the East Coast, so when he started working, I started working.*

Gary Solt

When I got out of school, I joined a band with a couple of older musicians [Frank Simes and Jennifer Condos] *who were pretty well known in L.A.* [and] *were touring with Don Henley at the time. Frank had a bunch of songs and was trying to get a record deal when he wasn't playing with Don. It was cool because they were much older than me—they were in their mid-30s and I was like 19—so I learned a lot from those people. I spent about five years in the band, and we did a record for Japan and Southeast Asia. When that ended around 1995, I started doing a lot of sessions and touring.*

Peter Thorn

I kept going to these parties and bashes and kept going around saying hello to the same people over and over. It got to the point that when they saw me coming, I looked familiar to them and they'd think, "He's always at these parties. He's got to be in the music business." At some point months later I'd go, "Hey, you still at Sony?" and they'd go "Yeah," and I'd pass him my card and he would pass me his and all of sudden I'm setting up meetings. That's how I did it.

Onree Gill

Now That You're There

You've got your first session—but now how do you keep them coming? First of all, here are the traits that you find in all studio musicians.

Let's go over these one by one. A studio musician

HAS GREAT CHOPS

Studio musicians are expected to be creative, be extremely versatile, and have a formidable skill set. They are usually the best musicians in town in terms of plain physical dexterity, and are able to play numerous styles convincingly. Your ability to read music will determine the type of sessions you can play on. For record dates, it's important to be able to read and transcribe lead sheets, and other types of sessions such as jingles and television and movie scores require exceptional sight-reading.

To illustrate the reading abilities of session players, here's a story about the late Tommy Tedesco, one of the most recorded guitar players ever, and a charter member of the famed Los Angeles studio band The Wrecking Crew during the '60s and '70s. Tommy was playing on a Jan & Dean date when, as a joke, singer Jan Berry turned Tommy's music upside down on the stand. The take started and Tommy proceeded to play the backwards score note for note. A frustrated Berry yanked the page off the stand and said, "You're just showing off!"

> *The town is full of guys who play great, so that's not even on the table. You have to find people who are doing what you want to do and connect with them, and when your shot comes, don't screw up! It's as simple and as cold as that.*
>
> Gary Solt

HAS GREAT GEAR

We'll go over this more in chapter 7, but having a wide variety of gear in excellent working order is a must. Having only one sound makes for a boring recording, so the wider the variety of sounds you can get or the more you can double on other instruments, the more valuable you become.

> *You've got to own the tools, or you can't go build the house.*
>
> Gary Solt

IS EASY TO WORK WITH

Your reputation among other musicians and those in our industry who make the recordings is what gets you hired and keeps you working. So if other session musicians, producers, and engineers like you as a person, like how you play, and like the feeling you bring to a session, then you're more likely to get calls for work. If you were cooped up in a submarine for a while, you'd sure want to get along with the other people in there with you. Obviously studio conditions are different than that in most ways, but the fact that you are working very closely with other players, engineers, producers, artists, and label and agency people (and who knows who else) usually means that the easier you are to work with, the more likely you'll get asked back. Playing comes first, and it always will, but if you make the people who are paying your check uncomfortable in even the slightest way, it will come back to haunt you. Smiles and a pleasant, accommodating attitude, as well as superb personal hygiene and an appropriate sense of style go really far in the session business. There are a lot of great players out there, and unless you're something unbelievably special, the people who pay the checks will always hire the easiest musicians to work with, all things being equal. No back talk, no sass, no snide remarks—nothing other than a wide smile and a "Tell me what you want" and "No Problem!" attitude.

HAS NO EGO

Everyone has their own idea of how they should sound, how the song should be played, how others should be playing it, and a host of other musical items both large and small. That all goes out the window when you're being hired to play on someone's recording. Some won't want your ideas at all, while others will listen with an open ear yet reject every opinion. You've got to have a thick skin while recording, and realize that even if the artist-producer-songwriter listens to your idea, it might not carry much weight or be acted upon. If they listen to you and actually use one of your suggestions, consider it a good day.

> *I would say an important thing for me is to serve the song at all times. Try to keep an open mind, and if someone has an idea in the room, then always let that idea be heard. If it involves you trying something different in the part that you're playing, you can't get defensive about it. You have to just let it happen, because that really goes a long way toward creating a good atmosphere in the room. When everybody drops their ego and just tries to serve the song, I find that the best idea will rise to the surface and everybody will recognize it. It's human nature to want our ideas to be the best ones, but if you can be open to others' suggestions, you can learn something and maybe do something that you wouldn't have thought of doing.*
>
> Peter Thorn

TAKES CRITICISM WELL

If you have a fragile ego, being a session musician is not for you. Except for the times when you're playing a written part, you can bet that every take is going to be examined under a microscope and picked apart with a fine-tooth comb. As difficult as that might seem, you can't take it personally, because the artist-producer-songwriter wants only what's best for the song. You may play a part with a bitchin' feel, but if the sound isn't right and doesn't mesh with the track, chances are you'll do it again. Play the same track again with a better sound, and this time the part in the bridge might not be happening—so you'll play it one more time. It's possible you'll keep playing it all day until the results meet the expectations of those in the control room that are in command (but if it takes you that long, you might not be asked to return). You can't ever fall in love with what you just played, because eventually you're going to get your heart broken.

> *You have to make it feel good. If you don't, you're going to get beat up from having to play it over and over again. I usually try to get stuff done in one or two takes. Hopefully, I can get it done in one* [laughs], *but if not, two or three is not bad.*
>
> Ricky Lawson

> *Be as flexible as you can be. Don't be stubborn and* [do] *trust the people you work with. If the engineer or producer has a suggestion, trust their advice.*
>
> Brian MacLeod

HAS PROPER STUDIO ETIQUETTE

There's a way to do things in the studio, and it differs from playing live. A studio musician's protocol exists, and you'll be expected to abide by it. We'll take a deeper look at this in chapter 10, but suffice it to say that if you like being the center of attention, then studio work may not be for you.

When the red light comes on, they're all perfectionists. Everyone is there to play their part as perfectly as possible. When the red light is off, the personalities are as diverse as you would see anywhere, but when it's time to make music, everyone's focus is 100 percent locked on the music. That's the one trait I see, always. I wouldn't say their focus is better, but their focus is aligned specifically for what that moment demands.

Gary Solt

CHAPTER 6

How Much Money Can I Make?

The vast majority of studio musicians love their work. For most, the practice of recording music is truly enjoyable because the work environment (the recording studio itself) is a comfortable and fun place to be, co-workers are most often amicable, and a spirited camaraderie usually flows in a roomful of quiet, confident smiles. On a "smoking" session in which the creative juices are flowing and everyone from the artist and producer to the musicians themselves feel the music cooking, time almost seems to stop. A real sense of satisfaction prevails when everyone knows the music is right. Even when challenges to one's technique and skill set arise, they're usually viewed as growth opportunities, so once someone has established him- or herself as a session musician, rarely do you hear them complain about the job. But studio work has always been accompanied by an air of financial uncertainty, and like those in most other career fields, we session denizens would always like to be paid more. After all, it's human nature!

The amount of money that a session musician makes can vary wildly depending on the frequency and types of gigs, and on the musician's track record. Those fortunate enough to play on bona fide hits and Grammy-winning recordings seem to get work more easily and can charge a lot more than the hitless jobbing journeymen. That being said, most gigs can be broken down into either union or nonunion gigs.

Union Gigs

The Musicians Union is called the American Federation of Musicians (AFM), which looks after recording musicians so that they are properly treated and paid. The advantage of working on a union gig is that, because all terms are fixed, you know exactly how much you'll make and how much time you'll spend on the gig. That being said, determining union rates can be somewhat of a maze. Since different scales cover different situations, rates are renegotiated every few years, and pay scales vary (though not that much) from union local to union local.

TYPES OF UNION PAY SCALES

Generally, the union pay scales for recording are broken down as follows:

Demo scale. This means that whatever you play on is used only to secure a master record deal and can't be sold commercially. This is the least expensive (to the producer) of all the scales. Demo scale is a relic from a time when having a demo was a necessity to take your project to a higher level in the business, and even though this scale still appears on the books, it has become outdated now that any recording is so easy to release commercially.

Limited-pressing scale. Another relic of the past (thanks to digital music), the limited-pressing scale allows the producer to make and sell up to 10,000 copies of anything you play on. The limited-pressing scale pays a bit more than the demo scale.

Low–budget scale. The low-budget scale was originally created to help small indie record labels that never had the large recording budgets that were typical of a major label product. The key here is that the budget needs to be submitted to the union for approval in advance before you can play on the project, but the label can sell as many copies of the product as they can.

Master-recording scale. This is the scale used to pay musicians to record a typical medium- or big-budget master recording for a major record label. It's the highest paying scale with the most perks.

Jingle scale. The jingle (commercial music) scale is a little different in that most jingle sessions are so short that everything is based on a single-hour pay with 20-minute increments. The number of jingles that can be recorded in that time period is limited to three (or three minutes of music), or else you must get paid for another session. When you play on a jingle, you get paid again for every 13-week run that the commercial airs. You also get paid if the producer takes the music bed that you played on and creates an additional commercial (called a dub fee) or a new commercial (called a conversion fee).

Motion–picture and film scales. This is a dizzying array of scales for orchestral recordings that vary depending on the size of the orchestra and budget, and on whether the performance is a "buyout" (you get paid only once, for the original performance) or you'll get paid for subsequent performances.

Typical local orchestral rates. The table on page 56 gives an idea of how much rates can vary depending on the type of session and where the session takes place. These rates do not include any mandatory union health-and-welfare or pension charges, nor do they include contracting fees, payroll taxes and fees, any federal or local taxes, doubling, cartage, travel costs, or any other associated costs. And they are approximate, because rate scales are renegotiated frequently.

Location	Scale	Hourly Rate	Additional
Los Angeles AFM (union)	motion picture scale—theatrical motion pictures	$87.31	No buyout available. Note: additional payments may be required for "new use" and "reuse" of music.
Los Angeles AFM	motion picture scale—TV film	$71.76	No buyout available. Note: additional payments may be required for "new use" and "reuse" of music.
Los Angeles AFM	low-budget theatrical film scale	$60.18	No buyout available. Entire film budget not to exceed $40,000. Notice required. Note: additional payments may be required for "new use" and "reuse" of music.
Los Angeles AFM	ultra-low-budget theatrical film scale	$51.75	No buyout available. Entire film budget not to exceed $12,000,000. Notice required. Note: additional payments may be required for "new use" and "reuse" of music.
London		$97.24	Complete buyout included
Seattle, WA		$60	Complete buyout included
Salt Lake City, UT		$55	Complete buyout included
Bulgaria		$23	Complete buyout included
Moscow		$30	Complete buyout included
Prague		$20	Complete buyout included

Fig. 6.1: Orchestral Rate Comparison

As you can see, the prices really change when you leave the union in Los Angeles for other cities, which is why so much of the orchestral recording is done overseas these days. That being said, the quality of the orchestras, studios, and recording equipment may not be equal to what can be found in L.A., which is a strong hedge against productions trying to save a little money only to find that their product isn't what they're used to.

ADDITIONAL FEES

There are other fees that you're entitled to under certain circumstances on a union date. If you're a leader, then you're always entitled to twice the scale rate regardless of what kind of session and which rate scale you're using.

If you double on a second instrument during the session, you will make an additional 20 to 30 percent (depending on the type of session and scale), and an extra 15 to 20 percent for each additional instrument played after that.

In some cases you may even get an additional bit for cartage of large instruments: for example, $12 for cello, baritone sax, bass sax, contrabass clarinet, tuba, drums, marimba, chimes, accordion, Cordovox, and each amplifier, and $30 for harp, keyboard, tympani, vibraphone, and acoustic bass.

There are other session fees paid to you on a union date that might not show up in your pocket right away. Besides the hourly scale amount, the producer will also contribute another 12 percent or so to your union pension fund, an additional 3 percent to your health-and-welfare fund, and, in some cases, 4 percent more to a vacation fund.

As stated before, the scales and rates are subject to change every few years, so it's best to check with your union local to find out exactly what those rates are today. We've given you just a thumbnail of the detail here, so check for all the particulars that might apply to your specific session well in advance of when you get there, and make sure that the session leader or contractor (who files the paperwork) is on the same page as you.

Musicians who play on film and TV sessions that yield music-to-picture have another source of revenue from the

Film Musicians Secondary Market Fund. This fund provides annual payments to musicians listed as performers on soundtracks for films and TV shows. It's a generalized fund in that the more soundtrack work you do, the more you're paid, so the "top dogs" get the biggest checks. Economic climates are always changing and money is always welcome, so if you do play on a legitimate film or TV date, more than likely the production company is registered with this organization and you'll see monies in addition to your session fees. These checks always seem to come when most needed, and unexpected funds (nicknamed "mailbox money") are always most welcome!

Here's a list of the union locals and Websites of the major U.S. media centers:

New York City Local 802; local802afm.org

Los Angles Local 47; promusic47.org

Nashville Local 257; afm257.org

Chicago Local 10-208; cfm10208.com

Nonunion Gigs

Now as anyone who has ever played club and bar gigs knows, the union doesn't help you much in most of those situations. While the union tries to set pay standards, if you want to work, you either take what a club owner is willing to give you or you stay home. This is somewhat the case with nonunion recording gigs as well. If you're not working on a Wednesday afternoon and you get a call to do a two-hour session for $100 "off-the-books," you'll most likely take it. While the union frowns on and even forbids such actions, it's a fact of studio life these days that if you want to work, you'll take whatever's offered.

Even the most well-known players might do a quick favor for a hundred bucks if the time is short, the hassle is small, and you can work around their schedule. So what's the going rate? It depends upon where you're based, what the competition is like, and what your stature is in the session community. And you may get paid either by the song or by the hour, or be given a flat rate for the session.

SET YOUR RATES

Whether it's a demo for a local singer-songwriter that's cut in a small-town garage studio, or you're being flown first-class to London to play on Tina Turner's comeback with a world-class producer in a world-class studio (and we've had both experiences in just the past few years!), you're best served to *mentally* set your own rates, hoping that your prospective employers—producers, artists, managers, and contractors—accept it graciously. On most recording dates, the paymaster (the person who controls the purse strings and therefore sets the musicians' pay rates) will have a figure in mind and will offer that up during the initial discussion. If they don't, *ask what they have in mind first!* Their figure may be higher than what you would first offer up. If the rate offered doesn't meet what you have in mind, negotiate from there appropriately. Some studio musicians also require a 50 percent "up-front" deposit to lock down the session. Those who ask for it get it about half the time, but you'll never get it if you don't ask.

Remember that session musicians are hired hands who, unlike members of bands, are generally paid a flat fee for a recording session and therefore don't benefit from any publishing royalties unless they've contributed to the songwriting process. Though they are entitled to performance royalties in certain situations, these tend to be far lower than the songwriting royalties. Infrequently, effective negotiations can sometimes involve "points" (a percentage of CD sales or other revenues), but this is rare and most unlikely unless you're willing to tour and promote the product that your artistry helps create.

YOUR INVOICE

Whether you're getting $100 for a backyard demo or $1,500 a day to help create Thom Yorke's next solo masterpiece, you have to generate a simple invoice in order to get paid.

During your rate negotiations, make sure to always get contact information for whoever will be paying you, then prepare and send an invoice (most often by email) immediately upon the session's completion. Make sure that you keep accurate records of date, time, instruments played, and songs recorded, and keep duplicates of these records (both on your laptop's calendar program and as a hard copy) just in case. Keeping good records is really important because facts can be forgotten and invoices lost, so the more you have to confirm what you did on the session, the easier it is to resolve any pay issues that may arise later.

GETTING PAID

Established session musicians are used to receiving two basic forms of payment: direct money (either cash or check) straight into their pockets from their employers or their accounting firms, and payment through the Musicians Union and its ancillary payroll companies.

To offer insight, let's look at the money flow for a session (See Fig. 6.2 A Typical Pay Stub). Here's a good nonmainstream example of how one gets paid to record.

Kellii Scott, an established L.A.-based rock drummer and songwriter, started getting more and more session work after 20 years in Los Angeles. Known best for his contributions to Liquid Jesus and Failure, two of L.A.'s most influential and groundbreaking late-'80s indie bands, Kellii welcomed the switch from touring to studio work, as it keeps him off the road and in town to pursue other interests. Most, if not all, of his studio bookings came and still come from direct artist and manager referrals, and he has *never once* been paid through the union for a session! Only when he appeared on television did he get paid through the union. Kellii wasn't even paid through the Los Angeles Local 47 Chapter of the Musicians Union for his contributions to the three major-label releases by his aforementioned bands, since both bands took control of their recording advances and paid themselves (a not-so-rare occurrence these days). This DIY approach influences Kellii's thinking to this day.

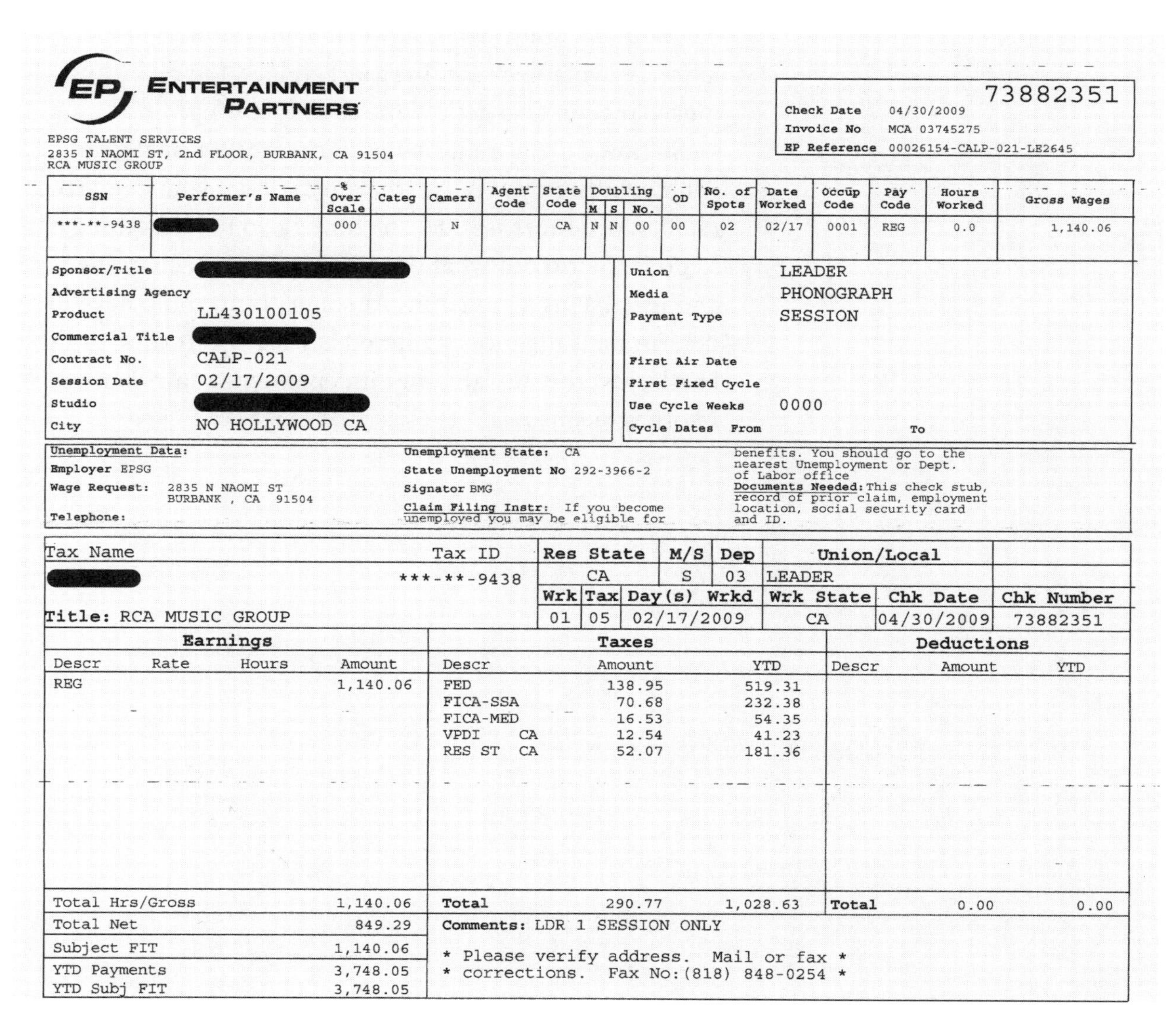

EP ENTERTAINMENT PARTNERS

EPSG TALENT SERVICES
2835 N NAOMI ST, 2nd FLOOR, BURBANK, CA 91504
RCA MUSIC GROUP

73882351
Check Date 04/30/2009
Invoice No MCA 03745275
EP Reference 00026154-CALP-021-LE2645

SSN	Performer's Name	% Over Scale	Categ	Camera	Agent Code	State Code	Doubling M	Doubling S	Doubling No.	OD	No. of Spots	Date Worked	Occup Code	Pay Code	Hours Worked	Gross Wages
***-**-9438		000		N		CA	N	N	00	00	02	02/17	0001	REG	0.0	1,140.06

Sponsor/Title
Advertising Agency
Product LL430100105
Commercial Title
Contract No. CALP-021
Session Date 02/17/2009
Studio
City NO HOLLYWOOD CA

Union LEADER
Media PHONOGRAPH
Payment Type SESSION
First Air Date
First Fixed Cycle
Use Cycle Weeks 0000
Cycle Dates From To

Unemployment Data:
Employer EPSG
Wage Request: 2835 N NAOMI ST
BURBANK , CA 91504
Telephone:

Unemployment State: CA
State Unemployment No 292-3966-2
Signator BMG
Claim Filing Instr: If you become unemployed you may be eligible for benefits. You should go to the nearest Unemployment or Dept. of Labor office
Documents Needed: This check stub, record of prior claim, employment location, social security card and ID.

Tax Name	Tax ID	Res State	M/S	Dep	Union/Local
	***-**-9438	CA	S	03	LEADER

Title: RCA MUSIC GROUP

Wrk	Tax	Day(s) Wrkd	Wrk State	Chk Date	Chk Number
01	05	02/17/2009	CA	04/30/2009	73882351

Earnings

Descr	Rate	Hours	Amount
REG			1,140.06

Taxes

Descr	Amount	YTD
FED	138.95	519.31
FICA-SSA	70.68	232.38
FICA-MED	16.53	54.35
VPDI CA	12.54	41.23
RES ST CA	52.07	181.36
Total	290.77	1,028.63

Deductions

Descr	Amount	YTD
Total	0.00	0.00

Total Hrs/Gross	1,140.06
Total Net	849.29
Subject FIT	1,140.06
YTD Payments	3,748.05
YTD Subj FIT	3,748.05

Comments: LDR 1 SESSION ONLY

* Please verify address. Mail or fax *
* corrections. Fax No:(818) 848-0254 *

Fig. 6.2: A Sample Session Invoice

When asked to record, like most contemporary session musicians, Kellii establishes a rate based on many factors, since today's session musicians are subjected to a very broad range of pay scales. With the decline of major-label projects and the rise of home studios, even in the major recording centers, studio musicians find themselves working for the widest range of rates since Edison invented the cylinder recorder! True, established "greats" with track records three decades long and many Grammys deep can still command rates as high as $2,000 to $5,000 per day, and "per song" rates between $500 and $2,500. But in today's volatile recording marketplace, top recording musicians can also get as *little* as $100 a song!

So how do you gauge what to charge? Regardless of what you think you're worth, you can't get your preferred rate if a producer just doesn't have it; so the best thing to do is to find out what your competition is charging and use that as a guideline. At some point, you'll have to determine if the money offered is worth your time or the hassle, just the way all other independent contractors do in other businesses.

CHAPTER 7

What Equipment Do I Bring to a Session?

Having the right equipment is a big part of being a session musician. For rhythm section musicians, the days are gone when you can show up with the bare minimum to get the job done. Sure, that can happen from time to time (like on a spec date), but for the most part you're expected to show up with gear that will provide at least a reasonable variety of sounds. Many dates will require you to bring as much of your gear as possible in the unlikely event that some piece of it might be needed. While it sounds like a drag to carry all that gear around, that's a big part of the gig. It's also why cartage companies exist. Some sessions provide additional funds for cartage, but nowadays most studio musicians provide transportation for their gear, although exceptions are made for drummers. In major recording centers like New York, London, and Los Angeles, companies like drum luminary Gersh Gershunoff's Drum Fetish and Ross Garfield's Drum Doctors provide cartage, maintenance, tunings, and rentals specifically for L.A.'s top session drummers.

Different Gear for Different Jobs

It's been stated many times before in this book, but playing a gig is distinctly different from playing at a recording session. What works on a gig won't always translate to the studio, either playing-wise or gear-wise. You choose your gear for a live gig based on its versatility, durability, and general ruggedness. The only thing that counts in the studio is the sound.

While one size might fit all on a gig, it will usually make for a boring recording, especially if you're recording more than one part or playing on more than one song. The sound issue doesn't necessarily apply if you're playing on a demo (where the performance is most important), but if you're playing most other serious recording dates, then gear makes a profound difference. You should make every effort to get a variety of the best-sounding gear, because it will not only make you sound better but will also increase the demand for your services.

Well-Maintained Equipment Required

Having well-maintained gear is essential for the musician who's serious about doing studio work. Everything is expected to work perfectly, with no tuning problems, no extraneous noises, and no intermittents (unexplainable deviations in sonic character). Not only does your gear have to work, but it also has to be in tip-top condition. The better everything works and sounds, the better the recording will sound and the better you'll look in the eyes of the people around you in the studio.

If you're a drummer, this means at minimum that you have new drumheads on all drums, your drums are in tune, and the pedals are oiled so they don't squeak. If you're a guitar- or bass player, it means your instrument is properly intonated so it plays in tune anywhere on the neck, none of your cables are crackling, and your amp (if you're using one) doesn't buzz or hum (and make sure your tuner is working, too!). If you're a keyboard player, you must know your way around each keyboard so well that you can easily get to any sound that's requested; further, as with guitar and bass players, your gear and cables should work flawlessly. If you're a horn player, it means that none of your valves or keys stick, and no extraneous noises come from the instrument. Like everyone else, string players should show up to a session with their best-sounding instrument(s) for that particular application.

And regardless of which instrument you play, make sure that you can set everything up quickly and that you cause as close to zero hassle to anybody, whether technically or personally.

These are the things that are not only expected but also required to even get in the game. Your instruments must sound great, first and foremost.

The Comfort Factor

Make sure that you are comfortable with your gear. If you just bought a new instrument, don't break it out on the session until if feels comfortable in your hands and you're aware of its capabilities and limitations. Remember that to be at your best, your playing must flow easily and effortlessly, and this can't happen if you're fighting your instrument for any reason.

The comfort factor also extends to the capabilities of an instrument. Until you're familiar with everything it can do as well as with its limitations, it's best to leave it at home or in its case (you might be able to break it out if you're into the experimental phase and you explain that you don't have your chops together on it). No one wants to hear you experimenting on the job, especially if it's seen as wasting time.

Tailor What You Bring

Now say you're lucky enough to have a gigantic collection of excellent-sounding instruments. Should you bring them to every session? That depends. Most players will get a feel for the session first, and then bring the gear that will fulfill the producer-specific requests. Even if it looks as though only one type of sound might be required, it's best to bring along a few options, just in case there's time to experiment or the producer changes his mind midsession.

> *Since I have the luxury of knowing the composer, he usually calls me and tells me what he wants. If it's someone that I don't know, I usually try to get some indication up front of what they'll need. If it sounds like the guy doesn't have a clue, then I'll get a cartage guy to take everything I own to the studio. If it's a session that I do for Jay* [composer Jay Chattaway], *it's usually some sort of electric guitar with effects, steel-string acoustic guitar, and nylon-string guitar. I've also played a lot of Dobro and banjo for him, as well as a little mandolin and baritone guitar.*
>
> Gary Solt

> *I don't bring much any more because if I'm working at* [producer/writer] *Linda Perry's, she has so much stuff there that it's sort of fun to go and just pick through the stuff that's there.* [Bobby Owsinski's note: Linda has the most fantastic collection of vintage gear I've ever seen in a studio, and I've been in hundreds of studios all over the world.] *If I am going to do a session on my own and I need to bring something, I'll bring the TC pedalboard and either a 1×12 or a 2×12 speaker cabinet with these little heads built by Suhr called Badgers; there's one that's 18 watts and another that's 30 watts. I really like them*

because they're versatile and sound great with pedals. For guitars, I'll try to bring a Les Paul, a Strat, a Tele, and maybe one acoustic.

Peter Thorn

If a producer is uncertain what he wants, then it's time to pack it all up and call the cartage company. Many players will bring their entire arsenal, even if there's only a remote possibility that a piece of gear might be needed, the school of thought being that you bring it anyway because you can bet it'll be the one piece that will hold everything up if you don't.

Other players bring much more gear than they'll use because that's part of the charm, the "oooh, aahh" factor, of hiring them. One thing's for sure, if you don't know what you're going to be doing or where the music is going to go, that one extra piece that you bring could make all the difference—so it's better to have it with you.

Generally, I try to get a heads-up from the producer or the producer's assistant as to what kind of song we're doing and what he wants it to sound like. Like if he says they're doing something that's a retro-'70s Led Zeppelin type of thing, then I know to bring my 26" kick and an old Radio King snare. If he says that it's a midtempo R&B kind of thing, then I'll know to bring my 20" or 22" kick. So I try to get as much information from the producer before the session and find out as much about the artist, the specific band, and the direction of the music.

Brian MacLeod

Here's the reality of today, at least with the stuff that I do. There are always budget considerations, so I generally bring six [snare drums]. *I could bring 30 snares, but then the cartage bill goes up and, to be honest, you're usually way covered with the six snares because no one is ever asking*

"What else you got?" past that. So I bring three different sizes of wood and three different sizes of metal drums. That's not including if I go to do an orchestral date, where I'd bring about eight different orchestral snares.

Bernie Dresel

First I'll ask if there's anything in particular they need me to do. They might say, "Just bring your congas and timbales," or "Bring your timpani," so that makes it pretty simple. If there's nothing in particular that I'm asked to bring, I end up bringing all my gear, which is a truckload of stuff.

Ronnie Ciago

Is Vintage Gear Necessary?

No one has ever said that you needed to own all the most desirable vintage gear to get a studio gig, but the most desirable gear does seem to have a way of sounding the best on a recording. That being said, even if you own a '57 Les Paul or a '62 P-Bass or a '72 Black Beauty snare or an original Mini-Moog, if it doesn't sound good or has an operating problem, you're much better off with something that's newer that actually works well. Just because an instrument is worth a lot of money doesn't necessarily mean that it sounds good or that it's going to work on a session.

But the fact of the matter is that a lot of the revered vintage instruments are revered because they do sound very good for recording, providing they're in top working order. Ever wonder why a vintage Les Paul or Strat or P-Bass, or a Plexi Marshall or 1959 Fender Bassman, or a 1960s Ludwig drum kit or Hammond B-3 or Mellotron are so coveted that they've all been reissued to be as similar to the original as possible? It's the sound, of course, and using one of these items can make you instantly get the sound that the producer is looking for and help your part fit better in the track. That's why you always see what seems to be some of the same gear from concert to concert, video to video, and article to article. Studio players learn what makes them sound their best, and certain instruments, amplifiers, effects, and accessory brands and models are just tried and true (when properly maintained, of course).

That's not to say that inexpensive gear isn't worth having, too. If it has a unique sound, it can have a place in a session! In reality, musical gear in any price range is a far better buy than it's ever been. In fact since about 1985 or so, it's become really difficult to purchase something that doesn't perform at a reasonably high level of quality. Automated manufacturing has driven prices down and raised quality up in a way we never could have imagined in the '50s, '60s, or '70s. That being said, the homogenization of manufacturing has also taken what might be called the "character" out of most of today's low-cost instruments, because they're all pretty much exactly the same.

One of the reasons that vintage gear is such a draw is that it's all a little different from instrument to instrument. That's because much of it was handmade, and the tolerances were much broader than they are now. As a result, sometimes a drift in tolerance because of human error (an instrument constructed on Monday morning or on Friday before quitting time, for example) resulted in magic that's still difficult to duplicate. And the fact that wood and metal that are aged can't help but have a different sound than something off the shelf that's new.

Okay, so what's tried and true that usually works? Here's a quick and very incomplete list of instruments, amps, and accessories that are prized for their sound (and the older they get, for their collectibility, too). We're not recommending that you run out and buy any of these, but it's worth knowing exactly why something is so sought after. If you get a chance to try one of these for just a couple of minutes, it'll give you a good reference point as to why they're so desirable.

GUITARS

Fender Telecaster (the '52 reissue is a good example of the Tele at its best)

Fender Telecaster Deluxe or Custom (with humbucking pickups)

Fender Stratocaster especially the models from 1957 through 1960)

Gibson Les Paul Standard (The 1957 to 1959 models are the most expensive instruments on the vintage market today.)

Gibson Les Paul "Goldtop" (the original Les Paul with a single-coil pickup instead of a humbucker)

Gibson Les Paul Junior (an entry-level Les Paul used by Billy Joe Armstrong and Leslie West)

Gibson Firebird (used by Johnny Winter)

Gibson Les Paul Special (with smaller humbuckers—extensively used by Pete Townsend during the '70s)

Gretsch 6120 (this hollow-body Chet Atkins-style guitar was used on a variety of huge hits, including The Who's "Won't Get Fooled Again")

Gretsch Silver Jet

Rickenbacker 360 (the guitar responsible for the sound of the British Invasion)

Rickenbacker 360-12 (a 12-string version of the 360)

Gibson ES-335 (the "dot neck" versions that use simple dots for position markers are the most desirable on the vintage market)

Epiphone Casino (used by John Lennon)

Martin D-28 (an acoustic standard)

Gibson J-45 (an acoustic standard)

Guild F412 (the only acoustic built from the ground up as a 12-string)

Coral/Dano Electric Sitar

GUITAR AMPLIFIERS

1959 Fender Bassman (some think this is the best guitar amp ever made!)

Any tweed-covered Fender

Any brown-covered Fender

Any blackface Fender (has a black control panel, hence the name)

Deluxe Reverb (a circuit design different from most Fenders makes it sound different when overdriven)

Marshall Plexi (has a control panel made out of Plexiglas, hence the name)

Marshall JMP head with model 1960 cabinet

Marshall 1968 Super Lead head

Marshall JTM-45 combo

Mesa/Boogie Mark II

Hiwatt Custom 100

Vox AC30 Top Boost (has extra factory-installed circuitry that gives it more overdrive)

Roland Jazz Chorus 120

BASSES

Fender Jazz Bass ('60s, '70s, even '80s)

Fender Precision Bass ('60s, '70s, even '80s)

Music Man StingRay

Rickenbacker 4001

Danelectro Longhorn

Höfner Beatle bass

Gibson EB-2 or 3

BASS AMPS

Ampeg B15A (the standard for the studio)

Ampeg SVT (the standard for touring)

Acoustic 360 (the sound of the '70s)

PEDALS

Fuzz Face (the original Arbiter version)

Electro-Harmonix Big Muff Pi

Ibanez Tube Screamer (the older TS-808 and TS9s are the most desirable for their sound)

Pro Co Rat

Octavia (the Roger Mayer version)

MXR Dyna Comp

Mu-Tron III (the Musitronics version)

Boss CE-1 Chorus Ensemble

MXR Phase 90

Uni-Vibe (the original Univox model)

Vox V847 Wah (the original, and some say still the best)

Cry Baby Wah

Electro-Harmonix Deluxe Memory Man

Digitech Whammy Pitch Effect

Maestro Tube Echoplex

Roland RE-101 Space Echo

KEYBOARDS

Hammond B-3 (or A-3 or C-3—same electronics, different cabinet) with either a Leslie 122, 145, or 147 (basically the same except for cabinet size and connecting cable)

Wurlitzer Model 120 or 200 electric piano

Fender Rhodes Stage 88 or Suitcase 73 electric piano

Hohner D6 Clavinet

Minimoog

DRUMS

Gretsch "Round Badge" (on the logo) kit ('50s/'60s)

Ludwig "Keystone Badge" kit ('60s)

Gretsch "Stop Sign Badge" kit ('70s)

Ludwig Supraphonic 6½-inch snare drum

Ludwig Black Beauty snare drum ('70s)

Ludwig Acrolite snare drum

Noble & Cooley 5½-inch maple snare drum

The broad reach of contemporary, vintage, and boutique gear that is appropriate for recording sessions runs from affordable entry-level instruments and pedals to the most expensive musical equipment on the planet. Most often you get what you pay for, and the pricier pieces sound best. There are exceptions—like that time when the cheap no-name snare you bought at a yard sale for $20 and accidentally left in your car the night before your first session with a huge producer really made a track come alive—so it's best to establish and maintain the best instrument and effects collection you can. Most session musicians are gear hoarders who rarely sell anything, fearing the day when a producer asks them, "Hey, you don't happen to have a cheesy '80s Casio keyboard you could bring along, now do ya?!"

CHAPTER 8

Before the Session Begins

Since most session work is booked through phone contact, the session really begins when you get the call from the contractor, producer, artist, engineer, or even the artist's management company.

Your outgoing voice-mail greeting is most often what makes your first impression with prospective employers, so if you're not available to take the call, be sure your message is understandable, pleasant, and professional. When you do speak on the phone to a prospective employer, make sure your phone demeanor is professional but friendly.

If you have a personal Website, a Facebook page, or a MySpace page, make certain that it represents you as a recording musician first and foremost. If you are serious about your career as a session musician, a good rule of thumb is to ask yourself, "Does this Web portal present me in the best possible manner to the people who might want to hire me for session work?"

Here's a list of questions to ask about the session so that you can be as prepared as possible for the session's downbeat.

What Kind of Session Is It?

You want to find out if you're going to be playing on a movie or television cue, a record date, a demo, or something more exotic like a television or music-video shoot or a live stream over the Internet. Again, this information tells you what kind of gear to bring and approximately how long the session will take. It also tells you if you'll be playing with other musicians or doing an overdub by yourself.

Who's the Artist (if it's a record date)?

You've got to have this information to help you determine the kind of music that you have to prepare for, so it helps if you familiarize yourself with the artists and their material. Again, this information determines the gear you might pack for the session, but it can also provide some useful tidbits that might come into use later during the session. For example, if you get called to do an overdub on a song for the highly anticipated next release by someone like PJ Harvey, you might want to do a little research to hear what she's been up to lately. both musically and personally. If you visit her Website and read that she's playing piano instead of guitar on her current recordings, or listening to a lot of Indian ragas, that will definitely help you later during the session, both musically and personally.

What Type of Music Will Be Recorded?

If you haven't gotten a hint by now after you've been told about the artist, now's the time to ask. Once again, the type of music might determine what gear you bring. For example, if you're booked on a date with Ziggy Marley and you've never listened to or played much reggae, its good to know as much about what you're getting into so you can prepare accordingly to best serve the situation. Keep in mind that Ziggy's producer may have hired you with the full knowledge of your unfamiliarity with reggae and may be looking for a fresh approach, so it's your job to bring exactly that. They may have seen you play live or heard something you've recorded and want your contribution and your "vibe" in their context.

What Direction Will the Music Go In?

This determines the subgenre of the music and refines your choice of gear even more. Even though you've been told it's a rock date, for instance, there's a big difference between rockabilly and metal, so it's best to get an idea of which subgenre you'll be working in. On a country date, there's a big difference between modern and traditional, and if it's a jazz date, there's a huge difference between "smooth" and "straight ahead."

If you have the time, it's also a good idea to listen to that subgenre before the date. If you are unfamiliar with the style of music, ask for help from friends or professional associates who play that music well. Whether it's a contemporary R&B date or a traditional bluegrass recording session, try to find out as much as you can about what they're going for. Specifics really help you to do your best work for them.

Who's the Producer?

The answer to this question can tell you a lot of things. Some producers take a lot more time than others, so if you know who the producer is, you'll know to adjust your schedule accordingly in case the session goes longer than planned. Some producers are more demanding than others, which will take more time as well. Some producers expect you to use their gear, and others depend on you to bring everything. Familiarize yourself with the producer's catalogue and listen to some recent recordings. If he or she is established, read their interviews in technical magazines beforehand so that you glean some insight into their studio techniques and methods of working.

Which Studio Is Being Used?

Not only is this a basic piece of information so you know where to go to, but it also will tell you whether you'll have to bring additional equipment. For instance, the studio might have headphones that you find uncomfortable, so you'll know to bring your own. Or it might have the best vintage amplifier, keyboard, or drum collection around, so you might not have to bring yours. Always call to see if the gear they have that you wish to use is available for your session. The session also might be at the producer's or artist's personal studio, which could mean that your own microphone or DI that you know sounds great might work better than what they have available.

Also, find out everything you need to know in advance about parking and getting your equipment into the recording environment. You may be playing in a large room that takes five or ten minutes to move all your gear into, or you may be walking straight from the street into a control room. Regardless, it's best to know as much as you can about the environment you'll be going to.

What Time Does the Session Begin?

Usually when a producer tells you the session starts at, for instance, 2 p.m., he or she means that that's when everyone should be set up and ready to play. Sometimes you'll be told something a little more vague, like "We're all getting there at 2 p.m." Does that mean everyone is getting there at 2 p.m. to set up, or is it the downbeat time? Make certain that you know for sure, and ask if the time given is the downbeat time or the load-in time. Everyone likes the session player who is relaxed and set up to play a half hour to 15 minutes before downbeat.

How Long Do You Expect the Session to Last?

This information will tell you if the client has some unrealistic expectations of you. If he says that he wants you to play on five songs but thinks it should take you only about an hour, now is the time to discuss how realistic that estimate really is. It could work the other way too: if the producer says he wants you for five hours for one song, that could mean a lot of overdubs, which might in turn require that you bring some additional gear.

How Many Songs or Cues Will Be Recorded?

This question not only gives you an idea about how much time the session could take, but also what type of equipment to bring. If you're told that you might be working on five songs, you'll know to bring a lot more gear to be ready to record them all (since different sounds might be required) than you would if you were specifically asked to bring certain gear for one song.

Who Are the Other Musicians on the Session?

When recording with an ensemble, it always helps to know if you're familiar with the other players, or you're walking in to a situation with new faces, which could be a bit colder than usual. If you know the players and have played with them before, the session will probably go faster since there's already some degree of tight playing between all of you. Also, it's a good idea to call your fellow sessionmates to let them know that you're on the upcoming session, and to find out if they have any additional info about it. Camaraderie goes a long way and can really help to establish a positive vibe in the studio.

What Is Expected of Me?

This question drills down even further than the others you've already asked, so that you can gauge both the time commitment and the necessary gear to bring. If you're a guitar player, for example, you could be told either that you'll be needed for only a couple of acoustic rhythm guitar part overdubs or that you'll be doing something like laying down basic tracks with a few other players. Given the information, you'll know if you should set up a few acoustic guitars when you get there, or just your regular electric setup. If you're a sax player and they tell you to bring your alto for a solo, you're already in that headspace when it's time to record.

Is There Any Particular Sound That's Desired?

Again, the answer to this question determines the gear you bring. If you're a guitar player and you're asked for a Smashing Pumpkins sort of sound, that'll tell you to bring along all your pedals and a modern amp like a Mesa/Boogie or a Diesel. If it's a Zeppelin sound they're going for, you'll know to bring either a Les Paul/Marshall or Telecaster/Supro setup (you're going to ask which one, right?). If you're a drummer and you're asked for a hip-hop sound, then you might bring a 20" kick drum that's tuned low. But if you're asked for a pop sound, you'd bring a 22" with a hole in the front head.

Are There Any Particular Instruments, Amps, or Effects to Be Used?

Many times the producer or artist has a specific sound in mind, either because they've heard it from you before or they just expect it from you. "Bring your Strat," "Bring your Black Beauty [snare]," "Bring your bari," or "Bring your white P-bass" tells you not only what to bring but also exactly what to set up to track with first.

How Much Are You Being Paid?

Find out how much you will be paid immediately. Don't wait until you get to the session, or even worse, when the session is over. Find out now how much the gig pays and if it's union or nonunion. If the price is not to your liking, you might compensate for a lower price by asking the producer to pay for your cartage, or ask if you can bring a limited amount of gear instead of your usual arsenal.

Yet another way to negotiate a more favorable rate is by offering to do the track at your home studio if it's just an overdub. Many of the more successful studio musicians are now doing sessions at their home facilities at reduced rates. This is a big advantage for the session musician in that you don't have to haul any gear, and you can make your own hours, usually working alone but offering one "revision" session. If you can play what you hear and feel on the track at your convenience, then charge your lowest rate. If the producer or artist attends the session, your rate should be a bit higher. Be aware that if you're just starting in the session business, this probably isn't an option, but it's something to shoot for after you build a solid reputation.

Take Care of Your Individual Needs

If you find that the session is expected to last more than four to six hours, it's appropriate to ask if there will be a break for a meal and how long you'll get.

CHAPTER 9

Session Musician 101

Now we get to the fundamentals of being a studio musician, which mostly reside within the player. You can have the best gear and the best contacts, have a winning personality, and be a joy to be around. But if you don't have the chops, feel, musicality, and mind-set that contribute to making a great musical product, you're probably not ready for this kind of work yet. That's not to say that you can't get there, but you have to know what's expected of you first.

> *There are many qualities: great ears, focus, dedication, ideas. It's a special breed of player. You have to bring a lot more than just your facility on your instrument to the date.*
>
> Leland Sklar

Your Roots

A recording session begins long before someone presses the Record button. In your journey as a session musician, you bring the sum total of all of life's experiences into every recording occurrence. Everything you've ever experienced comes up from your heart and soul, through your brain and ears, out of your fingers, feet, or mouth onto the recording medium. Every hour spent practicing scales, and every moment spent laughing or crying may eventually manifest in your recording work. As a session musician, you bring your whole person to a session: the musician, the personality, the artist, the diplomat, the follower, (sometimes) the leader, the consummate professional, the instrumental or vocal master. The goal is to be not only the best musician or singer you can be, but also the best *you* that you can be so that every recording session is a winner for you and all others involved.

Your Mind-Set

When you're playing live, it's really easy to get up for certain gigs, and be a little slacker on others. If you know that you'll be playing in front of a lot of people or someone who can help advance your career, it charges you up a bit. We'd all like to say that each gig is just as important as the next, but we all know that's not the case for the most part.

Playing in the studio is another notion entirely. Each session is as important as the next, because you are recording music that can last a lifetime. It will live far past when you've left the studio, so each note you play has to count. Playing a session requires your utmost focus, concentration, and ability to summon that magic from deep inside of you. You must be "on" at every moment.

> *Your focus must be aligned specifically for what that moment demands.*
>
> Gary Solt

> *Be in the moment, and that does not mean play everything you know.*
>
> Charlie Drayton

As a result, most studio musicians approach every session, whether it's in somebody's little cramped studio with Pro Tools LE or in a multi-million-dollar facility, the same as if it were at Abbey Road with the two surviving Beatles recording their comeback record. They're all equally important, and you have to be as enthusiastic and excited about coming over to somebody's house for $50 as you are for a triple-scale record date. As a result, artists, producers, and other musicians will sense that enthusiasm and excitement and will want you to play on their sessions as a result.

Your Musicality: Ears, Chops, and Feel

Studio musicians are known for their musicality, which consists of their ears, chops, feel, and judgment. Session players have enough experience to know what to play and when to play it. They know how to best interact with the artist, other musicians, the engineer, and the producer to make the session the most efficient and fun. They have an innate feel about how to make you and your song sound great. Let's take a look at some of the musicality attributes that you'll need.

YOUR CHOPS

Studio musicians are expected to be creative and extremely versatile, and have a formidable skill set. They're usually the best players in town. Overall, the session musician is playing to a recording medium where there is little or no entertaining involved. Playing live is all about entertainment, and finesse gives way to pleasing the crowd and experiencing the heat of the moment. The same musician will come from a different place in the studio and will need to utilize finesse and restraint to create a feel that's different from the one when playing live. And there is a completely different set of challenges on a session. Live music terminates in the air and is a series of snapshot moments. Sessions can be seen as opportunities to create musical "building blocks" that terminate on recorded media and are meant to be frozen in time forever. That's why session musicians fare just as well in the live idiom as everyone else. Sadly, the same cannot be said for the majority of musicians who cull most of their experience playing live.

> *Some great live players don't do well in sessions because of the precision required. Live you can play a little looser, enjoy yourself, and have fun. If you hit a flam or misfinger a couple of notes by accident, nobody's going to really care. In the studio you have to be precise, and everything has to be almost perfect.*
>
> Onree Gill

YOUR TECHNIQUE: PURITY, NOT PERFECTION

Successful session musicians all have an innate feel for their instruments. Their actual technique may not be textbook perfect, but they all have a way of sounding great when they play. Studio musicians know how to make their instruments sound "right" for the song, cue, or jingle. They know just which axe to use and are capable of responding to direction in a way that yields audible results that are more than pleasing to the ears of producers, engineers, and artists. Session players are also remarkably consistent in that they can play a part many times over without losing the fire or feel. There's a zone all session players strive for, where they're hitting the note and the groove just right and are capable of sustaining that moment and repeating a performance as many times as it takes until that voice from the control says, "We got it! Excellent!"

YOUR READING

Your ability to read music will determine the type of sessions you can play on. For record dates, the ability to read and transcribe lead sheets is essential, and many other types of sessions, such as jingles and television and movie scores, require expert sight-reading.

YOUR EARS

Among the most important qualities one needs to have to be a successful studio musician is what's known as "big ears." Having big ears is another phrase for having the ability to listen deep into the track to dissect parts, rhythms, and harmonies. Just like with your sight-reading, you have to work on your ear-training and transcription skills every day. When there is no written part, players are expected to quickly learn a part by ear. You don't want to be caught "out on a limb," unable to manifest a part on your instrument because you can't hear it.

When this does happen, it's only because the part is outside your musical language. Don't panic. It's important not to allow nerves or fear to overcome your connection with your inner ear. Ask to hear the part slowly, and sing along with it until what comes out of your mouth matches what's coming out of the speakers note for note. Try tapping out the rhythm, too. If you can do both of these operations but you still can't play the part, then it surpasses your physical abilities on your instrument. This is where the boys and girls are separated from the men and women. If you can sing it, then that means you musically understand the part. But if you still can't play it, you just don't have the chops yet. On most professional recording sessions—and most particularly on jingle, film, TV, and record dates there's little or no time to practice or get the part together. It can be a very unforgiving environment. But there's hope!

Even the best players sometimes have to take a minute or two to get a part under their fingers. Even the best sight-reading session singers sometimes need time to work things out. A good leader on any recording date will create a studio environment that is nurturing and creative, since all of us play best in low-stress, drama-free environments. If a player is having a hard time with a part, a few moments can usually be spent to work things out.

YOUR FEEL

Your "feel" is how you react to the groove of the song. *All* good music, regardless of whether it's rock, jazz, classical, rap, or some new alien space music that we haven't heard yet, has a strong groove. You always hear about "the groove," but what is it?

> The Groove is the Pulse of the Song
> and How the Instruments
> Dynamically Breathe with It.

To your audience, the groove is an enjoyable rhythm that makes even the people that can't dance want to get up and shake their booty. And while the concept of the groove is subjective, the idea is well understood by experienced musicians at a practical, intuitive level. Funk and Latin musicians refer to the groove as the sense of being "in the pocket," while jazz players refer to the groove as the sense that a song is really "cooking" or "swinging."

A common misconception of a groove is that it must have perfect time. *A groove is created by tension against even time.* That means that time doesn't have to be perfect, *just even*, and all performances don't have to have the same amount of evenness. In fact, timing that's too even or perfect, makes the groove feel stiff. This is why perfect quantization of parts and lining up every drum hit in a workstation when you're recording frequently takes the life out of a song. It's too perfect because there's no tension. *It's lost its groove.*

> *The groove can start from any element. You can build a groove off something like a rhythm guitar and build around it, but ultimately it comes down to the bass and drums being locked right there with it. It doesn't mean that it's square and machined out—it just means that there's some basic factor*

in the track that has this irresistible feel to it, and everybody in the band adheres to it.

Producer Frank Fitzpatrick

Just about every hit record has a great groove, and that's why it's a hit. But if you want to study what a groove really is, go to the masters: James Brown, Sly Stone, George Clinton, and Prince. Every song is the essence of groove.

We usually think of the groove as coming from the rhythm section, especially the drums, but that's not necessarily always the case. In the Police's "Every Breath You Take," the rhythm guitar establishes the groove, while in most of the songs from Motown's golden age that were by the Supremes, the Temptations, and the Four Tops, the groove was established by James Jamerson's bass. Every song has its groove—you just have to listen for it and always pay attention to it.

When you have to explain to someone how to make something feel better, it becomes a hard place to have it come from if you have to wrap your head around it first. As soon as you have to think about it, you're going to miss part of it anyway. But you can get there—you just have to listen and practice and always pay attention to it. For example, if I have Chad Wackerman on drums, I can tell him to lay back one more hair on the beat and he'll know what I mean. Where with younger players, there's only ahead of the beat, behind the beat, and on the beat. For advanced players, there's a hundred variations of all of those places.

Frank Fitzpatrick

STYLES

The studio musician has to be comfortable and able to play many styles convincingly to work consistently. Sure, you might get some work if you're a fantastic blues or jazz player (for instance), but your limitation to that style will also limit the work that's available to you. That's why you're best served by being familiar and at least passably proficient in as many styles as possible.

> *As time progressed, I saw the value in reading and playing different styles of music. I think today the best advice I could give to any young guitar player is if you want to be a success, first of all learn how to read, and second of all learn how to play styles convincingly. Don't make yourself a one-trick pony unless you've got something that is so magical that it will go out and take over the world. If you don't have that, learn to play styles, because then you can always function.*
>
> Gary Solt

Preparation

Everyone likes the session musician who offers to prepare in advance because everyone (especially you) benefits. If you have time to learn the material first, always offer to do so. Let's say you get the call for a recording date that's booked for six hours, and the goal is for you to complete your tracks on three songs. If you can, take a couple of hours beforehand to listen to the tunes and make simple charts. It's time well spent, and your efforts will be most appreciated.

Sometimes preparation isn't required or desired. The people hiring you may want your spontaneous musical response to the material. In that case, producers with prior knowledge of your style, skill level, and abilities often say, "No, you'll be fine. Just show up with your ears!"

Although it's best to find out as much as you can about the music you're about to create, realistically, most dates require little preparation. Often players walk in to the studio, listen to a demo, and make their own charts within the first few minutes. Sometimes they are provided with sheet music or a "Nashville style" chord and form chart (see Fig. 9.1). Sometimes a producer will ask the musicians to duplicate prerecorded parts note for note and expect the musicians to be able to do so quickly by ear. And sometimes there is preproduction—a process of familiarizing a session player or ensemble with the material before recording it. There are some great photos and some video of Tom Petty and the Heartbreakers with producer Jimmy Iovine (around the time of "Damn the Torpedoes") sitting in a circle while Tom plays acoustic guitar and sings as the Heartbreakers scribble notes and make their charts on the fly. That's preproduction.

Producer Linda Perry has been known to "campfire" songs. Sometimes she likes to sit on the couch in her lavish studio's tracking room with acoustic instruments, as if the ensemble were gathered informally around a campfire, playing the tunes loosely while everyone gets their parts together. This method most certainly works, but I don't know the last time anyone heard the sound of a grand piano anywhere near a campfire!

> *I try to find out as much as I can out front. If I know they'll want specific instruments, all the strings are changed and everything is ready by the time I get there. If it's a certain style they'll want, I try to work on that style to get it together. I did a movie that I had to play all Dobro on, and the composer didn't have a lot of understanding of what the Dobro could play so he didn't really write a lot for it. He said to me, "Come up with some stuff that gives this mood, and we'll go with that." If you have some clue before you go in, you can have it together. I had an idea beforehand of what the guy wanted, so I had worked out four or five thematic ideas, and it all ended up working out great. So to me, preparation is the most important thing.*
>
> Gary Solt

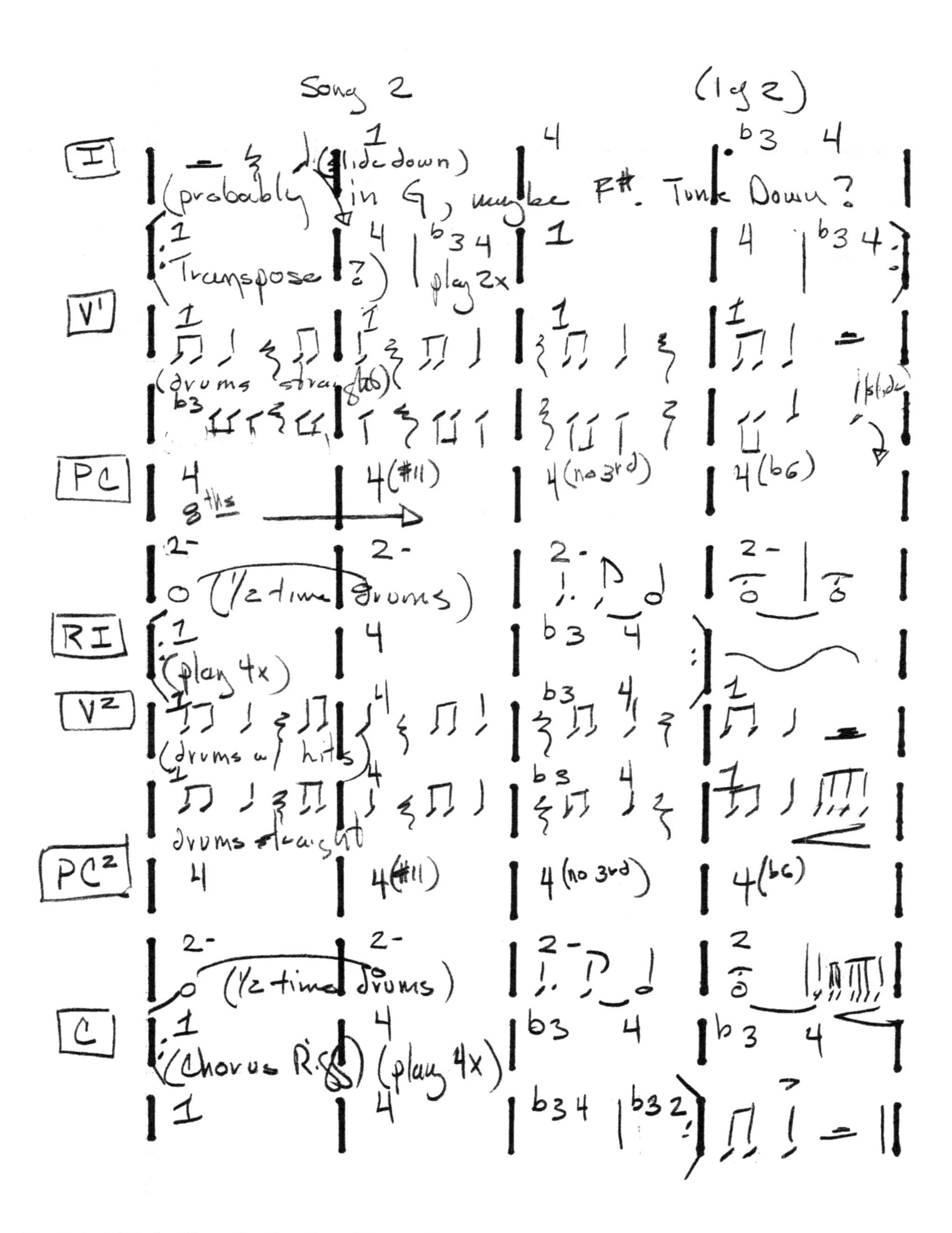

Fig. 9.1: A Nashville-style Chord and Form Chart

Serving the Muse: Playing the Music, Not the Instrument

All musicians seek inspiration from the world outside and from the inner emotional world. The best sessioneers can access a broad emotional and musical language and play what's best for the music at hand. If it's a record date, session greats have been known to say, "Hey, what if I lay out on the bridge? Maybe this song will have more emotional impact if I *don't* play on that part." Great studio musicians play in a way that not only makes the session run smoothly, but also makes the music come alive in a way that best serves it's emotional purpose. That means studio greats play *evocatively.*

Evocative playing means playing parts that create the most desirable emotional response within the listener. Case in point: back in the '70s singer-songwriter heyday, alto sax great Dave Sanborn had a knack for always laying down the "right" sax solo, whether it was for Carly Simon, Bonnie Raitt, or Michael MacDonald. His solos were the most lyrical moments of pure expression and were completely unlike the ripping solos on his acclaimed fusion recordings that harken from the same period. Same guy, same sound, totally different emotional content. Simon, Raitt, and MacDonald loved Sanborn's *sound and feel*. His formidable technique and knowledge of jazz and R&B allowed him to access his musical and emotional language. Dave played on those soft-rock classics in a way that was in his own unique and immediately recognizable voice, but with content that best suited the context created by the singer-songwriters who were among the best in their day. This is what the studio musician strives for: a unique, recognizable voice and feel that best suits as many musical situations as possible. Playing evocatively is how to best Serve the Muse.

> *I would say an important thing for me is to serve the song at all times. Try to keep an open mind, and if someone in the room has an idea, then always let that idea be heard. When everybody*

drops their ego and just tries to serve the song, I find that the best idea will rise to the surface and everybody will recognize it. It's human nature to want our ideas to be the best ones, but if you can be open to others' suggestions, you can learn something and maybe do something that you wouldn't have thought of doing.

Peter Thorn

What may link us all together [as studio musicians] *is our ability to put the ego in the back pocket and play for the song in a way that heads it in the right direction.*

Rami Jaffee

Leave your ego and your chops at home. One day you might build a shelf, and one day you might build a house. Just do the job that's required.

Denny Seiwell

CHAPTER 10

Session Etiquette

Recorded music is the result of so many ingredients, but it is made up chiefly of inspiration, musicality, technology, personal interaction, and most importantly, vibe. The feeling you create at a session is the context you create. That's your "vibe." You want people in the recording business to say this about you: "Great player, great vibe." Of course, what you play and how you play it are the most important building blocks in the context you create, but let's look closely at that "feeling in the room," and how you can always be at your best.

There is an expected way to carry yourself at a session that's gracious and professional while not being stiff. Here's a list of things to remember that, if observed, will greatly contribute to your vibe and the vibe of the session.

Before the Session Begins

▶ On any session, always know who your point of contact is.

▶ Always show up early. To be early is to be on time. To be on time is to be late. To be late is almost like not showing up at all! If the downbeat is for 2 p.m., show up at least a half hour early, at 1:30.

▶ Let the powers-that-be know you've arrived. Make your presence known at a session as soon you roll up on the studio property. If you're there and no one knows it, you can cause the session to start late if, say, you're hanging out in the lounge instead of the studio, where everyone else has been waiting for you because they were unaware that you're already there.

▶ Load your gear in quickly and quietly. Accept help with this if it's offered. If it's your first time there, introduce yourself to those you make contact with, and find out what the plan for the session is.

▶ You may be immediately welcomed in the studio or control room, or you may not. You may be asked to wait in the lounge instead. While you're waiting, use those people skills and find out what's going on. Be friendly and respectful, but don't be overly formal.

▶ After you're set up and ready to play, keep your warm-ups and noodling to an absolute minimum. Get your sound and follow the producer's or engineer's directions to a tee. If you're playing an electric instrument, it's totally cool to turn your volume all the way down and do your warm-ups.

▶ If there are headphones in use, try putting them on with the volume all the way down (studio headphones are capable of being loud enough to cause hearing damage), so don't hurt yourself, and slowly turn them up to see what's happening with the mix. If there are other people in the room, you might want to "keep one ear on, one ear off" until recording begins so you can hear if someone speaks to you. Always keep your focus on the music and do what's right here, right now.

While Recording

- If there's creative dialogue with the artist, songwriter, producer, or engineer, make sure that your opinions are wanted and warranted before you offer them.

- Stay relaxed and casual, but always be alert for cues.

- Be careful about musical references. You may think that the track you're working on is great because it reminds you of Dusty Springfield's classic "Son of a Preacher Man," only to find out on your mention that song's on the artist's "Ten Most Overrated Songs" list.

- Try to tune in to what it is the producer, engineer, and artist want from you, and do your best to give it to them better each time you play it.

> *Be as flexible as you can be. Don't be stubborn, and trust the people you work with. If the engineer or producer has a suggestion, trust their advice.*
>
> Brian MacLeod

> *Don't try to impress a producer with what you can do. You'll never get called back.*
>
> Denny Seiwell

- Once the session commences, everything you play or sing may be recorded. Be aware that many producers run a 2-track machine as soon as the musicians are making noise just to catch ad-libs or moments of thoughtless brilliance.

▶ Whether you're on your own or are part of an ensemble, focus on your work first. If you have input for other players, make sure it's warranted and you can actually help them out. Players often tweak each other's parts or help one another to understand a written passage, remember a song's form, or get a sound.

▶ Remember—always defer to whoever is in charge. That person is usually the producer, but you may be receiving guidance or input from a musical director, the artist, or the engineer.

▶ Keep an open mind. Greet suggestions with willingness and always respond positively. If you're receiving input from more than one source and they contradict each other, diplomatically point that out and let them resolve it.

▶ Producers love studio musicians who always work hard to make the music the best it can be and who bring their own "thing" to a recording session, which is usually musicality and an uncanny feel for the music at hand. Most studio greats also have a real gift for creating parts that are hooks that are memorable but don't draw attention away from the music's main motifs. The Funk Brothers are a perfect example of session "hookmeisters." Great studio musicians make any part or idea better through their unique playing or singing, so studio etiquette or behavior should always reflect that aspiration.

▶ And don't forget: if you can't keep your cell phone outside the studio, turn it off (not just on vibrate—that's a distraction, too).

▶ Put away the magazines, computers, iPhones, and anything else that can be a distraction. The last thing a producer wants to see is you updating your Facebook status in between takes!

▶ If you need time to check your messages, make sure you ask first. Most sessions have timed or natural breaks when you can meet your individual needs, but always be sure to ask if you wish to leave the recording environment while there's work being done, even if you're not directly involved at that moment.

- We studio musicians have our own golden rule: Serve the Muse. That means to always do what's in the best interests of the music, even if it sometimes means not playing what you want to play or what you hear in your head.

- Your behavior should always be positive, and you should strive to be "present for the moment."

- There's a time and a place for everything, but sometimes cajoling, goofing around, or humor doesn't belong at a session. Then on another day with the same people, the session may be all about the gags and laughs. Studio pros know how to go with the flow and are experts at reading people and situations.

- Studio musicians are known to be friendly, respectful, personable, and approachable. Discussions usually focus on the task at hand, and even though musicians always like to talk about music, off-subject discussions are generally kept to a minimum.

- If people are conversing, treat the session like any other workplace and try to avoid potential conversational hot spots: politics, religion, family, and money.

- Everyone likes a good conversation and a funny joke, but it's best not to risk being misinterpreted or misperceived as offensive.

- Earn and honor rank. That means if there are players on the session with more professional or personal history with the artist or producer than you have accumulated, let them lead. Everyone benefits when everyone gets along and knows his or her place.

▶ It's always best to offer to do a little more than what's asked of you. If they tell you it's an acoustic-guitar overdub date, bring an exotic instrument along like a 12-string, a mandolin, or a banjitar. Let the producer know you have it available for extras or experimentation if there's time.

▶ Always wait until the job is done before you ask the powers that be if they are open to your creativity. It's appropriate to do so before you offer your ideas. Always ask first if they are open to your input. If so, and you hear it in your imagination, let them know. You might hear that acoustic guitar in an open tuning and offer to do another overdub. Or you may want to capo at the fifth fret and play that key-of-G song in D position to get that classic country wire-choir sound going.

▶ If you really want to score points with the producer, provide a lot of options. Successful session musicians are known not only for their musicality (which in this context means an ability to play great parts immediately with great conviction), but also for their versatility and sonic options.

When the Session Ends

It's perfectly natural to develop relationships with people you meet on sessions, but make sure you don't ruffle any feathers or create more work for yourselfin your noble efforts to make new friends. You want to get called back for the next session, and you want the team you just worked with to refer you for more work.

▶ After your tracks are completed and you've basked in compliments during playback, let whoever hired you or your point of contact know how much you enjoyed the experience and how much you'd like to come back again.

▶ Remember to honor rank and be careful to defer to established relationships. If you just finished a synthesizer overdub for a producer but his engineer got you the gig, your best bet is thank the engineer for the referral at a time when the producer is present. Then let them both know you are available for more work.

▶ Just because you played on the session, don't assume that it's cool for you to stay and watch when you're finished. Unless you're specifically invited, assume that you're presence is unwanted. You'll quickly develop a keen sense of when it's cool to hang out, or if you should quickly be on your way.

▶ Be careful not to be overly friendly with the staff. This can be misinterpreted and come back at you later if you make someone feel the least bit uncomfortable.

▶ Be careful about making unsolicited referrals for your friends. A general rule of thumb is to refer someone only when you're asked to recommend a player or singer for work. If you're good at what you do and act professionally, producers, artists, contractors, engineers, and managers will inevitably ask you for recommendations, and then you'll have ample opportunity to create your own "A Team."

▶ Fast friendships and strong bonds can be made among recording musicians. Often a sense of "family" prevails, and often it's perfectly appropriate to hang out and socialize after sessions. Recording musicians often end up touring or doing media promo dates with artists for whom they've made records, and lifetime bonds can be formed. Just remember to acknowledge the individuals that create these opportunities.

It's always good to check in after a session via phone or email just to stay up on the radar. Many successful recording musicians make themselves available free of charge or at a reduced rate for callbacks—brief quick-fix sessions that involve little or no logistical hassle and usually take only a few minutes. It's always good to make sure your regular employers know when you're available, especially if you also tour.

The Session

Although no two sessions are exactly the same, there are similarities between them all. Below are a number of items that are common to any session, as well as a real-world example of a record date that culminates what's been illustrated in the previous chapters.

Your Studio Comfort

During a session, your immediate needs are always addressed so that you'll be at your best to play your best. Snacks and beverages are usually provided, but long gone are the days of studio debauchery! Except for celebratory moments at the end of a "killer date," rarely does one see open beers or cocktails on sessions, and recreational drugs are a thing of the distant past. This is a serious business, with reputations and money on the line, and it must be treated as such.

Studio temperature is always a factor, and you usually see studio musicians dressed for cool temperatures even on hot sunny days. It might be okay to ask for the temperature to be adjusted, but as soon as recording begins it's best to forget about changing it unless the heat or the cold really impairs your playing or the performance of your instrument.

Breaks are commonplace and a good producer will have a sense as to when to keep things rolling if the playing is especially together, or when taking a break might be appropriate. That being said, bathroom breaks or a "pause for the cause"—whether it's to clear your head, send a text, or check your voice mail—are all well within reason and are to be expected during the course of the session. As a result, session musicians usually cart their laptops around and are often seen snooping on eBay for good deals on more gear!

The Signal Chain

The signal chain refers to the order of the electronics that are connected from the microphone to the recorder (either a DAW or a tape machine) and/or monitor speakers, and back again. The signal chain usually includes a microphone or DI connected to a standalone microphone preamplifier or one in a recording console, maybe into an equalizer and/or compressor, and then into the recording device.

Generally speaking, the studio usually has a higher-quality audio signal chain than the setup that most session musicians can supply, and the engineer and/or the producer certainly have their preferences about what they like to use on certain instruments. That being said, if you have some parts of a signal chain that you know work particularly well with your setup or that might be higher quality than what the studio can provide, it's in your best interest to suggest using them to the engineer before the session begins. The engineer or producer might still want to use what they're comfortable with, but they might also jump at the chance to use your gear.

Among the gear that players commonly bring to a session are direct boxes (mostly from bass players) and microphones (horn players and vocalists). Occasionally a session player might bring an entire signal chain consisting of microphone or DI, mic preamp, and compressor, but this usually occurs when doing a session at a home studio, where the choices are limited.

The Headphone Mix

You deserve the sound that's best *for you* in your headphones. While many studio musicians travel from date to date with their own headphones, some are less concerned and will use anything available. If you're on a session with your own mixer that allows you to create your own custom mix, you may want to start by listening to the stereo bus mix (the mix they're hearing in the control room) if they are sending it to you. This helps you to hear things from the producer's and the engineer's perspective. Add in or turn down the other tracks as you see fit to optimize your performance, but be careful not to start with a listening level that's so high that it will lead to premature ear fatigue. Make sure you can really hear yourself, and make sure you can hear the control room talkback at all times, especially when you are playing, so you can respond to production input in real time.

If the engineer is creating a mix from the control room but it's individually tailored for you, tell him what you need to get it set up quickly. If the mix later requires changes, ask for them in between takes; try never to stop a session for any reason, especially while that red recording light is on! If your headphone mix changes while you are playing, finish the take and don't stop unless it's absolutely impossible for you to hear yourself. On that note, if you hear a mistake or you sense a technical audio problem like a ground buzz, don't stop playing. Let the leaders lead—multitrack magic may be happening even under conditions of duress, and no one wants to bear the responsibility of pulling the plug on that special take.

If you're working under limited conditions in which multiple musicians are on the same headphone mix, remember your golden rule and Serve the Muse! Defer to the common good. If it's a band tracking date with a live vocal, try to strike a reasonable compromise about the headphone mix by making certain that the vocalist and drummer are comfortable with it. Usually, each person can replay his or her part later if the performance suffers because of the mix. If you're a four-piece band and you're going for the drum track first and have only one headphone mix, let the drummer make the call on the balance. Everyone has different headphone mix needs, and session variables may require that your mix changes even while you're tracking.

If you're on a date and you have your own separate headphone mixer, don't be afraid to adjust your mix on the fly if you need to. Just don't ever do anything that has an adverse effect on your performance. Special note to singers and string players: Be careful with your headphone volume—you're usually close-miked with a lot of gain on the mics, so you may be asked to turn your overall headphone volume down because of leakage. Always comply and strike a compromise that doesn't adversely affect your performance, but don't forget to Serve the Muse!

Working with the Engineer

Being a session musician is similar to being a pilot flying a small aircraft, and your engineers are like your air-traffic controllers, so treat them well. You always want to have safe take-offs and landings, and you always want to know where you are. Sometimes you're flying alone (a solo overdub session), and other times it's a very crowded airspace (an ensemble tracking date), so it's always best to respect your engineer. After all, he's got your sound in his hands.

Most often, engineers are congenial professionals who are that rare breed of people who manage to combine artistry and technical expertise to create sonic beauty. Let the engineers do the job they're hired to do and give them the best sound that you can, but don't be afraid to tell them what you need. If you're doing overdubs and you need more preroll, just ask for it nicely. If your headphone mix isn't allowing you to perform at your highest level, be specific about just what you need to fix the problem. You and your engineer should easily make a great team. You both want the same results, and rarely should there be any dissonance between you and those on the other side of the glass.

Working with the Producer

Your producer is your leader. The artist's name may be "up in lights," but the producer takes the behind-the-scenes final responsibility for any session and answers to the powers that be about it. Sometimes people have multiple roles: artist-producer (think Peter Gabriel, Jay Z, Beck, and Jagger/Richards as the "Glimmer Twins"), producer-engineer (think Brendan O'Brien, Hugh Padgham, and Joe Chiccarelli), or someone like Prince who's comfortable in all three roles. Just remember that when it comes to final decisions, your producer gets your deference. If an artist or engineer has brought you in on a date and questions about creative choices arise between them and the producer where you are involved, remain quiet, honor loyalties, and trust your gut. Let them work it out, and remember that you are there to Serve the Muse and do what's in the best interests of the music. That being said, always take into consideration that the producer's aesthetics are the determining factor on any session.

The successful studio musician has to have the temperament, talent, and skill set that is roughly equivalent to a cross between a professional surfer and a professional footballer. Like a surfer, sometimes you sit quietly while there are only little ripples, but all of a sudden you look up into the face of a 40-foot wave. Regardless, you ride it and flow with the changes, always using your talent and accumulated life experience to help the producer get what he needs. That's really your primary purpose on any session: to help the producer win. In doing so, you not only give the producer his or her desired musical results, but you pay equity into your job-security bank with everyone involved.

Remember the golden rule: successful studio musicians Serve the Muse. As a group or individually, studio musicians can be seen to function as pro footballers in that they have to play for the team and follow the leader (think of the producer as a cross between the coach and the quarterback), but occasionally sessioneers also get to make the star play. On a session, a star play usually comes in the form of hooks, a group's great signature "feel" (think Muscle Shoals and the Swamp Rats), or stellar individual performances that gel together to create hits like the Wrecking Crew's seven consecutive Records of the Year. Now that's working with a producer!

Working with the Artist

The type of session at which the artist is usually present is the record date, although you can find yourself working alongside artists in the studio on demos, too. If it's a jingle date, view the client or anyone from the ad agency in the same light as you do an artist; and if it's a film or TV date, the director, producer(s), music supervisor(s), studio execs, or any of their representatives can be considered akin to an artist. With respect to all the tangential interactions that may occur on a session, also consider anyone (such as a spouse, family member, boyfriend or girlfriend, guest, driver, personal assistant, or staffer) associated with the aforementioned group an "artist," too. Treating them lightly can bring the scorn of the artist down upon you!

Simply put, show quiet, friendly respect to the artist during the session. While recording, you're a valued asset to their creative and business process, but you are not their peer. During your time involved in the sphere of activity with the record—be it for just that session for a few hours, or for a few weeks, or if you're invited to spend time outside the session (like for a group dinner)—you inhabit the artist's musical, professional, and social universe as a cross between an "honored guest" and a highly valued independent contractor.

Let the artist set the boundaries and determine the tone of your interaction. Very rarely are artists cold or unkind to session musicians. A casual friendliness usually prevails, but be careful not to get too "chummy" too quickly. Always be yourself and remain positive, friendly, and focused on the music. You are there to help them achieve the best recording possible, so let them know that through your professional demeanor and command of your musical skill set.

Also remember that quite often you're there because someone else (usually the producer) hired you, so you represent that person, too. Do all you can to ensure that the artist has the most positive and valuable experience possible. Ultimately, they take final responsibility for the session's outcome. It's their name, not yours, that is "up in the bright lights," so do your absolute best to make certain they are proud of your contributions. You want them to have a glowing smile on their faces as they write your checks, but most importantly, you want the artist to come away from any experience with you very happy and extremely proud of your musical contributions to their life's work. Much the same can be said of working with producers, and that brings us to our next section.

A Session Example: A Typical Record Date

Here's an example of the way a typical session with a recording artist might take place.

Al, the bass player who brought songwriters Mandy and Evan (the artists) to the producer's attention, was called on Monday morning for a date. He wasn't surprised to be asked to show up at producer Harriet's studio later that day at 2 p.m., because record dates are quite often booked on the spur of the moment. The producer wanted to assemble her regular recording team, and luckily everyone was in town and available. As usual, it was Al on bass, Nate on drums, guitarists Pete and Johnny, and Dave on keyboards. Mandy was slated to play piano on the songs, too. Harriet's engineer Drew and assistants Kyle and Mike were on board, so it was business as usual.

Upon arriving at the studio an hour early, Al was greeted by Harriet, who everyone calls "Harry." "Here's a CD of our first tune. Make a chord chart for yourself and the other guys. We're going to try to knock out two songs a day through Thursday, and then I'll spend Friday tightening things up."

All the musicians arrived by 2 p.m., and Al had the relatively easy pop tune charted by 3 p.m. Nate and Harry spent two hours creating drum sounds that she thought might be suitable for the song, and by 5 p.m. they were getting bass sounds. After auditioning two amps, a vintage Ampeg B-15 and a new JMI boutique Vox AC-100 clone, the decision was made to use both amps instead of the usual amp/direct-line combination.

As usual, everyone involved was positive in demeanor, following Harry's direction to the letter and going with the flow. Pete was first to start getting guitar sounds. They settled on using a vintage Fender Deluxe and a mid-'70s Les Paul. Microphone and signal-chain choices were left to Harry and Drew, but everyone present noted the additional "warmth" that was added to the sound when a Royer ribbon mic was added. As the team had recorded together so frequently, they all displayed an intuitive sense of when or when not to offer observations or opinions. All of them came to the Mandy sessions with enough experience to know that a good rule to follow on any recording session is to "Offer your opinion only when it is asked for, most especially when matters being discussed don't involve you."

However, over time most successful session musicians develop a keen sense of when it is appropriate to offer unsolicited advice or perspective, especially when someone comes up against a creative brick wall, needs help with a part, or has a technical problem that one can help solve. In most professional recording situations, the question "May I offer a suggestion?" is greeted with a "Yes!" answer.

Harry called Johnny from the lounge into the tracking room to get his guitar sound. "Pete's using a Les Paul," she opined, "so I am hearing a contrasting tone, like from a Tele through a small combo, breaking up just a little."

"Good idea, Harry," Johnny smiled, "whatever sound you need, I'm going to help you get." And with that one statement, he displayed the quiet but sincere enthusiasm and supportive initiative that is part of what should be the studio musician's "vibe."

After sifting through the sounds of an enviable trio of vintage Teles paired in various combinations with a handful of small combos, Harry and Johnny chose a Fender Custom Shop Tele with a rosewood fingerboard cooking through an ancient little Harmony amp that was never meant to be played outside a teenager's bedroom. "That's the sound I hear in my head," nodded Harry. Johnny replied, "Works for me," and the session proceeded onward to Dave and the Hammond B-3.

Intent on always pushing the creative envelope, Harry told Dave and her engineers, "Let's do it a little differently this time. Mandy's going to be playing piano, and she's got classical chops so she tends to play pretty busy, but that's her style. Let's go for a more ambient organ sound. Whaddya say we put the Leslie speaker in the Jacuzzi room and mic up the tiles? Close-mic it as usual, but put a PZM mic or a piezo on the wall, too. That's going to sound . . . different!"

Dave quizzically nodded his head in agreement. Even though he was looking forward to playing some in-your-face gospel organ, he chose to go along with the flow, and appropriately so. Less than ten minutes later, he was hearing a most unique organ sound in his headphones and grinning from ear to ear.

With all six musicians in place, Harry took her spot behind her beloved vintage Neve console and began to listen closely to all the musicians together as they started playing Mandy's song. After a few minutes of adjusting tones and levels in the control room, she started monitoring the musicians individually and in pairs or small groups.

"Al, I love what you're playing, but I don't like the way your bass sound is sitting with the drum kit. Nate is cooking, and the drums are sounding great. Does everyone like the drum sound? I know you're just hearing them in your cans, but what do you think?"

As everyone chimed in agreeing with her, she overrode the banter to say, "Al, we need a bass to 'pillow' the drums. I like their snap, but your sound is too bright. Will you try the old Kay with flatwounds, and play your part with one of your felt picks?"

Referring to the old bass and the obscure pick by nickname, Al exclaimed, "Carol Kaye and a 'felty.' No problem!" In less than three minutes, Harry was smiling again and she leaned on the talkback, "Now everything sounds great, but we have to move a bass mic back a little. Hold on guys, and no noodling because I don't want you to lose this vibe. Everyone's right where they should be, so stay there."

As the band fell silent, Drew scurried into the bass-amp isolation closet, moved the mic, and the band fired up, cooking right where they left off in exactly the same headspace. Mandy looked up, marveling at their precision and willingness to serve her song and their common muse. Her tune sounded great out of the gate, and everyone immediately knew it was going to be a successful day.

Three run-throughs later, and after offering input primarily to the rhythm section, Harry knew she had the band sitting right for the song. "Mandy, you're singing really well, but we need to work on your vocal sound, and I want to cut this with a click so that I can comp your vocals. Not only will we get our rhythm track today, we may get a keeper vocal out of you, too. Band, take a break. Kyle, get Jezzie [the new receptionist] to order these guys some dinner, and let's continue to make this record!"

The musicians didn't wander too far off, because they all knew they were close to getting a track. The smokers went outside while the others lounged around the kitchen, attempting to decide where to order from and what to eat. Before Jezzie could step outside to get the smokers' orders, Harry's voice boomed out of the control room, "Let's rock!" And the band members made their way down the hall to the tracking room and resumed their positions, tweaking headphone mixes and checking their tunings.

Harry beamed happily through the control room glass, "Johnny, I was thinking. Can you give me more skank on your rhythm parts in the verses and add a fuzz tone to the prechorus? Keep it on for the choruses as well, and can everybody hit a strong downbeat on the last bar of each chorus, like you're doing at the end of the song?"

Everyone nodded in agreement while Al and Pete notated their charts. Those two, as was their habit like many session musicians, almost always have some kind of chart or notes on the stand regardless of their familiarity with the material. Like Al and Pete, Dave, Johnny, and drummer Nate found Mandy's first song easy to learn and a joy to play, so they were not using charts. Whether it's a bedroom studio demo or a high-end record date with a world-renowned artist, most recording musicians strive to get "off the chart" as soon as possible. Charts, written music, and notes in one's own shorthand are never frowned upon during the recording process, and are often encouraged if the music or song is going through a lot of changes as a result of the creative process.

The day was moving along so well that Harry, Mandy, and the band had the track done by the time dinner was delivered. As they sat down to eat, Harry immediately started planning overdubs.

Part Two

Player's Guides

CHAPTER 12

Guide for Guitar Players

There's a burden on guitar players that other session musicians don't have, and that's the tone of their gear. Yes, you're hired for your fabulous technique and sparkling personality, but if you can't get the sounds that a producer or an artist has in his or her head, you probably won't get a return call. Luckily, it's easier than ever to get the standard guitar sounds that everyone asks for, and there are numerous avenues that can be taken to get there. Let's take a look.

Before the Session Begins

Of all the questions that you might ask when you get the call for a session (as outlined in chapter 8), make sure that you zero in on the following two:

Is there any particular sound that is desired? The answer to this question determines what gear you bring to the session. If you're asked for a Tom Morello/Rage Against The Machine sort of sound, that'll tell you to bring along all your pedals. If it's an Americana sound they're going for, you'll know to bring a Gretsch guitar and Fender Tweed amp. If you don't have the exact replica of the gear, then you'll at least know what to do to get your sound in the ballpark.

Are there any particular instrument(s), amps, or effects to be used? Many times the producer or artist has a specific sound in mind, either because they've heard it from you before or they just expect it from you. "Bring your blue Strat" or "Bring that Martin D-18" tells you not only what to bring but also what to set up to track with first.

Your Sound

You're being hired for the sound that you bring as much as for your playing, so you have to concentrate on getting that part of your game together, too. The first thing to understand is that your sound can be bigger without pedals or anything in between your guitar and your amp (and a big sound is what producers like).

Yes, it's true. That's the way it usually works. Most of those sounds that you've been hearing on recordings (especially on classic '60s and '70s recordings) have come from a guitar plugged straight into an amp, with no pedals (or one or two at most) in between. What gives it that big sound is the type of amp and the fact that it's turned up pretty high, if not to max.

Granted, your sound really depends on the amp. Most amps will work well, but a few just won't cut it in the studio except for in special circumstances (the '70s and '80s Yamaha amps sound great for jazz, but not much else, for instance). That's one of the reasons session guitar players traditionally prefer tube amps to solid-state amps. They have the right sound when you turn them up, while solid-state amps, for the most part, just don't. Likewise, if the amp has too much power, you just might never be able to turn it up to where you need in order to get the right sound, especially in small studios. That's why a 50-watt (or less) amp is a lot more versatile than a 100-watt, since you usually can't drive a 100-watt to where it needs to go without everyone in the studio wearing hearing protectors like the ones you see on an airport flight line. In fact, the trend for most session guitarist these days is to have an amp (or amps) with a wattage of between 15 and 35 watts.

Now I'm not saying to throw away all your distortion and overdrive pedals, because they certainly have their place; but get the sound from the amp first, then add your pedals. If you can't make the guitar sound great plugged directly into the amp, then consider a different amp that will get you where you need to go.

The second most important thing to learn is to play clean without the help of any distortion or sustain. This might sound like the same thing as just stated above, but it's not. Playing with distortion is fun, but the sustain gives you a false sense of security and can cover up a lot of mistakes and technique problems that you might have. Distortion and artificial sustain can give you a flawed sense of your ability, and the way to get around that is to learn to play completely cleanly. Yes, you might not like what you hear at first, but with some practice you'll find that it'll make you a much better player. That's because you'll be able to hear all the nuances that you're either playing well or need to work on because you just can't hear through the distortion. If you can sound great clean, you'll sound even better dirty!

But this is not only a technique issue it's a sound issue. More than half the time in sessions the track is going to require a clean sound, and even when you're asked to dirty it up, it still won't be as much as you might be used to. Surprisingly, a little distortion goes a long way in a track, and most players new to recording are always amazed by how what seems to be the right amount in the room is way too much on the recording.

LESS IS MORE

Expanding on the above, playing with fewer effects and less distortion helps your sound in another big way: it's a lot easier for it to fit into the mix. The more effects (reverb, delay, chorus, flange, vibrato, and so on) and distortion you use, the harder it is for the listener to discern exactly what you're playing. This means that the sound turns into a mushy din instead of an exciting mix of instruments greater than its parts. The engineer will usually ask you to try your effects pedals first, but he might have something in mind that he can add later that might sound better.

I'm not saying to stop using your pedals; set them up and have them ready to use. But don't be surprised if you use them a lot less than you think you will.

You might be thinking that your pedals are part of your sound, but unless you're a superstar guitar player already, you aren't being hired for your sound. As a studio musician, you're being hired to be a chameleon and imitate everyone else's sound (or at least any sound that the client hears in his head). A studio guitar player is egoless about sound and style. Save that for your solo project.

THAT'S WHAT TONE CONTROLS ARE FOR

Most players seem to have either questions about or a misunderstanding of why and how to use the tone controls on their amps, so don't feel bad if you do, too.

First of all, you want to adjust the tone controls so that all the notes of your instrument speak evenly. That is, no note or group of notes should be way louder or softer than any other. You might sound too boomy when you play a Les Paul or something with humbucking pickups through your amp setup, while it's nice and even with a Strat or something that has single-coil pickups. Or the other way around, with the Les Paul sounding balanced while the Strat sounds light on the low end. In this case, adjusting either the bass or the mid controls on the amp will ensure that all notes are equal in level.

Another situation might be one in which the midrange is so bright and strident that it tears your head off, but it's close to the sound you like. In this case, it's great to have the flexibility of a parametric tone control if available. Sweep the frequency until you find the band of frequencies that's too loud, narrow the bandwidth until just that frequency is affected, then lower it. Your tone will remain pretty much the same, but the offending frequency will be lowered so it's balanced with the rest. This is also a big thing with basses, where one note on the neck is much louder than the same pitch on a different string!

But where tone controls really shine is in the context of the mix of the song. You want to be sure that every instrument is distinctly heard, and the only way to do that is to be sure that each one has its own frequency space. It's especially important with two guitar parts that have similar instruments and amps (something like two Les Pauls and two Marshalls would be the worst-case scenario, but in the cases of Thin Lizzy and the Allman Brothers, they definitely found a way to make this combination work). Then you have to shape your sounds so that the guitars occupy a different part of the sonic spectrum. A good initial frame of reference can be where one guitar occupies a higher frequency register, and the other is in a lower register.

This might mean that one guitar has more high end, while the second guitar is fatter sounding. Or both guitars might have different midrange peaks. Plus, the guitars have to sit in a different frequency space than do the bass and drums (and keys, percussion, horns, and so on), so you either alter your tone controls or try another instrument to make this happen. The engineer can do this with equalization in the control room, but it's always better if you get as close to the sound as possible in the studio first.

All this might take a while to learn how to dial in, so don't get discouraged if it doesn't happen right away. Listen closely to some big-selling CDs or MP3s, and you'll hear how everything is layered and you'll get the idea. The producer, artist, and engineer will also have specific ideas about what's needed for the track and will guide you in that direction.

DIFFERENT INSTRUMENTS AND AMPLIFIERS

It's always easiest get the right sound for the track by using different guitars for different guitar parts, and that's the reason it's always advisable to bring a wide range of instruments to the session. Sure, you could make the sound different by adjusting tone controls on the amp and equalizers in the control room, but another guitar will instantly provide a different sonic texture. The same goes for different amplifiers, too. Bringing several different types of amps opens up the opportunity to take everything to yet another place where it's easy to differentiate between parts. Basic amp sounds could include a Marshall, a Fender, and a Vox, although there are models within each brand that sound different from the general sound of the brand. The idea is to make each track sound different so the engineer doesn't have to spend a lot of time trying to do the same thing later.

CLASH OF THE GUITAR TRACKS

Most recordings have more than one guitar track, so it's important to learn how to refine your sound to make the track bigger and fatter instead of just loud and thin. Although this might sound like the producer's job, it's good to know the tricks so you can suggest them if appropriate.

As stated above, the tone controls on your amp are the first place to start to carve out your sound so that it isn't covered up by another guitar track (or other band instruments, for that matter)—or so that you don't cover anyone else up either. But with multiple guitar tracks on the recording, you have to take things to the next level. You have to make sure that the songs are arranged so the guitars stay out of each other's way. If you listen closely to just about any recording by a popular artist, you'll see that this is just what's happened in the studio already. If you can hear within the song (which isn't always easy with certain types of music or with data-compressed MP3s), you'll hear the following:

Each guitar is playing something completely different. One guitar might be playing full chords, while the other is playing a line. Going back to early Motown for an example (during their peak era, The Funk Brothers always used three guitar players on each record), listen to the Supremes' "You Keep Me Hangin' On." One guitar plays the lead line, the second guitar strums the whole-note chords, and the third guitar enters in the B section. Another example is Eric Clapton's (actually, Derek and the Dominos') "Layla," with the first guitar playing the opening bar, the second guitar playing the chords going down, and the lead guitar playing the signature line up high near the 12th fret. Yet another example would be Lynard Skynard's "Sweet Home Alabama," with the first guitar playing the signature intro line, the second guitar playing the lead line in the middle of the neck, and the third line playing a line against the first when the band comes in. Lynyrd Skynyrd's music is a great example of interplay between three guitars, and just about anything by them is worth studying.

Each guitar is playing in a different register or voicing. If one guitar is playing an A chord on the 2nd fret, the second guitar is playing it on the 5th fret. If one guitar is playing a line on the 5th and 6th strings, the second guitar is playing the same thing only up an octave on the 1st and 2nd strings. For a good example of this, listen to Lenny Kravitz's "Are You Goin' My Way," with the signature line being played in the open-E position, with the other guitar one octave higher on the 12th fret. On country and pop sessions, rhythm guitarists will frequently capo and play the same chord progression, but with (obviously) different chord shapes to create a "shimmering" sound. If the song is in G and the primary rhythm part is played in a folk style in 1st position, another guitarist on the session can capo at the 4th fret and play it in a folk style in D.

Each guitar is playing a different rhythm. If one guitar is playing long, sustained chords (called "power chords" or "footballs," because they're whole notes that look like footballs when transcribed), the second one is playing a faster rhythm, made up of, say, quarter or eighth notes. You'll find that this occurs a lot in hard rock and metal music, although two guitars can also just be playing different lines in which the two rhythms seamlessly integrate together, like in the Eagles' "Hotel California" or the verse sections in "Sweet Home Alabama."

These techniques must be employed so that the guitars will lay in better with the track and better support the vocals and rhythm section. Using them will make the song a lot more interesting to boot.

LAYING IN WITH THE RHYTHM SECTION

Regardless of if you're hired mostly to play solos and lead lines, more times than not you'll have to play some chordal rhythmic part that will require you to lock in with the rhythm section. Yes, the producer can always edit the part in a DAW to make it lay in better with the bass and drums, but that's not why you're being hired. You're expected to do a lot better than that. Playing rhythm and locking in with the rhythm section is an essential part of your studio-playing technique and is a superessential part of getting the track to sound great, so let's take a look at just how to do this.

Locking in with the rhythm section means that you're playing in rhythm with the drummer, in particular. It doesn't mean you're playing exactly the same rhythm as he is playing, but it does mean that you're exactly with him on every quarter note (the 1–2–3–4 of the beat) of the part that you're playing. Metallica does this a lot in their music, with "Master of Puppets" being a good example.

The easiest way to lock in with the drummer is to watch him as much as you can. Whenever he hits the snare drum, you have to be with him as closely as possible. Even a small amount before or after is too much. It has to be exactly on!

If you're lucky enough to play with the same drummer for a while and you get to know one another, you'll naturally lock into each other's rhythms. Under those circumstances, watching all the time becomes unnecessary, but it's still important to watch during recording, since it's the absolute easiest way to lock in as closely as possible.

> *Set up so that you can see all of the drummer's appendages, so that you watch his feet and hands as well as listen. It's a visual idiom sometimes. Watch his body. Watch his face. When he grimaces, maybe you can lean into a note with your body. It's choreography almost, but it makes a difference.*
>
> Paul Ill

So that takes care of 2 and 4. How about the 1 and 3 with the kick drum? The kick drum usually isn't that easy to hear, whether it's live on stage, in rehearsal, or while recording. A trick that experienced studio players use is to put your foot against the kick drum so you feel the vibration and play to that.

What to Bring

As stated above, a recording is made interesting by using multiple layers of different-sounding instruments or by the unique tones created by individual instruments and how they combine. You just never know when a piece of gear, even one that you haven't used in years, will give you just the right sound for a song. Until you know that you can cover every type of sound likely requested in a session by using a certain limited amount of gear, bring every amp that you can, regardless of how small it is (some of the best recording amps are the smallest), as well as every effect and guitar. If you're limited to what you can easily bring because there are space limitations, bring pieces of gear that are distinctly different from each other, like, for example, a Les Paul, a Strat, and a hollowbody electric like a Gibson ES-335 or a Gretsch Tennessean. The exceptions here are if the studio is so small that you can't fit everything in it, or the producer or engineer specifically asks you to bring or not to bring something.

I'll bring the TC pedalboard (that contains a Trinity overdrive, a Boss Fuzz, a Line 6 rotary simulator, and a Peterson tuner) and either a 1×12 or a 2×12 speaker cabinet, with these little heads built by Suhr called Badgers; there's one that's 18 watts and another that's 30 watts. I really like them because they're versatile and sound great with pedals. For guitars, I'll try to bring a Les Paul, a Strat, a Tele, and maybe one acoustic.

Peter Thorn

I have a great rack that I really love using that's built by David Freedman of Rack Systems Ltd. here in L.A. It includes some vintage pedals like an Electro Harmonix Memory Man and a MicroSynth, a Cornish pedal that's fantastic, a DigiTech Experience pedal, and a blue Boss VB2 vibrato pedal that's really rare. It also has these great Randall preamps and amps that have a convertible preamp system and a MIDI-switchable power section. They can sound like a great blackface Fender, a great Plexi Marshall, an AC-30, and then a sort of rectified Mesa, all with MIDI-switchable power sections between EL-34s (like a Marshall) and 6L6s (like a Fender) so you can have any combination of presets. There's also a Rocktron Replifex, which works great in the post-preamp position before the amps. The rack also has an auxiliary amp send, so I can use a different head together with the different preamps—so I usually bring an AC-30 or my Divided by 13 [JRT] 9/15 head along. Then I have baritone guitars, lots of different Les Pauls, and lots of vintage stuff that I don't bring out on the road much but [that] *I'm happy to bring to sessions in town* [Los Angeles].

Brian Ray, guitarist with Paul McCartney

Standard Session Procedure

Here's a routine that will stay much the same from session to session, regardless of the type of music, artist, or studio. While many of the following items below also apply to playing live, there's a different emphasis when playing sessions that centers on professionalism. All items apply to every recording session, with the possible exception of recording in your own studio.

Arrive early. You should always arrive at least a half hour before the downbeat of the session. This means that if your session starts at 7 p.m., you need to be there by 6:30 p.m. or earlier to be ready to play at 7 p.m. You can't expect to get there at 6:55 and for everything to be cool. If the session starts at 7 p.m., find out if that means load-in time or actual downbeat time. Remember that if you keep your employers waiting, you probably won't be asked to work for them again.

Turn off your cell phone. The session should be your main priority, and there should be as few distractions as possible. One of the easiest ways to achieve this is to turn off your cell phone. If you leave it on, you risk not only ruining a good take if the ringer goes off but also stopping the momentum of a session in its tracks. Further, it's so disrespectful to every else who is at the session. Don't even bother to put your phone on "vibrate," since a vibrating phone will cause you to lose your focus just as easily as when the ringer goes off. Turn your phone off, and then leave it outside the studio in the lounge so you won't be tempted to use it.

Make sure your guitars are in tip-top shape. This means that you should have the intonation professionally checked so that you can play in tune anywhere on the neck. The thing that brings down a session faster than anything else is a guitar player who either can't get his instrument in tune or can't get it to stay in tune.

Bring extra strings, picks, tubes, cables, and batteries. You must have backups in case you break a string, lose your pick, or your battery dies so that the session can keep going as soon you're up and running again. Even if you think you have everything in your case or gig box, double-check to make sure. It's easy to forget about that last time you broke an E string on a guitar you don't use that much, and that you never replaced the replacement.

Have your amp tuned up. While you might be able to get away with it onstage, you'll never be able to successfully record with an amp that is buzzing, farting, or randomly spitting and quitting. For recording, everything has to be in great, not just good, working order. If not, the tracks you put down will only have to be redone later, probably by someone else. Plus, you want the recording to sound the best it can, don't you?

Make sure your cables are working. It's easy to keep playing with a guitar cable that cuts out or makes noise occasionally. We all do it. But using anything less than a perfect cable is a definite no-no when recording. Having to redo the perfect take because your cable cut out is bound to upset not only you, but also everyone else in the studio. Cables are cheap. Buy a new one if you have any doubts about the one you're using. By the way, if you're used to going wireless onstage, you'll probably find that your guitar sounds a little better with a cable in the studio. Also, unless you have a really expensive wireless setup, it's susceptible to outside interference from police and fire stations at or near the same frequency. Be prepared to use a cable, since most producers don't even want to take the chance.

Warm up quietly. You've got to warm up and everyone expects you to, but try to be quiet as you can so you're not a distraction. The more quietly you can warm up, the more everyone will appreciate it.

Don't make any unnecessary noise. The less talk, the better. Don't leave your earphones uncovered, or turn them down when you don't have them on your head. A little courtesy like that can go a long way.

Don't complain about the air conditioner. The temperature is never going to be perfect for everyone, so it's useless to even bring this up as it will just become a distraction. The only exception is if it's so cold that it physically impedes your playing or adversely affects your instrument's tuning.

Stay awake! Listen to everything that's going on and be ready to play at all times. If you're playing with other studio musicians, watch the leader and stop playing when the leader stops.

Don't talk after a take until the engineer or the producer says it's okay to do so. Nothing can ruin a take or make a lot more work for the production team than someone thoughtlessly making a comment at the end of a take. Even if you think the take will have to be done again, keep all comments to yourself. Sometimes a take that feels bad to you can feel great to everyone else.

Always seem interested in the music. It's easy to get complacent when your chops exceed what you've been called to play on, but try to get beyond that feeling. It's best to have only enough chops for that particular job—nothing more and nothing less. Showing off is a good way not to be asked back. And try not to look ahead in the chart when you're playing; doing so can be a good way to lose your place.

Stay out of the control room. Unless you're specifically asked to do otherwise, stay in the studio. And if you are asked to come in to listen to a playback, don't eat the booth food unless it's offered to you. It's not necessarily there for you!

Make any charts, notes, or cheat sheets beforehand. Once again, this comes under the heading of being prepared. If you have some time before the downbeat of the session, ask to hear the song or songs you will be recording (if there's a demo or you're going to be doing overdubs) so you can make a chart or notes. You don't want to be wasting anyone's time doing something on the clock that could so easily have been done beforehand. Also, if you have to mark your charts, do it so anyone can read them later—make all your notes legible. Top studio musicians do develop their own shorthand techniques and always figure out ways to jot down necessary notes or reminders (most particularly about content or form changes that evolve as the music takes shape) on the fly, without slowing down the session.

Don't pack up early. Don't leave until you're officially excused, and be sure to clean up your area when you are finished.

The Guitar Player's Utility Kit

As Murphy's Law states, "If something can go wrong, it will go wrong!" so you have to be prepared during recording for any eventuality, so that you can get back up and running again as soon as possible. Things break, but a pro is always ready. The following list will help you prepare for just about anything. Each item should be considered just as essential to bring to a session as your guitar and amp are.

2 spare power tubes (if you use a tube amplifier)

2 spare 12ax7 preamp tubes (if you use a tube amplifier or a preamp)

A package of fuses for each amp that you bring

2 spare sets of strings for each guitar (if you use different gauges on different guitars)

Spare E strings

A string winder

A digital tuner (with a backup just in case)

Wire snips

Needle-nose pliers

A Phillips screwdriver

A flat-head screwdriver

A set of Allen wrenches

A light source (like a flashlight or a clip-on book light)

Gaffer's or duct tape

Super Glue

At least 2 extra 10' instrument cables (¼"-to-¼")

An extra 5' instrument cable

Extra RCA cables or various cable adapters like ¼"-to-RCA, RCA-to-¼", ¼"-to-XLR (if you're using equipment that uses these)

An extra AC cable

An AC extension cable

An extra power strip

Different kinds of picks

A spare guitar strap

A slide

A capo

Any special microphones that you like to use

A spare mic-stand adapter (if the mic uses something unusual)

Any special DI (if it's part of your sound)

Your own headphones (if they help you hear better)

Spare 9V batteries (if you use pedals or have a preamp built into your guitar)

Spare AA batteries

Spare universal 9V wall wart

A small notepad

A pen

A couple of pencils

A Magic Marker

A pair of earplugs

Band-Aids

Throat lozenges

Aspirin or Advil

A towel

Guide for Bass Players

Like session guitar players, session bass players have their own set of unique challenges. First and foremost is to anchor the rhythm section and drive the groove of the song. Studio bassists are also often called upon to create a bass line that not only moves the track, but also is unobtrusive to the rest of the music. No short order! But the bass sound is also a big part of session work. Many players, especially those new to studio work, take their bass sound for granted and don't give it much thought, but a bass player who's able to offer a producer several sonic alternatives in order to find the one that best fits a song will get a call back every time. That being said, let's look at what's expected of a session bass player.

Before the Session Begins

Of all the questions that you might ask when you get the call for a session (as outlined in chapter 8), make sure you zero in on these two.

Is there any particular sound that is desired? This question determines what gear you should bring. If you're asked to get a grungy modern rock sound, that tells you to bring along a bass with roundwound strings and a good overdrive pedal. If it's a classic Beatles sound they're going for, you'll know to bring either a Höfner or a Rickenbacker strung with flatwounds (you're going to ask which one, right?). If you don't have the exact replica of the gear, then you'll at least know what to bring to get your sound in the ballpark.

Are there any particular instrument(s), amps, or effects to be used? Many times the producer or artist has a specific sound in mind, either because they've heard it from you before or they just expect it from you. "Bring your vintage Kay" or "Bring your white P-bass" tells you not only what to bring but also what to set up to track with first.

Your Sound

Besides anchoring the rhythm section, the bass anchors the low end of the recording, and so its sound is important. If the low end is thin, then the recording doesn't seem as powerful. There's a reason that most recording bass players choose to use a Fender Precision bass and an Ampeg B-15. It's the sound! Even more so than with a guitar, the bass can make such a huge contribution to the sound that when you finally hear a fine example of one of these instruments, your first reaction is, "Oh, now I get it."

While every guitar manufacturer also makes basses, there are only a few that consistently see time in the studio. They are the Fender Precision or the Fender Jazz bass, the Rickenbacker 4001, and the Music Man StingRay. While you might see famous bassists play other models, you'll most often find that they use these to record with.

Generally, the bass used will be the one that, for the context of that particular track, offers the most fundamental tone, that is to say, the best low end when the recording is mastered while sitting correctly with the drum sound.

Occasionally, a bass is chosen for its unique character or voice to give the track a definable sound. Listen to Pino Palladino's masterful fretless bass on Paul Young's '80s hit "Every Time You Go Away" or Don Henley's "The Boys of Summer" for appropriate examples.

Make sure that you are comfortable with your gear, everything is functioning perfectly, and your basses are adjusted so that all the notes of your bass speak evenly—that is, no note or group of notes is noticeably louder or softer than the others (this is a common occurrence somewhere on the neck of just about every bass). If the notes are quiet or are lacking in fundamental pitch, they are called "wolf tones"; they are usually found on Fender-style basses on the G string, somewhere between the 4th and 9th frets. Some of the loud or dead notes can be fixed with proper nut and bridge adjustment and intonation, but sometimes you have to resort to equalization. Either way, you can expect a note or two to be softer than the rest, and a couple might just roar. The idea is to limit it to only those few places if you can't totally fix the problem.

The type of strings you use is important as well. Many players will bring nearly identical basses to a session, with one having roundwounds and the other flatwound strings. The difference is appreciable and worth the extra effort, since nothing cops the sound of '60s Motown (among other genres) like flatwounds! With the advent of Rotosound's roundwound "piano sounding" bass strings, flatwounds were out of vogue with most players by the late '60s. Case in point: 1973's *Houses of the Holy* was the first Led Zeppelin album cut with a bass using roundwound strings. Up until that album, John Paul Jones did all his '60s session work and cut the first four Led Zeppelin records with a 1964 Fender Jazz bass strung with Rotosound flatwounds. Roundwounds do offer a higher "fidelity" and are, for the most part, easier to play than flats, but since the early 2000s, flatwounds have made a noticeable comeback in the recording world.

Amplifiers are another important aspect. There's a reason you see Ampeg SVTs on stage after stage and hear Ampeg B-15s on record after record—it's their sound.

While both of these amplifiers are expensive items (and using the SVT can be overkill in many applications, since it's extremely loud, powerful, and heavy), it's worth doing everything you can to play through one for five minutes. Just having that point of reference will make a big difference in how you shape your sound from that point on.

Locking In

The bass player's job is as a support player, but good support can come only from locking in with the drummer. Laying in with a drummer requires more than listening; it's watching the drummer as well. It's watching his arms and feet so that you can see where he physically puts the beat. It's watching his face for grimaces to know where you maybe can lean into a note with your body. It's putting your foot up against the bass drum to feel his pulse. It's all about locking in with your rhythm mate.

What to Bring

As stated in various previous chapters, a recording is made interesting by multiple layers of different-sounding instruments, and in the case of record work, a group of songs is made more interesting by incorporating different sounds from song to song. As a result, you just never know when a piece of gear, even one that you haven't used in years, will give you just the right sound for the song. Until you know that you can cover every type of sound that is likely to be requested in a session by using a certain limited amount of gear, bring as much as you can, from basses to pedals to amplifiers. If you're limited to what you can easily bring because there are space limitations, bring pieces of gear that are distinctly different from each other, like a P-bass, a Rick, and a maybe something with flatwound strings. The exceptions here are if the studio is so small that you can't fit everything in it, or the producer or engineer specifically asks you to bring or not to bring something.

Standard Session Procedure

As you'll read throughout this book, the approach and mind-set needed for a recording session is somewhat different from what's needed for a live situation. While many of the following items also apply to playing live, there's a different emphasis when playing on sessions that centers on professionalism. All items apply to every recording session, with the possible exception of recording in your own studio.

Arrive early. You should always arrive at least a half hour before the downbeat of the session. This means that if your session starts at 7 p.m., you need to be there by 6:30 p.m. or earlier to be ready to play at 7 p.m. You can't expect to get there at 6:55 and for everything to be cool. If the session starts at 7 p.m., find out if that means load-in time or actual downbeat time. Remember that if you keep your employers waiting, you probably won't work for them again.

Turn off your cell phone. The session should be your main priority, and there should be as few distractions as possible. One of the easiest ways to achieve this is to turn off your cell phone. If you leave it on, you risk not only ruining a good take if the ringer goes off, but also stopping the momentum of a session in its tracks. Further, it's so disrespectful to every else who is at the session. Don't even bother to put your phone on "vibrate," since a vibrating phone will cause you to lose your focus just as easily as when the ringer goes off. Turn your phone off, and then leave it outside the studio in the lounge so you won't be tempted to use it.

Make sure your instruments are in tune. This means that you should have the intonation professionally checked so that your instrument plays in tune anywhere on the neck.

Also, check your tuning with a tuner rather than doing it by ear. The tuning of the bass is really easy to overlook when you're tracking, because sometimes the lack of tuning isn't that obvious. But it will bug the heck out of you every time you hear a tune played back if it's out of tune because you didn't take the time to fix it.

Bring all your basses to the session. All basses sound different (even two that are the exact same models, like Fender Precision basses, for instance). You never know when something that you haven't used in years will have just the right sound for the song you're recording. Bring every bass that you can, but if you have to limit the number because of limited space, just bring the ones that are really different from each other, like a Rickenbacker and a Fender, or a Fender Precision and a Fender Jazz bass, or a P-bass and a Höfner.

Bring extra strings, picks, tubes, cables, and batteries. You have to have backups in case you break a string or a battery dies. Even if you usually only play with your fingers, bring several kinds of picks, since using one could give you the perfect sound for the track. On that note, if you are primarily a pick player, get your finger chops up to speed. If you are primarily a finger player, work on those pick chops. Practice playing both ways until you can execute parts with the same facility and are able to switch on the fly between fingers and a pick. Stylistically, thumb slapping, while a signature sound for '70s funk and disco, is usually frowned upon on a contemporary session. But you never know—you may be asked to "slap and pop," so dust off those chops, too. Even if you think you have everything in your case or gig box, double-check to make sure. It's easy to forget about that last time you broke a string, and then never replaced the replacement.

Have your amp tuned up. Bringing a small amp with you to the session is never a bad idea, since the studio may not have one or it might not sound that great, while your amp just might have the sound (either by itself or mixed with the DI) that perfectly fits the track. And in line with a current trend in modern recording, you may be ask to forgo the DI and just use an amp or a combination of two amps. Just make sure that it's in good working order with no buzzing, humming, farting, or other unwanted noises. You also might want to check with the studio first to see if they have a bass amp that you can use (they usually do), and that it's working properly. Two of the best investments a studio bassist can make are in a vintage Ampeg B-15 and a vintage-sounding Fender Precision bass. Together, they create the industry standard for professional recorded bass sound.

Make sure your cables are working. Using anything less than a perfect cable is a definite no-no when recording. Having to redo the perfect take because your cable cut out is bound to upset not only you, but everyone else in the studio. Cables are cheap. Buy a new one if you have any doubts about what you have.

Warm up quietly. You've got to warm up and everyone expects you to, but try to be as quiet as you can so you're not a distraction. The more quietly you can warm up, the more everyone will appreciate it.

Don't make any unnecessary noise. The less talk, the better. Don't leave your headphones uncovered, or make sure that you turn them down, when you don't have them on your head. A little courtesy like that can go a long way.

Don't complain about the air conditioner. The temperature is never going to be perfect for everyone, so it's useless to even bring this up; it will just become a distraction. The only exception is if it's so cold that it physically impedes your playing or adversely affects your instrument's tuning.

Stay awake! Listen to everything that's going on and be ready to play at all times. If you're playing with other studio musicians, watch the leader and stop playing when the leader stops.

Don't talk after a take until the engineer or the producer says it's okay to do so. Nothing can ruin a take or make a lot more work for the production team than someone thoughtlessly making a comment at the end of a take. Even if you think the take will have to be done again, keep all comments to yourself. Sometimes a take that feels bad to you can feel great to everyone else.

Always seem interested in the music. It's easy to get complacent when your chops exceed what you've been called to play on, but try to get beyond that feeling. It's best to have only enough chops for that particular job—nothing more and nothing less. Showing off is a good way not to be asked back. And try not to look ahead in the chart when you're playing; doing so can be a good way to lose your place.

Stay out of the control room. Unless you're specifically asked to do otherwise, stay in the studio. And if you are asked to come in to listen to a playback, don't eat the booth food unless it's offered to you. It's not necessarily there for you!

Make any charts, notes, or cheat sheets beforehand. Once again, this comes under the heading of being prepared. If you have some time before the downbeat of the session, ask to hear the song or songs you will be recording (if there's a demo or you're going to be doing overdubs) so you can make a chart or notes. You don't want to be wasting anyone's time doing something on the clock that could so easily been done beforehand. Also, if you have to mark your charts, do it so anyone can read them later, and make all your notes legible.

Don't pack up early. Don't leave until you're officially excused, and be sure to clean up your area when you've been dismissed.

The Bass Player's Utility Kit

As Murphy's Law states, "If something can go wrong, it will go wrong!" so you've got to be prepared during recording for any eventuality. The following list will help you prepare for just about anything. Each item should be considered just as essential to bring to a session as your bass and amp are.

2 spare power tubes (if you use a tube amplifier)

2 spare 12ax7 preamp tubes (if you use a tube amplifier or preamplifier)

A package of fuses for each amp that you bring

A spare set of strings for each bass that has a different gauge or type

Wire snips

Needle-nose pliers

A Phillips screwdriver

A flat-head screwdriver

A set of Allen wrenches

A light source (like a flashlight or a clip-on book light)

Duct tape

Super Glue

At least 2 extra 10' instrument cables (¼"-to-¼")

An extra 5' cable if you use a pedal

Different kinds of picks (guitar picks of different thickness, felt)

A spare guitar strap

A digital tuner

Any special DI that you like to use if given the choice

Any special microphones that you like to use if given the choice

A spare mic-stand adapter (if the mic uses something unusual)

Your own headphones (if they help you hear better)

Spare 9V batteries for your bass electronics, tuner, or pedals

Spare AA batteries

A spare universal 9V wall wart (if you have an electronic piece that uses one)

A small notepad

A pen

A couple of pencils

A Magic Marker

A pair of earplugs

Band-Aids

Throat lozenges

Aspirin or Advil

A towel

CHAPTER 14

Guide for Drummers

Contrary to what you might think, being a great session drummer doesn't necessarily mean having great chops and the ability to play great polyrhythms. In fact, sometimes having too much technique can actually get in the way of your ability to drive a band during a session. Great session drummers are "song oriented," not "chops oriented."

In modern music, drums are the pulse of the song and the heartbeat of the band, and this is the drummer's major priority. Listen to just about any record and you'll see: the drummer drives the band and complements the song the same way that any other instrument does.

Simple Is Best

No matter what kind of music you're asked to play, the drummer's first and foremost role is to function as timekeeper. You may have the greatest chops on the continent, but if you can't play time with a great feel, none of your skills matter in the studio. It's true that most musicians (especially drummers) want to get better technically and then implement those skills and show them off, but playing in time and on tempo is the first order of business if you sit on that drum throne. Drummers practice forever trying to be as good as Neil Peart, yet it's not about technique, but rather the feel: nothing extra played, just hits in all the right places. Simplicity, yet perfection.

> *A lot of drummers miss the boat because they're not concerned with playing time and playing simple basic beats and being able to clone that beat over and over again like a drum machine, but with soul. A lot of drummers are into the flash and are constantly looking for stuff to play and where they* [can] *put the kitchen sink into every tune. I heard a story once where Miles Davis told someone, "When you think you want to play something, don't." That story is kinda funny, but it's also true. Don't try to be always playing something. Lay back, play the groove, and wait for your spot. They won't be as often as you think. A lot of times drummers try to play too much, and I'm not talking stylistically, either. Whether you're a fusion drummer or a groove drummer, a lot of young drummers are looking to play too much too often. If you have amazing chops, wait for that right moment to use them. It will mean a lot more.*
>
> Bernie Dresel

> *As far as advice, the first thing is to play good time. Secondly, you have to make it feel good. If you don't, you're going to get beat up from having to play it over and over again.*
>
> Ricky Lawson

THE CONCEPTS OF FEEL AND INTERNAL TIME

So what does playing "in time" actually mean? We can break the concept down into feel and internal time. "Feel" means an intuitive ability to know where the beats are placed in a given type of music. This is something that can be learned to some degree, but for the most part, you either have a great feel for a type of music or you don't. A drummer who has a great feel for one type of music might not have it for another. For instance, a drummer who has a great feel for a blues shuffle might not have it for bebop, while another drummer with a great feel for polyrhythmic progressive jazz might not have it for world music, or a drummer with a great R&B feel might have none for metal. If you don't have a great feel for a type of music, you either have to play and listen to it enough until you do, or play some other kind of music that you have a natural feel for. Either way, the music can feel good to everyone else (your audience and the mates you play with) only when it feels good to you first.

As for the concept of "internal time," having it is what makes the difference between a drummer who sounds as though he's moving furniture and a drummer whose playing makes people want to get up to shake their booty. Even though you might be keeping a steady tempo, you can still have bad internal time. Internal time means how evenly you play individual drums. For instance, you may be steady with your kick drum on beats 1 and 3, but a little ahead or behind on beats 2 and 4. Or always steady timewise with your snare drum but unsteady on your hi-hat. Now it's okay if you're steadily consistently behind with your time, but wavering in time makes you lose the feel and groove. For instance, going back to the kick drum, if you're always the same amount behind the beat on 2 and 4, that might actually be the perfect feel for the music. It's when you waver—sometimes ahead, sometimes behind, always by a different amount—that everything falls apart (see Fig. 14.1).

Fig. 14.1: Good and Bad Internal Time

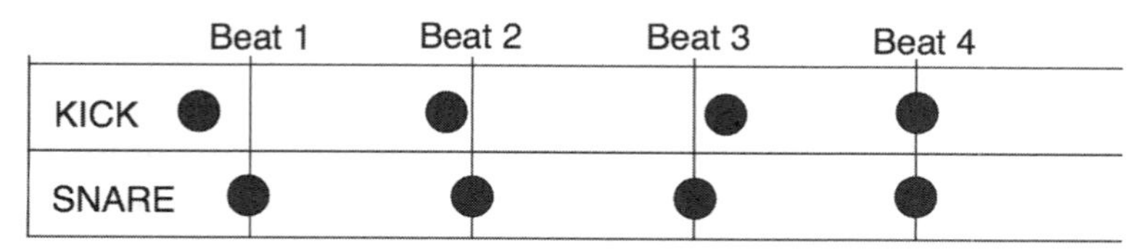

BAD INTERNAL TIME - Snare is on the beat. Kick is sometimes in front of the beat, sometimes behind.

Beat 1 Beat 2 Beat 3 Beat 4

KICK

SNARE

GOOD INTERNAL TIME - Kick is on the beat. Snare is behind the beat always by the same amount.

Although it seems that the best drummers are born with an innate sense of internal time, it can be learned. The problem is that studying it is relatively boring, and not many drummers want to spend the time required. You have to concentrate on playing as steadily as possible with each limb first, and then gradually add them all together. You should constantly record yourself, both with a click or loops and without, to gauge how much you've improved. Most drummers aren't even aware of the concept of internal time. But if you concentrate on it, you'll most certainly get better, since it's the one thing that can give you the biggest jump in feel and groove.

RUSHED OR LAZY FILLS

Perhaps the one area that plagues drummers, amateurs, and pros alike, is the problem of rushed or lazy drum fills. This is any fill that drifts out of time with the rest of the song and, once again, is a destroyer of groove and feel. There's really no excuse for this breakdown, and it can be overcome by practicing to a click or a loop, and recording the results. The big trick is to be aware that you're doing it.

A lot of drummers have great time except for when they do fills. I've heard from producers, "So and so has such a great feel, but his fills are always out of time." Rushing the fill is a really common thing for a lot of drummers. The way to cure that is just practicing to a click track a lot.

Brian MacLeod

ARE YOU PLAYING TOO LOUDLY?

Sometimes it's not the guitar player that's playing too loudly in a band—it's the drummer. This is usually the case with a drummer that's a heavy hitter and has a big, loud drum kit to begin with, and has no conception of dynamics or how to lay in with the band. While it's true that the drummer drives the band, a drummer who only thrashes at his loudest volume level sounds like he's moving furniture instead of playing and will usually cause the neighbors or the audience to get the "turn it down" signs out.

While feel usually applies to where the beats are put within the music, it also has to do with the volume level of the drums within the band and the recording. Being able to feel the right volume and intensity to drive the band is something that you can learn; it's called "dynamics" and is one of the basic keys to making a recording sound great.

What Makes a Drum Kit Sound Great?

Playing well is only half the equation to becoming a studio drummer; the other half is having a great-sounding drum kit. Although a great drummer can usually make a bad-sounding kit acceptable, you're really expected to deliver the sound as well as the chops.

So what does "great sounding" actually mean? While the definition of "great" is different to different people on a general level, to a pro it usually means a kit that is well tuned and free of buzzes and sympathetic vibrations. This means that when you hit the rack tom, for instance, the snare doesn't buzz and the other toms don't ring along with it. Or if you hit the snare, the toms don't ring along. So how do you achieve this drum nirvana? It's all in the tuning and the kit maintenance.

Tuning the Drums

Many drummers don't know much about why their kit sounds the way it does, and unfortunately, that also applies to drum tuning. All drummers are taught the basics of drum tuning at some point during their education, but knowing how to do it and knowing what to listen for are two different things. Here are some tips from Ross Garfield, the world-famous Drum Doctor, to get you started.

TUNING TIPS FROM THE DRUM DOCTOR

If you're doing a recording session in Los Angeles and want your drums to instantly sound great, then your first call should be to the Drum Doctor to either rent a fantastic-sounding kit or have your kit tuned. Ross Garfield is the "Drum Doctor," and you've heard his drum sounds on Platinum recordings from Alanis Morisette, the Black Crowes, Bruce Springsteen, Rod Stewart, Mettalica, Marilyn Manson, Dwight Yokum, Jane's Addiction, Red Hot Chili Peppers, Foo Fighters, Lenny Kravitz, Michael Jackson, Rage Against the Machine, Sheryl Crow, Nirvana, and many, many more. Not many people know as much about drums and drum tuning as Ross, and the following tips were learned after years of experience working closely with the likes of drum greats Jeff Porcaro, Jim Keltner, Charlie Watts, Terry Bozio, Jeff Hamilton, Steve Jordan, Charlie Drayton, and Peter Erskine (to name just a few), so check out his suggestions. You can also find out more about the Drum Doctor at www.drumdoctors.com.

HOW LONG DOES IT TAKE TO TUNE A DRUM KIT?

If I have to change all the heads and tune them up, it'll take about an hour, and that's even on a cheap starter set. I try to tune them to where I think they should be—a little on the high side for starters—then after we open up the mics and hear everything magnified, I'll modify the tuning more to the song.

PREPPING THE DRUMS FOR NEW HEADS

In order for drums to sound their best, the edges of the drum shell have to be cut properly, and this is something that no one ever checks, or even thinks of checking, until it's time to change the heads. When you take the heads off, all the edges of the shell should lie exactly flat against a flat surface. I'll put the shell on a piece of glass or granite and shine a light over the top of the shell; then I'll get down to where the edge of the drum hits the granite. If I see a light at any point, then that means there's a low spot on the edge of the shell and the drum will be hard to tune and probably have some funny overtones. So the first thing to do is make sure that your drum shells are "true." The next thing is for your shell edge to have a bevel to it, and not be flat on the bottom, because again, this affects the tuning and overtones.

If you have either of these problems with a drum, send it back to the manufacturer. Don't try to cut the edges of your drum shells yourself, since it doesn't cost that much money for the manufacturer to do it, and it's really something that should be done by someone who knows exactly what they're doing. Once your drum shells are in good shape, then tuning is a lot easier to do.

NEW HEADS

The first thing I do when I tune my drums is put a fresh set of top and bottom heads on. Nine times out of ten, I'll put white Remo Ambassadors on the tops, clear Remo Ambassadors on the bottoms, and a Remo clear Powerstroke 3 on the kick drum. I'll use a white Ambassador or a coated black-dot Ambassador on the snare top, and either a clear Diplomat or a coated Ambassador on the bottom.

A lot of the decision about what type of head to use depends on how deep the drum is. If it's five inches or less,

I'll usually go with an Ambassador, and if it's six and a half inches or more, I'll usually go with a Diplomat. Just this little bit of information really makes a difference in how the kit sounds.

A heavy hitter will get more low end out of a drum that's tuned higher just because of the way he hits, so as a result I usually tune a drum a little tighter if the drummer is a heavy hitter. I might move into different heads as well, like an Emperor or something thicker.

> *I just kind of move the combination of drum heads around to get different things. If I want a heavier sound, I'll use a thicker head. If I want it brighter with more attack, I'll use a thinner head. I usually don't go any thinner than an Ambassador, and I usually don't go any thicker than an Emperor.*
>
> Ricky Lawson

THE TUNING TECHNIQUE

Most drummers don't know the correct way to tune their drums, but it's really not that hard. For a proper tune job, you've got to keep all of the tension rods even so they have the same tension at each lug.

You hit the head an inch in front of the lug, and if you do it enough times you'll hear which ones are higher and which are lower. What you want is for the pitch to sound the same at each lug. When the pitch (the tension) is the same at each lug, then when you hit the drum in the center you should have a nice even decay.

Tune the top and the bottom heads to the same pitch at first, then take the bottom head down by a third to a fifth below the top head.

> *What I try to do is to tune to where the drum sounds good. You can take a drum and you can tune it out of the range of what it likes to be in, so I just try to find the sweet spot for that drum with the combination of heads that I'm using. I*

like the top head a little bit tighter, and then I use the bottom head just to bring in some tone.

Ricky Lawson

There's a lot of different theories about how a drum should sound, but the one that works best for me is when the top head is not exactly the same pitch as the bottom. The top head I tune about a minor third above the bottom head when you're just barely tapping it right on the edge near the lug.

Bernie Dresel

TUNING THE SNARE

The snare is probably the most important drum in the set because it's the voice of the song, since you hear it on at least every 2 and 4. So it's important to get the snare tuned to where you want it first.

SNARE-DRUM-TUNING TIPS

I like the ring of the drum to decay with the snares. If the snare drum has too much ring,

- Tune the heads lower.
- Use a heavier head like a coated CS with the dot on the bottom or a coated Emperor.
- Use a full or partial muffling ring.
- Have the edges checked and/or recut to a flatter angle.

If the snare drum doesn't have enough ring,

- Tune the head higher.
- Use a thinner head like a coated Ambassador or a Diplomat.

▶ Have the edges checked and/or recut to a sharper angle.

If the snares buzz when the tom-toms are hit,

▶ Check that the snares are straight. Replace as needed.

▶ Check that the snares are flat and centered on the drum.

▶ Loosen the bottom head.

▶ Retune the offending toms.

▶ Use an alternate snare drum.

> *I don't think it's good to tune the snare drum on the snare stand. It's better on a table or floor so it's laying flat. You make sure you get your head on flat if you have to change one, then tighten each lug so that it's barely touching the rim, then just finger-tighten the lugs (crisscrossing as you go) so you make sure that you don't overtighten one. Then you can start using the drum key.*
>
> Bernie Dresel

TUNING THE KICK DRUM

If the kick drum isn't punchy and lacks power when played in the context of the music, you can try the following:

▶ Increase or decrease the amount of muffling in the drum, or try a different blanket or pillow.

▶ Change to a heavier, uncoated head like a clear Emperor or a PowerStroke 3.

▶ Change to a thinner front head or one with a larger cutout.

▶ Have the edges recut to create more attack.

TUNING THE TOMS

The kick and snare are the two most important drums in a kit, and I tune the toms around them to try to make sure that the rack toms aren't being set off by the snare.

I like the toms to have a nice even decay. Usually I'll tune the drums so that the smallest drums have the shortest decay, with the decay getting longer as the drums get bigger.

I tend to tune each tom as far apart as the song will permit. It's easy to get the right spread between a 13- and a 16-inch tom, but it's more difficult to get it between a 12- and a 13-inch. What I try to do is to tune the 12 up a little, and the 13 down.

If one or more of the tom-toms are difficult to tune, don't blend together, or have an unwanted "growl," try the following:

- Check the top heads for dents, and replace as necessary.
- Check the evenness of tension all around on the top and bottom heads.
- Tighten the bottom head.
- Have the bearing edges checked and recut as required.

If the floor tom has an undesirable "basketball-type" after-ring, try this:

- Loosen the bottom head.
- Check the top heads for dents, and replace as necessary.
- Loosen the top head.
- Switch to a different type or weight top or bottom head, like a clear Ambassador or an Emperor.

- Have the bearing edges recut to emphasize the lower partials.

> *So what I try to do between my three toms—the 12", 14" and 16"—is to have them maybe a fourth apart in pitch; that way you don't get an octave between the highest tom and the lowest, and they sound musical together. Now if you have a lot of toms, then maybe tuning them a major third apart could work, but with three toms I think a fourth is good because all three are tuned within the same octave. A fifth is too much, because then they're not.*
>
> Bernie Dresel

CYMBALS

For recording, you have to be careful when you mix cymbal weights. For example, if you're using thin Zildjian A Custom crashes, you don't want to mix in a medium rock crash, because a thinner cymbal would probably disappear in the mix.

Thicker cymbals are made more with a live situation in mind. They're made to be loud and to cut through the band, but they can sound a little gonglike when recording. On the other hand, if you're playing all rock crashes and the engineer can deal with the level, that's not so bad either because the volume will be even.

If the cymbals are cracking or breaking with greater frequency, try the following:

- Always transport the cymbals in a top-quality, reinforced cymbal case or bag to avoid nicks that can become cracks.

- Use the proper cymbals felt, washers, and sleeves at all times.

- Avoid overtightening the cymbal stand.

- ▶ Use larger or heavier cymbals that you won't have to overplay to hear.

Standard Session Procedure

If you've read the previous chapters, you know that the approach and mind-set needed for a recording session is different from what's needed in a live situation. While many of the following items also apply to playing live, there's a different emphasis when playing on sessions that centers on professionalism. All items apply to every recording session, with the possible exception of recording in your own studio.

Arrive early. This goes without saying, but I'll say it again to reinforce it. You should always arrive at least an hour before the downbeat of the session because it takes that much time to not only set your kit up but also mic the kit. This means that if your session starts at 7 p.m., you need to be there by at least 6 p.m. to be ready at 7. You might even want to get there earlier (if they'll let you) to have some extra time to change your heads and tune your drums. If the session starts at 7 p.m., find out if that means load-in time or actual downbeat time. If you keep your employers waiting, it might be the last time you're asked to work with them.

Turn off your cell phone. The session should be your main priority, and there should be as few distractions as possible. One of the easiest ways to achieve this is to turn off your cell phone. If you leave it on, you risk not only ruining a good take if the ringer goes off, but also stopping the momentum of a session in its tracks. Further, it's so disrespectful to every else who is at the session. Don't even bother to put your phone on "vibrate," since a vibrating phone will cause you to lose your focus just as easily as when the ringer goes off. Turn your phone off, and then leave it outside the studio in the lounge so you won't be tempted to use it.

Change your heads. Nothing will help the sound of your drums like new heads. Get a set of new heads (at least the top ones), and either change them before you get to the studio or make sure that you have enough time to do so before recording.

Make sure your drums are in tune. Tune your drums as described above or hire someone that really knows how to do it. Not only will you learn something, but you'll also get a much better end result. For more information on drum tuning and drum sounds, check out the book The Drum Recording Handbook (Bobby Owsinski and Dennis Moody, Hal Leonard, 2009).

Bring all your snares to the session. You never know if and when a particular snare is right for a song until you try it. Sometimes you can be surprised at how good or how bad a drum sounds in the context of a recording. So to be safe, bring as many snares as you can to the session.

> *There are always budget considerations, so I generally bring six. I could bring 30 snares, but then the cartage bill goes up and, to be honest, you're usually way covered with the six snares because no one is ever asking "What else you got?" past that. So I bring three different sizes of wood and three different sizes of metal drums.*
>
> Bernie Dresel

> [I bring] *usually anywhere from five to six. At my studio I have about eight that I'll regularly choose from. You'd be surprised—different drums bring out different spirit in the music.*
>
> Ricky Lawson

> *I have two trunks that I generally bring that contain ten snare drums, plus I have an old vintage '70s Black Beauty that I hand-carry with me. I*

generally don't use a piccolo, but I have one in my arsenal. You have to make sure that you have everything, because whatever it is that you don't bring to the session, that's what the producer will ask for. So I like to be prepared and have plenty of options.

Brian MacLeod

Bring extra heads, sticks, beaters, cymbals, and batteries. You have to have backups in case you break a head or the battery on your metronome dies. Even if you usually play with only a certain type of stick, bring several kinds (plus mallets and brushes), since one of those sizes could have the perfect sound for the track you're recording. Even if you think you have everything in your case or gig box, double-check to make sure. It's easy to forget about that last time you broke a head on a little-used snare drum, and then never replaced the replacement.

I definitely bring a lot of different sticks, and brushes, and mallets, too, because someone will always ask, "Can you do a cymbal swell?" If you look in your stick bag and you don't have them, that's the part of being a session drummer where you have the most anxiety. It gets embarrassing if you have to tell them, "I can make some with some tissues and duct tape [laughs hard]*." I like to make sure that my stick bag is loaded with hot rods, brushes, different-size sticks, and mallets.*

Brian MacLeod

Bring the right cymbals. Most drummers choose heavier cymbals for playing live, because they're not only louder but they also last longer. Unfortunately, heavy cymbals usually don't sound as good as thinner cymbals do when under the close scrutiny of recording. You should have some lighter cymbals in your arsenal for recording. Be careful not to mismatch weights though, since the uneven balance will make the engineer's job a lot more difficult because of the volume differences.

If you use electronics, make sure that everything is working. If you use a drum machine as a click track or you're using electronic pads as a trigger, make sure that everything is in working order before you arrive at the studio. That includes making sure you have extra batteries, power supplies, and cables just in case something breaks in the course of the session.

Warm up quietly. You've got to warm up and everyone expects you to, but try to do so as quietly as you can so you aren't a distraction. The more quietly you can warm up, the more everyone will appreciate it.

Don't make any unnecessary noise. The less talk, the better. Don't leave your headphones uncovered, or make sure to turn them down, when you don't have them on your head. A little courtesy like that can go a long way.

Don't complain about the air conditioner. The temperature is never going to be perfect for everyone, so it's useless to even bring this up, it will just become a distraction. The only exception is if it's so cold that it physically impedes your playing.

Stay awake! Listen to everything that's going on and be ready to play at all times. If you're playing with other studio musicians, watch the leader and stop playing when the leader stops.

Don't talk after a take until the engineer or producer says it's okay to do so. Nothing can ruin a take or make a lot more work for the production team than someone thoughtlessly making a comment at the end of a take. Even if you think the take will have to be done again, keep all comments to yourself. Sometimes a take that feels bad to you can feel great to everyone else.

Always seem interested in the music. It's easy to get a little complacent when your chops exceed what you've been called to play on, but try to get beyond that feeling. It's best to have only enough chops for that particular job—nothing more and nothing less. Showing off is a good way not to be asked back. And try not to look ahead in the chart when you're playing; doing so can be a good way to lose your place.

Stay out of the control room. Unless you're specifically asked to do otherwise, stay in the studio. And if you are asked to come in to listen to a playback, don't eat the booth food unless it's offered to you.

Make any charts, notes, or cheat sheets beforehand. Once again, this comes under the heading of being prepared. If you have some time before the downbeat of the session, ask to hear the song or songs you will be recording (if there's a demo or you're going to be doing overdubs) so that you can make a chart or notes. You don't want to be wasting anyone's time doing something on the clock that could so easily have been done beforehand. Also, if you have to mark your charts, do it so anyone can read them later by making all your notes legible.

Don't pack up early. Don't leave until you're officially excused, and be sure to clean up your area when you've been dismissed.

The Drummer's Utility Kit

As Murphy's Law states, "If something can go wrong, it will go wrong!" so you've got to be prepared during recording for any eventuality. The following list will help you prepare for just about anything. Each item should be considered just as essential to bring to a session as your kit is.

A spare snare head

A spare kick drum head

A spare snare strainer

A spare kick drum pedal

A spare kick drum beater

A few tuning keys

Lots of sticks

Mallets

Brushes

Wire snips

Needle-nose pliers

A Phillips screwdriver

A flat-head screwdriver

A set of Allen wrenches

A light source (like a flashlight or a clip-on book light)

Duct tape

Super Glue

If you provide your own click or use electronic pads, also bring the following:

At least 1 extra 10' instrument cable (¼"-to-¼")

At least one extra ¼"-to-XLR cable

A set of headphones that you like

Spare 9V batteries

Spare AA batteries

A spare universal 9V wall wart

A small notepad

A pen

2 pencils

A Magic Marker

Band-Aids

Throat lozenges

Aspirin or Advil

A towel

Earplugs (just in case)

CHAPTER 15

Guide for Keyboard Players

If you're playing keyboards on a session in which the subject material is modern music, you will be called upon to play at least one of the five categories of keyboard sounds: piano, organ, lead sounds, pads, and nontraditional instruments (Optigon, Ondes Martinot, and so on). As a recording keyboardist (as opposed to a live keyboardist or accompanist), you will find that, with the exception of recordings requiring standard piano technique, sometimes the left-hand part rhythmically and sonically gets in the way of the bass player and maybe even the rhythm-guitar player. A left-hand part may be unnecessary and even harmful to a track's sound.

While piano is a minor exception, most schooled pianists have a naturally active left hand, which can really get in the way of the rest of the band and cause the low end to get muddy. By simplifying the left hand (sometimes by just playing root octaves), the piano sounds powerful yet still stays out of the way, and even that can sometimes be improved by playing the left hand up an octave.

All that being said, simple pads are powerful and are used a lot during recording. If you're an educated player, the last thing that you want to do is play a simple triad. It's boring and way beneath the talents of any knowledgeable musician. On the face of it, that's true, but simple triad pads are the glue that holds together modern popular music. So what's a pad? It's a chord with long sustaining notes, which are sometimes called "footballs" because they're written as whole notes, which look like footballs on staff paper. Pads are what musicians other than keyboard players tend to play when they play keyboards, but no matter who plays them they're very powerful.

Pads can be very subtle. Usually they blend into the background where they don't stand out but hold everything together (listen to "Clocks" or almost anything else by Coldplay for good examples of pads). In early rock music, pads were played initially by an organ (usually a Hammond); later on, they were also delivered extensively by the Fender Rhodes and Wurlitzer electric pianos. Soon afterward, synthesizers took over the pad-maker job, as a whole new world of sound opened up (synths ended up emulating the organ and electric piano, too).

Regardless of the sound or the instrument, most pads are built around simple triads since, like many other things in modern music, simplicity usually works the best in the context of a song. But keyboard pads are found in all forms of contemporary recorded music—most particularly, in nontraditional film scores. The day a keyboard player learns the power of the simple pad, he or she experiences a most powerful and defining moment.

Your Sound

As stated above, there are five basic families of sounds that most modern keyboard players are called on to play: piano, organ, lead sounds, pads, and nontraditionals. Maybe you'll have to play all five, or maybe just one or two in the context of your session work, but this is basically what there is to choose from.

The piano has always been a rock 'n' roll mainstay, whether it's the real thing or it's a variation of a grand-piano sample that's from a keyboard, a dedicated sampler, a plug-in, or a sound library. There's a ton of different versions available, though none sound exactly like the real thing. While most major recording facilities have a real piano, many smaller studios or home studios either can't fit one in the studio or can't afford to have a good one. In that case, the closer you can get to the real sound, the better (keeping in mind that whatever works best for the track is what you want). Note that we're not referring at all to an electric piano here. Because of the way it sonically lays into a track and can sustain notes, we can usually categorize electric piano as pads. However, most studio keyboardists will play electric piano in a very nonpad style, too, especially in its traditional applications. Most recognizable stylists like perennial Rolling Stones sidemen Ian MacClagan (ex-Faces) and Chuck Leavell (ex–Allman Brothers) are masters of both applications.

Most organ sounds are based on a Hammond organ with a Leslie or a Vox or a Farfisa speaker going straight into a full-range amplifier. Once again, while you might find a pretty close simulation, it's no match for the real thing. Hopefully, you'll be recording in a studio with a real Hammond and Leslie, Vox, or Farfisa, but if not, you'll be again called upon to get a sound that's as close to the real thing as possible.

Before you go to a session that requires you to play either the studio piano or the Hammond, it's best to give a call to the studio to see when the piano was last tuned (ask to have it tuned if the piano is critical to the session) and whether the Hammond and Leslie are in good working order and free of noises.

As stated a few paragraphs earlier, pads originated with an organ sound, then expanded to electric pianos, and then finally to synthesizers. Early synths were initially trying to emulate strings and horns, and did a really poor job of it. But a bad string sound actually makes a pretty good pad, and as synths got more sophisticated, so did the pad sounds, to the point where anything you buy today has a great many not-found-in-nature sounds that do a glorious job at the task (take a listen to Coldplay's "Clocks" again). Once again, pads are glue. They're subtle, they stay in the background, but they're essential in today's music.

Lead lines originally came from the grandfather synths like the *f* Odyssey and Bob Moog's classic Minimoog, both of which, for the most part, played only one note at a time (listen to Steve Miller's classic "Fly Like an Eagle" or ELP's "From the Beginning" for a great Minimoog sound). Once again, these old synths have a sound that today is only emulated and not truly captured, and almost all currently manufactured synths are polyphonic. But the sound used for lead lines, solos, and fills for the most part remains the same.

While it might be tempting to buy a vintage keyboard like an Arp 2600, a Minimoog, or a Mellotron, they each present a problem in that most vintage pieces are very unstable tuning-wise and require constant maintenance. Since their electronics are ancient by today's standards, finding a technician who knows how to work on one is no easy task, and being able to pay for the repair might not be easy, either. They still sound great on records, though.

Hauling Your Gear

Depending on the session, you may be asked to bring a lot of gear. If you don't have a cartage company or a tech to get your gear to the session, do yourself a favor and get a hand truck, or at least a furniture dolly, to minimize back strain and the number of trips to your vehicle. Don't depend on the studio having one.

An even better way to go is with the Rock 'n' Roller Mulitcart (see Fig. 15.1), which is built for moving musical equipment. The carts adjust in length, have fold-up brackets on each end to keep the gear on the cart, and even have inflatable tires. Once again, the idea is to do whatever you have to in order to get loaded in and set up on time so you don't keep anyone waiting. A good dolly or hand truck will really help you a lot (and your back, too).

Fig. 15.1: Rock 'n' Roller Multicart

The Quick Setup

Usually keyboard overdubs are done using one keyboard at a time while each one is set up in the control room, but if you're doing a tracking date for a movie (for instance), you might be asked to set your entire rig up in the studio. If you have an extensive keyboard setup that requires a lot of time to connect everything together, try these tricks to make things go a lot faster and more reliably.

▶ Before you even take your boards out of their cases, place all your power strips and extension cords at the point where you'll be setting up in the studio.

▶ If all your keyboards are usually connected to your own mixer, set that up next.

▶ Run any cables from the mixer to where the keyboards will be. You might consider either buying prefab snakes or making one by bundling together the cables that you normally use with plastic cable ties, or using a plastic cable conduit (like the ones Audioskin makes) to make your cable runs easier. Avoid running audio cables and power cables together in the same bundle, since that could cause noise or hum in the audio. Make sure that you label everything so you know which cable goes to which keyboard.

▶ Place your keyboards on their stands. To make this go faster, make sure you mark exactly where the height adjustment on the stand is for your playing style, so you'll always come back to the same place.

▶ Connect the cables to the keyboards. Avoid winding your cables around the stand like a barber's pole, since doing so will cause you to take a lot of extra time to break down and you'll hate yourself if you have to replace a cable during the session. Some Velcro straps like the ones used for mic cables can attach your cables nicely.

▶ Have a few pedals? Make your life easier by taking a cue from guitarists the world over and mount your pedals on a pedalboard. That way setup and teardown will be easier, and your pedals will always be in the same place, and they'll stay there. You can make one yourself, or you can just buy one from any number of vendors.

▶ Don't be afraid to hire a tech, a cartage company, or a helper. Whoever is paying you is used to hearing this request, and no one expects you to move a mountain of gear on your own. If there's no budget for cartage, a tech, or a helper, ask for help from the studio staff, since there may be "loaders" available, most often in the guise of assistant engineers or studio runners. But always remember: plan ahead and call first with any particulars or requests.

Standard Session Procedure

As stated in other chapters, the approach and mind-set needed for a recording session is different from what's needed in a live situation. While many of the following items also apply to playing live, there's a different emphasis when playing on sessions that centers on professionalism. All items apply to every recording session, with the possible exception of recording in your own studio.

Arrive early. You should always arrive at least a half hour before the downbeat of the session. This means that if your session starts at 7 p.m., you need to be there at 6:30 or earlier to be ready by 7 p.m. You can't expect to get there at 6:55 and for everything to be cool. If the session starts at 7 p.m., find out if that means load-in time or actual downbeat time. Remember that if you keep your employers waiting, you probably won't be asked to work for them again.

Turn off your cell phone. The session should be your main priority, and there should be as few distractions as possible. One of the easiest ways to achieve this is to turn off your cell phone. If you leave it on, you risk not only ruining a good take if the ringer goes off, but also stopping the momentum of a session in its tracks. Further, it's so disrespectful to every else who is at the session. Don't even bother to put your phone on "vibrate," since a vibrating phone will cause you to lose your focus just as easily as when the ringer goes off. Turn your phone off, then leave it outside the studio in the lounge so you won't be tempted to use it.

Know your gear inside out. It's important that you know your gear so well that you're able to get a sound up as soon as it's asked for. Nothing stops a session cold like a keyboard player hunting and pecking around looking for a sound.

Turn the effects off unless you're specifically asked to add them. Reverb, delay, compressor, and limiter effects or plug-ins should be avoided while recording, unless the engineer or producer asks you specifically to dial one up. Most of the time the engineer has a better-sounding one available and is more proficient in dialing up a sound than you are.

Make sure the piano is in tune. If you're going to a studio that has a real piano that you intend to play, call ahead and make sure that it's been recently tuned. If it hasn't, request it be tuned specifically for your session and make sure that it's tuned to A-440. This is an investment well worthwhile if the piano is to be an integral part of the sound of the recording.

Bring all your keyboards to the session. A recording is made interesting by multiple layers of different-sounding instruments. You'll never know when a keyboard or sound module that you haven't used in years will be the one with just the right sound for a song. Even though most modern keyboards have a wide variety of sounds, they tend to contain the same tonal quality within each keyboard due to using the same analog-to-digital converters and output circuitry that the sounds flow through. Each keyboard has at least one patch that's unique, and you'll never know when it'll be just the right thing to make a song special. To get a truly distinctive sound on the recording, bring all keyboards that you have, even if you don't normally use them. The exception here is if the studio is so small that you can't fit everything into it, or the producer or engineer specifically tells you what to bring or not bring.

Bring extra pedals, tubes, cables, and batteries. You have to have backups in case a volume pedal gets scratchy or a battery dies. Even if you think you have everything in your case or gig box, double-check to make sure.

Make sure that your cables are good. Under ordinary circumstances it's easy to keep playing with a cable that cuts out or makes noise occasionally. But using anything less than a perfect cable is a definite no-no for recording. Having to redo the perfect take because your cord cut out is bound to upset not only you, but everyone else in the studio as well. Cables are cheap. Buy a new one if you have any doubts about what you have.

Warm up quietly. You've got to warm up and everyone expects you to, but try to do so as quietly as you can so you aren't a distraction. The more quietly you can warm up, the more everyone will appreciate it.

Always seem interested in the music. It's easy to get a little complacent when your chops exceed what you've been called to play on, but try to get beyond that feeling. It's best to have only enough chops for that particular job—nothing more and nothing less. Showing off is a good way not to be asked back. And try not to look ahead in the chart when you're playing; doing so can be a good way to lose your place.

Stay out of the control room. Unless you're specifically asked to do otherwise, stay in the studio. And if you are asked to come in to listen to a playback, don't eat the booth food unless it's offered to you.

Make any charts, notes, or cheat sheets beforehand. Once again, this comes under the heading of being prepared. If you have some time before the downbeat of the session, ask to hear the song or songs you will be recording (if there's a demo or you're going to be doing overdubs), so you can make a chart or notes. You don't want to be wasting anyone's time doing something on the clock that could so easily have been done beforehand. Also, if you have to mark your charts, do it so anyone can read them later—make all your notes legible.

Don't pack up early. Don't leave until you're officially excused, and be sure to clean up your area when you've been dismissed.

The Keyboard Player's Utility Kit

As Murphy's Law states, "If something can go wrong, it will go wrong!" so you've got to be prepared during recording for any eventuality. The following list will help you prepare for just about anything. Each item should be considered just as essential to bring to a session as your keyboard is. Don't forget the hand truck or furniture mover to save the backs of both you and the studio runner or assistant.

An extra volume pedal

An extra sustain pedal

A spare keyboard stand

A hand truck or furniture mover

A light source (like a flashlight or a clip-on book light

Gaffer's or duct tape

Super Glue

1 extra MIDI cable if you don't usually use MIDI; 2 cables if you use MIDI all the time.

An extra USB cable

At least 2 extra 10' instrument cables (¼"-to-¼")

An extra 5' cable

RCA-to-RCA cable

Various cable adapters like ¼"-to-RCA, RCA-to-¼", ¼"-to-XLR

2 direct boxes, each with a ground-lift switch (always best to bring your own if you have some that you like)

An extra power cable

An extra power strip

An AC extension cord (or 2)

Any special microphones that you prefer to use (like on piano or organ)

A spare mic-stand adapter

Spare 9V batteries

Spare AA batteries

Spare universal 9V wall wart

A small notepad

A pen

2 pencils with erasers

A Magic Marker

Band-Aids

Throat lozenges

Aspirin or Advil

Earplugs

A towel

CHAPTER 16

Guide for Vocalists

Like most musicians, vocalists gain most of their experience and chops singing out in public. But what can get you by onstage sometimes won't cut it in a typical recording session; the studio is an unforgiving place, with every note magnified. Luckily, there are a lot of simple things that can really help your performance, but let's shine some light on them, since they are usually taken for granted or just overlooked.

The Three Ps: Pitch, Pocket, Passion

In the studio, the three Ps are what a producer lives by. You've got to have all three to have a dynamite vocal. And while pitch and pocket problems can be fixed by studio trickery, if you don't have passion, you don't have a vocal. Let's take a look inside the three Ps.

PITCH

Staying on pitch means singing in tune. And not just some of the notes—every single note! They're all equally important. Singing in tune requires having either real concentration and awareness or the very rare gift of being able to naturally sing in tune *all of the time*. If you know you have a constant pitch problem of singing either sharp or flat, there are some simple things you can try that might help.

▶ Singing sharp is usually caused by the power of your voice blanking out any background pitch reference. You're singing too hard to hear yourself! The fix is easy. Just ask for more vocal in the headphones.

▶ Singing a touch flat is easily fixed by simply lifting your eyebrows or smiling. Smiling is not only recommended but is also required because it provides proper relaxation of the facial, cranial, and neck muscles.

▶ Correct head position and correct position of the abdomen are needed for you to have enough air to stay on pitch. It's beyond the scope of this book to show you how to achieve correct positioning. If you aren't sure how, then now is the time to consult a vocal coach.

▶ The more relaxed you are, the easier it will be to hit the higher notes in your range. Yawning is a recommended warm-up, because it promotes relaxation.

Staying on pitch also means following the melody reliably. There's a trend these days to scat-sing around a melody, and while that might be desirable in some genres, it doesn't work in *any* genre if you do it all the time. Scatting might show off your technique and ability, but a song has a melody for a reason. The melody is what people know, that's what they can sing to themselves, and usually that's what they want to hear. Very rarely does the "civilian" or "man on the street" sing along with vocal histrionics, no matter how trendy they may be. That being said, when you're hired for a vocal session there is usually a very specific part (for example, a background part) that you're asked to sing, and scatting is deviating from that part. In a session, don't do it unless specifically asked!

In order to stay in tune, you've got to hear yourself. How much you hear yourself will actually determine if you stay on pitch or not.

As stated previously, some vocalists sing sharp when they sing too hard. They push themselves over the top of the correct pitch when they can't hear themselves in their headphones. *The secret is to have either more vocal or less of everything else in the phone. But be aware that pitch and timing problems can also occur if you hear too much of yourself in the mix.*

If you're singing flat, get a little less of yourself or more of everyone else in the mix, since it's not unusual for pitch to change with intensity. Less vocal makes you want to sing harder (and possibly raise your pitch slightly) and vice versa.

Sometimes there's too much in the mix, and thinning it out a little can help with pitch problems. First, ask for more bass (the root of all chords) and kick (the root of all rhythm) to help with pitch and pocket. Next, turn down anything that is heavily chorused (like effected rhythm guitars) and turn up anything that has a more centered tonal frequency (like a piano). Sometimes listening to only the rhythm guitar instead of two guitars (if there are two in the mix) can be helpful, because some singers can hear their pitch better from a simple tonally centered instrument than from screaming guitars or airy synth patches.

POCKET

Staying *in the pocket* means singing in time and in the "groove" (the rhythm) of the song. You can be on pitch, but if you're wavering ahead or behind the beat, it won't *feel* right. All of the things that help instrumentalists that are advocated elsewhere in this book apply to vocals as well. Concentrate on the downbeat (on beat 1) to get your entrances. Concentrate on the snare drum (on 2 and 4) to stay in the pocket.

> *Quincy* [producer Quincy Jones] *used to say that some singers have it in the pocket of their voice. Supposedly Michael Jackson has such an amazing pocket that he could sing a line and you could build a groove around it.*
>
> Frank Fitzpatrick

PASSION

Passion is not necessarily something that can be taught. To some degree, you either have it or you don't. What is passion? It's the ability to sell the lyrical content of a song through performance. It's the ability to make the audience believe in what you're singing—that you're talking directly to an individual listener and not anyone else.

Passion can sometimes trump pitch and pocket. A not-all-that-great singer who can convey the emotion in his voice is way more interesting to listen to than a polished singer who hits every note perfectly but with little emotion. Bob Dylan, Willie Nelson, Chet Baker, Mick Jagger, and Sarde illustrate this point. In fact, just about any vocalist you'd consider a "star" has passion, and that's why he or she is a star.

In the studio, a singer is never on "cruise control." You've got to give all the passion you can give for every song. A few paragraphs ago we said that you either have passion or you don't, but sometimes you really have it and you don't know it, and it's the producer's job to pull it out of you. That could mean getting the singer angry to stir some emotion, buildingher up by telling her how good she is, or making him laugh to loosen him up. Producers often coach singers the way that directors lead actors, offering suggestions for emotional context, asking for references to personal experience, all in an effort to provide more authentic feelings. Anything to sell the song! But once you know how to summon it up from inside you, you can do it again and again.

You're telling a story that's real to you. Do you believe in what you're singing about? You have to convey it from a place other than your memory of a bunch of words and chord changes.

Frank Fitzpatrick

Take Care of Yourself

Since vocalists are the only musicians who cannot put their instrument away in a protective case after the gig or rehearsal, it's important that they take very good care of it. Eventually, every singer has some vocal trouble or challenge, and if you're not careful, it can lead to long-term damage. That's why it's important for a singer to learn to be especially aware of the need to take care of him- or herself.

Aside from being sick, the number 1 cause of vocal problems is not getting enough sleep. When you're tired, all the parts of your body needed to support your vocal cords tend to weaken a bit, which leads to improper breathing; thus, throat problems can occur shortly after you begin singing. Get as much sleep as you can (preferably seven or eight hours) the night before a session, or take a brief nap on the day of the gig so you can feel somewhat refreshed.

The next thing is to avoid milk (and all dairy products, for that matter) for from three to six hours before you sing. Anything with milk in it will cause an excess production of phlegm around your vocal chords, so that's a definite no-no. The old remedy of milk and honey for a rough throat is very soothing after the gig, but not before!

If you're hungry before a session, don't be afraid to eat, but just eat until you're satisfied and don't stuff yourself with a seven-course meal. Try not to eat in the last hour before you record in order to avoid that excess phlegm again. If you do feel phlegmy, you'll have the strongest temptation to clear your throat (which can be harmful) immediately after eating; but if you finish eating an hour before you go into the studio, you'll usually have enough time for your meal to settle and the phlegm to subside.

And speaking of clearing your throat, there are some vocal coaches that say you should never try to clear your throat, because it can cause damage. But it's usually necessary to do so, because excess mucous really inhibits your singing. The trick is to find a way to clear your throat without irritating it, and the best way to do that is with a gentle "whispered cough," and then swallow and repeat. If that doesn't work, you need to deal with the excess mucous production. Squeeze a quarter of a lemon into a tall glass of water and sip it over a period of about 20 minutes. This should cut through a lot of the excess mucous.

Other things to avoid are alcohol, tea (despite popular belief), coffee, cola, and anything else with caffeine, since these actually have a dehydrating effect, which is quite the opposite of what you really need.

One thing you should do is drink lots and lots of water (ideally two to three quarts a day—the more the better), because a dry throat leads to a sore throat. If you live in an arid climate like Arizona, sleep with a humidifier next to your bed and try to warm up your voice in the shower. The moisture can be an incredible help for your voice. Also, learn to breathe in through your nose as much as possible. This will help moisten the air before it reaches your vocal cords.

Finally, some singers swear by Entertainer's Secret (see Fig. 16.1), a spray mixture developed by an ear, nose, and throat specialist that lubricates the vocal cords. You can get more information at www.entertainers-secret.com.

Fig. 16.1: Entertainer's Secret

If you have to go to the studio to sing but find that you have a sore throat from a cold or you just sang too much the previous night, you're going to have to take some precautions to be able to get through the gig. Here are some things to try as soon as you feel yourself getting sore:

- Drink warm liquids (they act as decongestants)
- Consume fruit and fruit drinks (but make sure they're not too acidic)
- Use your voice as little as possible (that includes speaking and singing)

Try this little mixture to make your voice feel better: squeeze one fresh lemon into a glass, and add a couple of teaspoons of clear honey and a little bit of water to mix. Gargle, then swallow. The honey coats the vocal chords and the lemon makes you salivate, thus stopping your cords from drying out.

Another remedy that you can use to help ease a sore throat (and other cold symptoms as well) is to make some hot water, but then add a mixture of honey and apple cider vinegar. Alone, the vinegar would probably hurt your throat because of its acidic nature, but mixed with the honey it becomes a source of energy. The mixture's exact ratio depends on your taste and the size of the cup. First add the honey to the water until it tastes sweet enough, and then add the vinegar until it tastes like a hot apple cider (more or less). Take it a few times a day, the more the better.

And again, avoid tea, coffee, cream, and alcohol before singing, because they can have a dehydrating effect. And above all—rest!

Take Some Lessons

All the successful studio singers that we know are either currently taking vocal lessons or have at one time or another, so don't be afraid to take some lessons to help you get your vocal chops together. Many pro singers see vocal coaches as frequently as once a week. It's not uncommon for vocalists (especially hard-rock singers) to be terrified that a singing coach will try to change them into an opera singer, but that's not what's going to happen. A good singing coach only wants to get you to use the proper technique to enhance your range and sing free of throat damage, not to change your style. There are a lot of benefits to having a good coach, not the least of which is being able to sing for long periods of time with ease. No one wants to lose his or her voice before a session ends (that might well be the end of your callbacks). A good coach can also give you some tips to cope with those times when your voice is not up to par because you're under the weather. As we said before, that's the time when you're most vulnerable to long-term vocal damage.

A vocal coach helps you to develop

- More power with less effort.
- Better pitch.
- Higher range.
- More stamina.
- A healthier voice.
- The best warm-up technique for your voice.
- A warm-up/practice CD or mp3 for warm-ups on nonlesson days.

So give it a try. Even just a few lessons can make a big difference.

Mic Technique

Many of the microphone techniques that are perfectly acceptable in a live environment (such as holding the microphone away from you when starting a sustained note, and bringing it closer to the mouth as the note diminishes to hide a lack of sustained breath control) just don't cut it in the studio. Every note is expected to be perfect, and you can't use mic technique to cover up any inadequacies that you might have.

Having good studio mic technique means that you know how to stay at the same distance from the mic at all times. This is to make sure to keep the vocal level consistent and, if you're singing in a group, to keep any harmony blend the same throughout the song.

Many times an engineer will mark a spot on the floor with tape to give you your ideal spot. The trick is that that's where you keep your head, not your body. You'll still drift in volume if you're head is drifting back and forth, even if your body stays right on the spot. Many engineers are hip to this problem and will ask you to stand a number of hand lengths away from the mic (see Fig. 16.2). This is easier to remember, and it centers your head instead of your body.

Fig. 16.2: Hand Technique

It's also not uncommon for an engineer or producer to tell you to "lean in" or "lean back," or "take a step in" or "take a step back," especially when singing harmony vocals in a group. This is to tweak the harmony blend. Again, the key is to remember where your head is, not your body.

Phrasing Is Everything

Singing together in a group really means that you have to sing together—exactly together. All vocalists in the group have to sing the same way, using the same inflections, slurs, attacks (starts), and releases (stops). Usually this means that one vocal part will be the reference part, and all others will follow that. The way that I've seen great background singers work is for one to say, "Sing it to me. Show me what you're doing." Then they'd try to match it exactly. It works for them, and it will work for you, too.

ATTACKS AND, ESPECIALLY, RELEASES

Attacks and releases are the secret to tight music, whether you're playing it or singing it. While it's usually easy to get the attack part (where everyone starts at exactly the same time), the release part (everyone ending at the same time) is usually overlooked. The releases are just as important as the attacks, and tightening up just this one area will make the group sound so tight that you won't believe it. So remember, everyone starts and stops at the same time. A great example of a background vocal with a tight release is at the very end of the theme song for the television show *American Dad*. Listen to how tight "Good Morning USA" is. That's what you're going for.

Standard Session Procedure

As stated in the previous chapters, the approach and mindset needed for a recording session is different from what's needed in a live situation. While many of the following items also apply to playing live, there's a different emphasis when playing on sessions that centers on professionalism. All items apply to every recording session, with the possible exception of recording in your own studio.

Arrive early. You should always arrive at least a half hour before the downbeat of the session. This means that if your session starts at 7 p.m., you need to be there at 6:30 or earlier to be ready by 7 p.m. You can't expect to get there at 6:55 and for everything to be cool. If the session starts at 7 p.m., find out if that means load-in time or actual downbeat time. Remember that if you keep your employers waiting, you probably won't be asked to work for them again.

Turn off your cell phone. The session should be your main priority, and there should be as few distractions as possible. One of the easiest ways to achieve this is to turn off your cell phone. If you leave it on, you risk not only ruining a good take if the ringer goes off, but also stopping the momentum of a session in its tracks. Further, it's so disrespectful to every else who is at the session. Don't even bother to put your phone on "vibrate," since a vibrating phone will cause you to lose your focus just as easily as when the ringer goes off. Turn your phone off, then leave it outside the studio in the lounge so you won't be tempted to use it.

Make sure you warm up before singing. Make sure that you've properly warmed up your voice before you begin to record, especially if you're going to sing aggressively or scream (good advice for singing live, as well). If you don't warm up, you can cause serious damage to your vocal chords as well as blow yourself out before you get a good take.

Have something handy to moisten your throat. Warm water, some mild fruit juice, or Entertainer's Secret are always good to have on hand. Warm water with a little honey and lemon will both coat your cords and cause you to salivate. Stay away from beer, cola, tea, and coffee, because they will actually dehydrate you.

Be sure to get your headphone mix right. The phone mix is really important to your overall performance. Your pitch can suffer if you can't hear yourself enough; but if you hear too much of yourself, you might not sing aggressively enough. Try listening with one earphone off your head to see if it helps.

Don't make any unnecessary noise. The less talk, the better. Either cover your earphones or turn them down when you don't have them on your head. A little courtesy like that can go a long way.

Don't complain about the air conditioner. The temperature is never going to be perfect for everyone, so it's useless to even bring this up because it will just become a distraction. The only exception is if it's so cold that it physically impedes your playing or adversely affects your singing.

Stay awake! Listen to everything that's going on and be ready to sing at all times. If you're singing in a group, watch the leader and stop singing when the leader stops.

Don't talk after a take until the engineer or producer says it's okay to do so. Nothing can ruin a take more or make a lot more work for the production team than someone thoughtlessly making a comment at the end of a take. Even if you think the take will have to be done again, keep all comments to yourself. Sometimes a take that feels bad to you can feel great to everyone else.

Always seem interested in the music. It's easy to get a little complacent when your chops exceed what you've been called to sing on, but try to get beyond that feeling. It's best to have only enough chops for that particular job—nothing more and nothing less. Showing off is a good way not to be asked back. And try not to look ahead in the chart when you're playing; doing so can be a good way to lose your place.

Stay out of the control room. Unless you're specifically asked to do otherwise, stay in the studio. And if you are asked to come in to listen to a playback, don't eat the booth food unless it's offered to you.

Make any charts, notes, or cheat sheets beforehand. Once again, this comes under the heading of being prepared. If you have some time before the downbeat of the session, ask to hear the song or songs you will be recording (if there's a demo or you're going to be doing overdubs), so that you can make a chart or notes. You don't want to be wasting anyone's time doing something on the clock that could so easily have been done beforehand. Also, if you have to mark your charts, do it so anyone can read them later—make all your notes legible.

Don't pack up early. Don't leave until you're officially excused, and be sure to clean up your area when you've been dismissed.

The Singer's Utility Kit

The utility kit for a singer isn't nearly as extensive as for the other session musicians, but it's just as vital.

A light source (like a flashlight or a clip-on book light)

A small notepad

A pen

2 pencils with erasers

A Magic Marker

Headphones (if you have a pair that helps you sing better)

Entertainer's Secret

A mild fruit drink (nonacidic)

Honey

A lemon or lemon substitute

Tea

Throat lozenges

Aspirin or Advil

A towel

Guide for Horn Players

In some ways, horn players have it a bit easier than other session musicians (except for singers) in that they don't have as much gear or as broad a range of sonic choices to contend with. But as with everything in the studio, what's not immediately obvious can be the part that trips you up during a studio gig. Learning some of the tricks can be really helpful as you head toward your first paying sessions. Traditionally, studio horn players are known to be among the best sight-readers, the most exciting soloists, and the quickest on-the-spot arrangers, and so they're expected to bring a high level of musicianship with them to the date. It's great to have a reputation as a killer soloist, but it's even better to become part of a section with your favorite other players in the spirit of the Memphis Horns or the Tower of Power Horns. Horn players work, but horn sections work *a lot*. Real music played by real players is never going to go away, and there is almost nothing as exciting as a world-class horn section playing live on a track. Established horn sections are engineers' and producers' dream teams—you come in already cookin' like a greased machine ready to add your flavor and make hits. And that is what recording is all about.

Mic Technique

Microphone technique is really important for the studio horn player, just as it is for vocalists. Having good studio mic technique means that you know how to maintain the same distance from the mic at all times. This is to make sure that the level and tone of the horn stays consistent and, if you're playing in a group, any blend with the other players remains the same throughout the song.

Many times an engineer will mark a spot on the floor with tape to give you your ideal spot. The trick is that that's where you should keep your horn, not your body. You'll still drift in volume if your horn is pulling back and forth or you're leaning back and forth in your chair if you're sitting, even if your body stays right on the spot. If you want to earn a place in the engineer's heart, keep the level of your horn consistent, and keep it at that same spot as much as possible. Remember that every note you play is expected to be perfect, and you can't use mic technique to cover up any inadequacies that you might have.

You've Got to Hear Yourself

Let's face it—you can't play in tune and be precise with the rest of the section (if there is one) if you can't hear yourself well. So here are some tricks.

In order to get the best blend with the other horns in a section, try taking one earphone off or using a one-sided headphone. This lets you hear the track yet set the balance acoustically while also helping with the section phrasing.

In a not-so-live room, it helps to be closer to a wall so you can dampen your horn's reflections and therefore hear yourself a little better to prevent overblowing. Ask the engineer if you can move if you think it might be helpful.

Standard Session Procedure

As you have heard throughout this book, the approach and mind-set required for a recording session is somewhat different from what's needed in a live situation. While many of the following items also apply to playing live, there's a different emphasis when playing on sessions that that centers on professionalism. Everything below applies to every recording session, with the possible exception of recording in your own studio.

Arrive early. You should always arrive at least a half hour before the downbeat of the session. This means that if your session starts at 7 p.m., you need to be there at 6:30 or earlier to be ready by 7 p.m. You can't expect to get there at 6:55 and for everything to be cool. If the session starts at 7 p.m., find out if that means load-in time or actual downbeat time. Remember that if you keep your employers waiting, you probably won't be asked to work for them again.

Turn off your cell phone. The session should be your main priority, and there should be as few distractions as possible. One of the easiest ways to achieve this is to turn off your cell phone. If you leave it on, you risk not only ruining a good take if the ringer goes off, but also stopping the momentum of a session in its tracks. Further, it's so disrespectful to every else who is at the session. Don't even bother to put your phone on "vibrate," since a vibrating phone will cause you to lose your focus just as easily as when the ringer goes off. Turn your phone off, and leave it outside the studio in the lounge so you won't be tempted to use it.

Make sure your instruments are in good working order. This means that you should have them professionally checked so that every note plays true without any unwanted noise.

Make sure your instruments are tuned to a real "A." If the song isn't tuned to the standard A-440, there'll be a tuning note recorded on the track for you to tune against. The tuning of your instrument is easy to overlook when you're tracking, because sometimes being out of tune isn't that obvious. But it will bug the heck out of you (not to mention the producer and the composer) each time you hear it played back if it's out of tune because you didn't take the time to fix it.

Bring all your horns to the session. You never know when something that you haven't used in years will have just the right sound for the song or cue.

Bring extra reeds, cork grease, mutes, straps, and so on. You have to have backups for everything, just in case.

Warm up quietly. You've got to warm up and everyone expects you to, but try to pick a nice quiet corner so you're not a distraction. The more quietly you can warm up, the more everyone will appreciate it.

Don't make any unnecessary noise. The less talk, the better. Either don't leave your headphones uncovered or turn them down when you don't have them on your head. A little courtesy like that can go a long way.

Don't complain about the air conditioner. The temperature is never going to be perfect for everyone, so it's useless to even bring this up because it will just become a distraction. The only exception is if it's so cold that it physically impedes your playing or adversely affects your instrument's tuning.

Stay awake! Listen to everything that's going on and be ready to play at all times. If you're playing with other studio musicians, watch the leader and stop playing when the leader stops.

Don't talk after a take until the engineer or producer says it's okay to do so. Nothing can ruin a take more or make a lot more work for the production team than someone thoughtlessly making a comment at the end of a take. Even if you think the take will have to be done again, keep all comments to yourself. Sometimes a take that feels bad to you can feel great to everyone else.

Always seem interested in the music. It's easy to get a little complacent when your chops exceed what you've been called to play on, but try to get beyond that feeling. It's best to have only enough chops for that particular job—nothing more and nothing less. Showing off is a good way not to be asked back. And try not to look ahead in the chart when you're playing; doing so can be a good way to lose your place.

Stay out of the control room. Unless you're specifically asked to do otherwise, stay in the studio. And if you are asked to come in to listen to a playback, don't eat the booth food unless it's offered to you.

Make any charts, notes, or cheat sheets beforehand. Once again, this comes under the heading of being prepared. If you have some time before the downbeat of the session, ask to hear the song or songs you will be recording (if there's a demo or you're going to be doing overdubs), so that you can make a chart or notes. You don't want to be wasting anyone's time doing something on the clock that could so easily have been done beforehand. Also, if you have to mark your charts, do it so anyone can read them later—make all your notes legible.

Don't pack up early. Don't leave until you're officially excused, and be sure to clean up your area when you've been dismissed.

The Horn Player's Utility Kit

Just about every horn player brings most of these items to sessions already, but it's always good to have a list.

Your own headphones (if they help you hear better)

Any special microphones that you like to use (if given the choice)

A spare mic-stand adapter (if the mic uses something unusual)

A digital tuner

Horn mutes, including straight, harmon, cup, bucket, and plungers

Valve oil

Extra straps

Cork grease

Swabs

Oils, powders, and maintenance materials

Horn stands

Reed holders

A couple of mouthpiece patches

A small notepad

A pen

2 pencils

A Magic Marker

Band-Aids

Throat lozenges

Aspirin or Advil

A towel

Earplugs (just in case)

CHAPTER 18

Guide for String Players

For a string player to be successful in the studio, one thing is paramount: intonation. Regardless of any of your personal attributes or technical skills, if you're not in tune, you just won't cut it; that's because nothing sounds worse than a solo string player out of tune with the track, or a string section out of tune with itself. In fact, this is one of the reasons that sample libraries have become so popular. Historically, producers and composers (especially those not located in the large media centers) had difficulty finding suitable (in-tune) sections for recording, so they resorted to using libraries (which were cheaper, too). That's not to say that excellent players aren't out there; they just aren't readily known and reachable or used to recording.

The secret to achieving good intonation, whether you're a beginner or a virtuoso, is consistent finger placement, and this precision comes from doing it correctly over and over until muscle memory makes achieving perfect intonation second nature. While some players are taught that good intonation comes from having a good ear, by the time you've heard your intonation drift, you're too out of tune for recording, so practice is the only way to perfect it. As a way to measure your intonation, half steps and whole steps should have clear delineation (which can be more difficult than it seems), and each note in a fast run has to be exactly on the mark. Of course, every note should be heard and exactly phrased no matter how fast or difficult the run is.

Live string dates are some of the most aurally pleasing and emotionally evocative studio experiences. Nonstring players often drop in on string tracking sessions because of the natural beauty—the "ear candy" as we like to say—that results when pro string players get together in an acoustically pleasing room with respectable gear and the right engineer. And like horn players, string players who do sessions are known to be some of the best sight-readers in the business. As a studio string player, you will work a lot of film and TV dates and pop record dates. Make friends with section leaders and contractors, and get ready for real top-shelf recording experiences.

During the Session

Bow control is an essential attribute of the recording string player. At the end of a note, if the bow bounces or stutters even the slightest amount, it will be heard clearly under the microphones. What's needed is to have a steady bow with no extra bounces, no rough bow changes, no unintended accents, and no ugly scratches. Lyrical lines require precise bow technique, so it helps to figure out how much of the bow will be used for each stroke. That way phrasing remains consistent and unintentional accents are avoided. You should also maintain the same power and strength at the tip of the bow as you do when you draw at the frog (the grip of the violin bow, for readers who aren't string players), and any bow changes made in midtrill should be inaudible.

Consistency of tone is also important for the recording string player. Your sound must be as pure as possible, regardless of how loudly or softly you're required to play. Vibrato can also become an issue during a long session when the left arm begins to tire. It's easy to forget, but you have to make sure that each note's vibrato starts well and stays consistent.

Consistency in playing is another issue. When repeating a take, you have to be able to play a part almost identically to the way you played the previous one. It's also important to be able to let the sound of your instrument decay far longer than seems normal. That's because the mics are very sensitive and will pick everything up, so try not to make any extraneous noises during fades.

Headphones

You may or may not use headphones during a session, depending upon how large the section is. With a small section of four to eight players, headphones are usually available for every player. With a larger section, only the concertmaster or the first chairs will use 'phones, since not everyone needs them to provide a great performance.

If you are using headphones, the mix is very important, just as it is for every other recording musician. Some studios will have only a single-phone mix available, which means that you'll have to compromise with the other players as to what works best for most of you. Many facilities now offer the ability for each player to set up his or her own 'phone mix, which can be confusing if you've never done it before. If a click track is available, you might want to hear a little, but you definitely need kick and snare drums for the rhythm (if they're used on the track), bass for the fundamental, and a chordal instrument like a piano or guitar to help with pitch (avoid anything with a flanger or chorus on it). Some players like a lot of vocals, and some players don't. Experiment with both.

Many players find that they can't find the right section blend while using headphones, so they'll take one earphone off. If you do this, be sure to alternate the earpiece from one ear to the other occasionally, dividing exposure between both ears to prevent ear fatigue in a single ear. Single-cup headphones are also available from Shure (the SCL2 ear-bud), Stanton (the DJ Pro300), and Beyer (the DT 102 and DT 252), but you'll probably have to bring your own to the session because most studios have only standard dual-cup phones (see Fig. 18.1).

Fig. 18.1: Beyer DT 102 Single-Cup Headphone

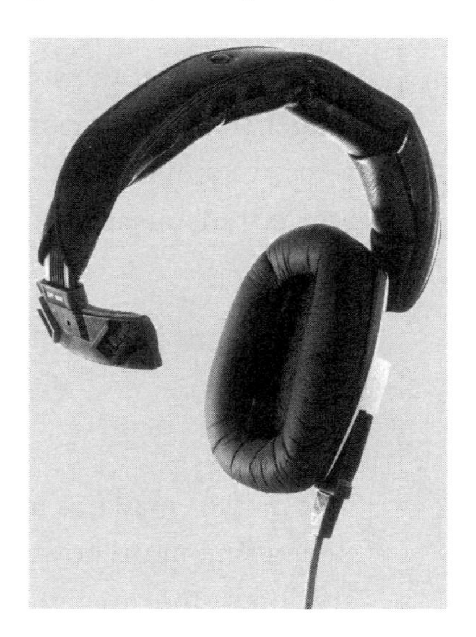

> *I like to have plenty of rhythm* [kick and snare are crucial], *a good amount of bass, enough of the chordal instruments for pitch, and just a little bit of vocals. If I'm playing solo, then I like having myself in the mix, but if I'm playing along with other string players, then I prefer to leave the live strings out of the headphone mix.*
>
> Eric Gorfain

If you aren't using 'phones, you'll be taking cues from the conductor or concertmaster, as usual. Many composers and conductors would rather listen from the control room than the studio, and while they can still speak to you through the talkback mic, it might be difficult for them to cue entrances and endings. Most players prefer to have the conductor in the studio not only for that reason, but also for reassurance and confidence.

Standard Session Procedure

For a string player, the approach and mind-set required for a recording session is very different from what's needed in a live situation. While many of the following items also apply to playing live, there's a different emphasis when recording that centers on professionalism. All the following items apply to every recording session, with the possible exception of recording in your own studio.

Arrive early. You should always arrive at least a half hour before the downbeat of the session. This means that if your session starts at 7 p.m., you need to be there at 6:30 or earlier to be ready by 7 p.m. You can't expect to get there at 6:55 and for everything to be cool. If the session starts at 7 p.m., find out if that means load-in time or actual downbeat time. Remember that if you keep your employers waiting, you probably won't be asked to work for them again.

Turn off your cell phone. The session should be your main priority, and there should be as few distractions as possible. One of the easiest ways to achieve this is to turn off your cell phone. If you leave it on, you risk not only ruining a good take if the ringer goes off, but also stopping the momentum of a session in its tracks. Further, it's so disrespectful to every else who is at the session. Don't even bother to put your phone on "vibrate," since a vibrating phone will cause you to lose your focus just as easily as when the ringer goes off. Turn your phone off, and leave it outside the studio in the lounge so you won't be tempted to use it.

Make sure that your instruments and bows are in good working order. This means that you should have them professionally checked so that every note plays true without any unwanted noise.

Wear the right clothing. The microphones are powerful in the nuances they pick up, so it's important to wear quiet clothes. Since your shoes affect the alignment of your body, which in turn affects the way you play, make sure that you wear something comfortable.

Make sure you retune your instrument to the "A" of the track. If the song isn't tuned to the standard A-440, there'll be a tuning note recorded on the track for you to tune against. The tuning of your instrument is easy to overlook when you're tracking, because sometimes being out of tune isn't that obvious. But it will bug the heck out of you (not to mention the producer and the composer) each time you hear it played back if it's out of tune because you didn't take the time to fix it.

Warm up quietly. You've got to warm up and everyone expects you to, but try to pick a nice quiet corner so you're not a distraction. The more quietly you can warm up, the more everyone will appreciate it.

Don't make any unnecessary noise. The less talk, the better. Either don't leave your headphones uncovered or turn them down when you don't have them on your head. A little courtesy like that can go a long way.

Make the producer aware of the best temperature, but don't complain about the air conditioner. It's important that the temperature be consistent to keep your instrument in tune, so let that be known as soon as you feel uncomfortable. But when the red light goes on, it's best to keep a tight lip about the air conditioning. It's never going to be perfect for everyone, so don't bring it up unless it's so cold that it physically impedes your playing.

Stay awake! Listen to everything that's going on and be ready to play at all times. Always watch the conductor/concertmaster/leader, stop playing when he or she stops, and never hang over on an ending.

Don't talk after a take until the engineer or producer says it's okay to do so. Nothing can ruin a take more or make a lot more work for the production team than someone thoughtlessly making a comment at the end of a take. Even if you think the take will have to be done again, keep all comments to yourself. Sometimes a take that feels bad to you can feel great to everyone else.

Always seem interested in the music. It's easy to get a little complacent when your chops exceed what you've been called to play on, but try to get beyond that feeling. It's best to have only enough chops for that particular job—nothing more and nothing less. Showing off is a good way not to be asked back. And try not to look ahead in the chart when you're playing; doing so can be a good way to lose your place.

Watch your left-hand wrist alignment. In order to prevent straining the left arm during a long day of recording, it's a good idea to keep an eye on your left-arm alignment. Any strain can affect your tone or technique.

Stay out of the control room. Unless you're specifically asked to do otherwise, stay in the studio. And if you are asked to come in to listen to a playback, don't eat the booth food unless it's offered to you.

Don't pack up early. Don't leave until you're officially excused, and be sure to clean up your area when you've been dismissed.

The String Player's Utility Kit

Just about every string player brings most of these items to sessions already, but it's always good to have a list.

Your own headphones (if they help you hear better)

A digital tuner

Rosin

An extra bow

A small notepad

A pen

2 pencils

A Magic Marker

Band-Aids

Throat lozenges

Aspirin or Advil

A towel

Earplugs (just in case)

CHAPTER 19

Guide for Percussionists

A percussionist's contribution to a record may sometimes be so subtle that the listener doesn't notice until it's pointed out, but it's crucial to so many records nonetheless. That being said, many producers consider percussion the final, yet essential, icing on the cake: the cake is still good cake without it, but with it the cake is fantastic.

Motion, Dynamics, and Texture

Producers like percussion for three basic reasons: motion, dynamics, and texture. Most people (even percussionists) can't define the addition of percussion tracks as such, but it's helpful if it's broken down in the following way.

Adding motion means that the tempo of the song seems upbeat and "brighter," but not faster. For motion to happen, a percussionist must be deeply tied to the groove of the drummer and the groove of the track, without sounding stiff. The double-time maracas and the congas on the Stones' "Sympathy for the Devil" and Jack Ashford's tambourine on just about anything from the Motown of Detroit are prime examples of how percussion can add motion to a song. If you were to take the percussion away, these songs would feel completely different.

> *I guess number one would be to learn to swing with the click instead of being afraid of it or just staying with it. You've got to be able to groove with the click but still make it sound musical and not stiff. Your playing has to still be on time, but it has to groove with the click, too. That's the first thing that any drummer or percussionist needs to learn, aside from learning the technique of the instrument.*
>
> Ronnie Ciago

Likewise, percussion can easily add dynamics (the way the song builds) to a song. A popular technique is to begin a song with a simple rhythm or even single hits on beats 2 and 4 (with a tambourine, for instance) and, by the end of the song, have the instrument playing in double time. In this case, both the motion and the dynamics of the song are uplifted. Another way is to begin the song with a single percussion instrument and add more as the song goes along. This could be something like a shaker on the verse, another instrument (maybe congas) at the chorus, and a tambourine added at the outro in double time.

Finally, percussion can add an interesting sonic texture to a song. Tambourines, shakers, bells, cabasa, chimes, and triangles can add some missing high frequencies to a song that might have been lacking. Congas, bongos, and tablas provide a nice midrange addition, while djembes, udu, or cajon can add low frequencies to the track.

Standard Percussion Items

Although there are hundreds of percussion instruments available, there are standard requests from producers. These include mostly Latin percussion items (congas, bongos, timbales, cabasa, shakers, cowbell, and so on), although African percussion like the djembe and Indian percussion like tablas have become more popular in recent years. While drums like congas, timbales, and bongos are high on the frequently requested list, an assortment of shakers (both soft and loud), scrapers (like a guiro), tambourines, cowbells, bells, triangles, woodblocks, and claves are necessary to have available at a moment's notice as well. In fact, it's best to bring instruments that cover the whole audio spectrum as outlined above.

> *First I'll ask if there's anything in particular they need me to do. They might say, "Just bring your congas and timbales," or "Bring your timpani," so that makes it pretty simple. If there's nothing in particular that I'm asked to bring, I end up bringing all my gear, which is a truckload of stuff. I have an assortment of tambourines, shakers from all over the world, different udu drums, and lots of other things.*
>
> Ronnie Ciago

All that being said, percussionists are a resourceful group who have an uncanny knack for seeing how many inanimate objects can become instruments. Anything can make a sound if shaken or hit, and many percussionists have the ability to understand how the resulting sound can be used in the context of a recording. Case in point: years ago I hired a percussionist who, no matter how hard he tried, couldn't find the right sound for the track despite his trunks of gear. After surveying the studio, he removed a ceiling tile from the drop ceiling (this was a pro studio, but back in the '70s room acoustics were somewhat challenged in many cases) and began to scrub it with a small mallet. Lo and behold, it was the perfect sound for the song.

Another example of some studio inventiveness that's used a surprising number of times is to put salt or sugar in a couple of Styrofoam coffee cups, the open ends of which are then duct-taped together to make a nice soft shaker. These shakers are easy to play and fit nicely in many tracks.

Just Owning the Instrument Isn't Enough

A mistake that many neophyte percussionists make is to acquire an instrument and try to play it without knowing how it's played or used in its normal environment. This is a critical element in percussion, since just owning the instrument isn't enough to make it useful in the studio. Most producers are fully aware of what the most popular instruments can do and which rhythms make them useful, and that's why a producer or engineer may have asked specifically that you bring certain instruments with you in the first place. If you can provide only the sound without the indigenous rhythm, or the rhythm is played badly, you risk not being hired for a later date.

> *Just having the instrument doesn't really mean anything. You have to know how it's played and where and why it's used, so that requires some research and sometimes even a teacher.*
>
> Ronnie Ciago

Standard Session Procedure

If you've read the previous chapters, you know that the approach and mind-set needed for a recording session is different from what's needed in a live situation. While many of the following items also apply to playing live, there's a different emphasis when playing on sessions that centers on professionalism. All items apply to every recording session, with the possible exception of recording in your own studio.

Arrive early. This goes without saying, but I'll say it again to reinforce it. You should always arrive at least *an hour* before the downbeat of the session because it takes that much time to not only set your kit up but also mic the kit. This means that if your session starts at 7 p.m., you need to be there by at least 6 p.m. to be ready at 7. You might even want to get there earlier (if they'll let you) to have some extra time to change your heads and tune your drums. If the session starts at 7 p.m., find out if that means load-in time or actual downbeat time. If you keep your employers waiting, it might be the last time you're asked to work with them.

Turn off your cell phone. The session should be your main priority, and there should be as few distractions as possible. One of the easiest ways to achieve this is to turn off your cell phone. If you leave it on, you risk not only ruining a good take if the ringer goes off, but also stopping the momentum of a session in its tracks. Further, it's so disrespectful to every else who is at the session. Don't even bother to put your phone on "vibrate," since a vibrating phone will cause you to lose your focus just as easily as when the ringer goes off. Turn your phone off, then leave it outside the studio in the lounge so you won't be tempted to use it.

Warm up quietly. The more quietly you can warm up, the more everyone will appreciate it.

Don't make any unnecessary noise. The less talk, the better. Don't leave your earphones uncovered, or make sure to turn them down when you don't have them on your head. A little courtesy like that can go a long way.

Don't complain about the air conditioner. The temperature is never going to be perfect for everyone, so it's useless to even bring this up because it will just become a distraction. The only exception is if it's so cold that it physically impedes your playing.

Stay awake! Listen to everything that's going on and be ready to play at all times. If you're playing with other studio musicians, watch the leader and stop playing when the leader stops.

Don't talk after a take until the engineer or producer says it's okay to do so. Nothing can ruin a take or make a lot more work for the production team than someone thoughtlessly making a comment at the end of a take. Even if you think the take will have to be done again, keep all comments to yourself. Sometimes a take that feels bad to you can feel great to everyone else.

Always seem interested in the music. It's easy to get a little complacent when your chops exceed what you've been called to play on, but try to get beyond that feeling. It's best to have only enough chops for that particular job—nothing more and nothing less. Showing off is a good way not to be asked back. And try not to look ahead in the chart when you're playing; doing so can be a good way to lose your place.

Stay out of the control room. Unless you're specifically asked to do otherwise, stay in the studio. And if you are asked to come in to listen to a playback, don't eat the booth food unless it's offered to you.

Make any charts, notes, or cheat sheets beforehand. Once again, this comes under the heading of being prepared. If you have some time before the downbeat of the session, ask to hear the song or songs you will be recording (if there's a demo or you're going to be doing overdubs), so that you can make a chart or notes. You don't want to be wasting anyone's time doing something on the clock that could so easily have been done beforehand. Also, if you have to mark your charts, make all your notes legible so that anyone can read them later.

Don't pack up early. Don't leave until you're officially excused, and be sure to clean up your area when you've been dismissed.

The Percussionist's Utility Kit

The percussionist's utility kit differs a lot from other musicians' kits in that the range of instruments is so vast and the majority of studio percussionists can make most inanimate objects work in a pinch.

That being said, there are some items that can prepare you for just about any eventuality. Each item should be considered just as essential to bring to a session as your kit is.

A tuning key

Drumsticks

Mallets

Wire snips

Needle-nose pliers

A Phillips-head screwdriver

A flat-head screwdriver

A set of Allen wrenches

A conga or timbale tuning wrench

A light source (like a flashlight or a clip-on book light)

Duct tape

Super Glue

If you provide electronic percussion, also bring the following:

At least one extra 10' instrument cable (¼"-to-¼")

At least one extra ¼"-to-XLR cable

A set of headphones that you like

Spare 9V batteries

Spare AA batteries

Spare universal 9V wall wart

A small notepad

A pen

2 pencils

A Magic Marker

Band-Aids

Throat lozenges

Aspirin or Advil

A towel

Earplugs (just in case)

Part Three

The Interviews

CHAPTER 20

The Interviews

Ronnie Ciago—Drummer and Percussionist

Ronnie Ciago is the very image of a modern percussionist in that he's equally as proficient on drums as he is on percussion. In fact, Ronnie has many clients that know him only for his percussion abilities and don't even realize he has other skills, although he does sessions for both instruments. With musician credits like Ricki Lee Jones, Bill Ward (of Black Sabbath fame), Brand X, Randy Stonehill, Mick Taylor (ex–Rolling Stone), Patrick Moraz, The Riverdogs, and Robert Downey Jr., and high-profile producer credits like Jack Douglas and Linda Perry, and movie and television tracks as well as jingle sessions under his belt, there are few more qualified to speak about the role of the percussionist in the studio.

How did you start doing sessions?
I got in the same way everyone does: by just being out there and playing with people. You keep getting recommended for better and better gigs and play with better and better players, and the next thing you know you're recording. That's how I started to play with Bill [Ward]. I started to play with the guys who played on Bill's first solo CD, and when he was looking for somebody, I got the call. Then it went from there.

What do you usually bring with you to a session?
First I'll ask if there's anything in particular they need me to do. They might say, "Just bring your congas and timbales," or "Bring your timpani," so that makes it pretty simple. If there's nothing in particular that I'm asked to bring, I end up bringing all my gear, which is a truckload of stuff. I have an assortment of tambourines, shakers from all over the world, different udu drums, and lots of other things. When I did the film *Elmo in Grouchland* for Sony Pictures, the producer said, "Bring all your stuff, and we'll find out what we want to use." He'd tell me what kind of sound he was looking for, and then I'd start auditioning instruments until he found something that he liked.

A lot of the time people will bring in a percussionist but they don't know exactly what they want. I'll hear the groove and after a while understand the context of the music, and then the light will come on and I'll go, "I know what they want. I'm going to need this instrument to do this and that instrument to do that, and then it will sound great." For me, that's the defining moment of any session I go to.

How long does that process usually take?
Since the studio is costing them money, they don't want to spend too much time. But if they can give me some sort of an idea, then I'll usually zero in on what they want pretty quickly.

You usually end up doing more than one part, right?
Oh, yeah. Sometimes I'll end up doing 10, even 15, different tracks during the same session. They'll all be different instruments with different rhythms that complement each other. One might be a simple pattern, while another one might go in between that pattern. Sometimes I'll put down a bed of maybe four different percussion instruments just to play the groove, then I'll use other textures over it. It might be just one note or an assortment of rhythms.

How did you get into playing percussion? A lot of drummers never get really good at playing anything other than drums.
It was almost like a necessity. There's only so much work for drummers some times. *[Laughs.]* I was always interested in percussion from the time I was a teenager. I started playing tablas a long time ago because the Indian rhythms are so interesting. When I was about 15, I was studying drums with Narada Michael Walden, and he told me to go see John McLaughlin's new band, Shakti. They were actually recording their first album that night [the recording is called *Shakti with John McLaughlin*], and Zakir Hussain was the tabla player. That night inspired me the rest of my life. The music and the playing was light-years ahead of its time. That, to me, is really interesting.

There's so much music that can come out of percussion instruments because they all have a different sound. So as I went along, I began collecting and learning about their heritage and how each instrument is used and played.

How big is your collection of instruments?
Wow, I never counted. I have hundreds and hundreds of different percussion instruments from India, Africa, Brazil, Ireland, South America, Turkey—just about from anywhere in the world.

Are you interested in the rhythms or in the instruments at first?
I usually get the instrument first, but just having the instrument doesn't really mean anything. You have to

know how it's played and where and why it's used, so that requires some research and sometimes even a teacher. These days it's easier, because you can find out a lot from the Internet, but it's better to get one on one with a teacher or a pro who really knows the instrument and can show you a few things.

Take tablas, for instance. They're probably one of the hardest instruments to learn how to play. You can study tablas for ten years before you start using them well—there's that much to learn. But each instrument has its own texture and technique of how to play it; so whenever I pick up an instrument, I learn what it is I need to do to play it the right way.

Congas are another one. It takes a couple of years just to learn to slap them the right way. It took me a long time before I finally got it. It's almost like a drummer playing a beat but not being able to hit the 2 and 4 right. That's what happens with congas when you first start off.

Back when I was first doing stuff for Bill Ward, he liked a lot of the African rhythms, so I started honing in what the djembe is about and how to orchestrate it against other percussion and other djembe tracks. I remember saying to myself, "Okay, I've got to really look into this," so I started to learn a lot of the African rhythms. Of course, the djembe alone is another instrument where learning the right way is important—from the slaps to the rhythm.

And then there's learning to play the tambourine the right way, too. You don't just hit it. There are a lot of different ways to play it.

It's harder than it looks.

Yeah, especially the bandero, which looks like a tambourine but is shaped a little bit differently and has a head on it. That's another instrument that you can study for years just to play it the right way. In some of the old Motown songs the tambourine carried the groove of the whole tune. A drum set in a recording is just a part of the music. The percussion sometimes carries the whole tune even more than the drums.

Who are your influences?
First was Zakir Hussain and second was Airto Moreira. Airto was so rounded in that he could play with Miles and Chick Corea, and then just as easily do a pop record with somebody. Alex Acuña is the same way. He can play in any situation. That's what I like. I'm not a big fan of any one-trick pony. I like the guys who can make any situation sound great.

What do you see that all great percussionists have in common?
There's a handful of things, but knowing dynamics would be first, and [then] time and texture. Those are the three major things in terms of percussionists. Luis Conte is a good example. Sometimes you see or hear him playing just a tambourine, but he knows that maybe that's all the song needs.

What do you know now that you wish you had known when you were first starting out?
Everything! *[Laughs.]* You learn as you go along. I've probably played on over 300 releases with different artists and different styles, but there's still more to learn. It's never over. You always want to get better or get into some other instruments just to see what they're about. There are so many that it takes a lifetime.

Do you have any advice for someone just starting out in session work?
Sure. Listen to all different styles—don't just stay in one. If you're a percussionist, listen to all the great percussionists to see where they put their sounds and how that works against the other tracks.

Do you have any session tips?
I guess number one would be to learn to swing with the click instead of being afraid of it or just staying with it. You've got to be able to groove with the click but still make it sound musical and not stiff. Your playing has to still be on time, but it has to groove with the click, too. That's the first thing that any drummer or percussionist needs to

learn, aside from learning the technique of the instrument. The second thing is to have big ears and listen to what's happening in the music and the session.

What was the worst session you ever did?
I've done some really bad sessions where I wished I wasn't there. I remember one I did that was a double-album session but they didn't have much time to finish it, so I was there for 12 hours straight for two days. I think I came home and had a panic attack after it was done. No matter how good or bad it is, you still want it to be right. At least I got some good reviews of my playing on the record.

What was the best one you ever did?
The one I did a couple of weeks ago with Frank Stallone was probably the greatest thing I've ever done. It was with a 60-piece orchestra playing big-band jazz. Sammy Nestico arranged all the music, and it was fantastic stuff. Sammy was also there as guest of honor that night. He has arranged for Count Basie, Buddy Rich, Frank Sinatra, Quincy Jones, Phil Collins, and so many other artists of that caliber. Mr. Nestico was one of the nicest, most humble gentlemen I've ever met. I was honored to be able to work with him!

What kind of sessions are the hardest for you to do?
Sessions where the time signature's changing a lot, so you're always counting and trying to figure out what the phrasing is instead of grooving. Instead of playing free with the music, you're just counting every measure.

What kind are the most fun?
The ones where you come in and they say, "Do whatever you think the track calls for." Those are really the best sessions, because if you're a percussionist, you know what will fit best. In those kinds of sessions you're not even working, really—you're just having fun.

What do you like to hear in your headphones?
A lot of times I play to songs that are already finished, so I don't need the click that much; I just need the full mix. On the other hand, if I'm playing on something with just a piano player and bass player, I need a lot of click as a reference point to make sure that everything is tight. You really have to use your imagination in a situation like that to figure out how you're going to orchestrate everything against the existing music.

What's your greatest strength as a player?
I think being able to play a lot of styles. Also being able to play dynamically within a song to make it build and be more exciting.

What's your weakness?
Definitely within the Indian context. I was actually fired one time because I wasn't expert enough on the tablas. It wasn't like I was fired . . . it was more like, "We can't use you, because you're not as proficient as we need you to be." In my defense, the guy that hired me thought that because I own tablas, I must be an expert. I try to be the best that I can be on each instrument, but some instruments require a lifetime to master. Most of the stuff I'm asked to play tablas on isn't that intricate.

What do you hate about recording?
Recording is almost like my favorite thing to do, so it's hard to say what I hate about it. I do hate when I go to a session and hear everything in the track's out of time or not done to a click, and they want me to play to it. If things aren't already in the pocket, bringing me in isn't going to magically make it that way. Sometimes it can work, but most of the time it doesn't.

As I go along, I learn more about my playing and more about what I should and should not do. Actually, it's really more of what I should not do. That old statement of "less is more" is really true. When I first started, I thought that

I had to play everything at every minute of the track, but you don't get called back when that happens. The artist or producer will say, "That was great. You really played your ass off," but then they never call you again.

Charlie Drayton—Bassist and Drummer

Charlie Drayton is a unique and special player in that he's equally adept and in demand as both a drummer and a bass player, so his perspective is that of a total rhythm section. Charlie's long and eclectic list of credits includes such names as Herbie Hancock, Keith Richards, Johnny Cash, Chaka Khan, Mariah Carey, Michelle Branch, Seal, Iggy Pop, Neil Young, Janet Jackson, and Courtney Love, among many others.

Give me some background on how you got into session work?
My father guided me toward the studio at an early age, [when I used to watch] him produce jingle sessions in NYC. He would occasionally have me sing on spots that featured a young voice—either in a group chorus or [as a] solo performance.

Before a session would begin, I would usually find a seat between the drum booth (this was back in the '70s) and the bass chair and B-15 amp (which was the standard bass amp in any NYC studio back then). It only took sitting through a few sessions to know that being in the studio was like being in the best classroom you'd ever walk into, and your dad is the principal. My father then took the band I was playing in into the studio to nurture us and [help us] grow in the studio environment. What a trip it is to hear yourself played back in high-quality audio for the first time! I can still remember the first-time experience, *vividly*.

If I remember correctly, my first professional recording session was playing drums for John Sebastian. He was brilliant and a huge supporter. Walking into the studio was easy, but that first day of tracking was one hell of a ride in my life! The scary part was trying not to be too overwhelmed that the bass player was Anthony Jackson [a highly regarded New York session player] and the guitar player was Steve Khan (I think Steve recommended me for that session). Needless to say, I was hooked and still am.

What do you bring with you to a session?
It depends on what the music or the producer requires and what hat I'm wearing on the session, but I'll just list some of the items at random: I come with a sense of humor, an open heart and mind, and a great deal of patience. If I'm a principal player or producer on a session, a song is also a wonderful thing to bring with you.

I also bring a hot-water kettle and an assortment of herbal and black tea, an endless amount of sugarless mint candy, some incense, chopsticks, cayenne pepper, hot English mustard, crushed red pepper, and fresh ground cardamom.

Also, there's nothing better then having your own gear on a session. For me, that could consist of drums, cymbals, rags, hockey tape, a bullet mic, a Line 6 Bass Pod, an iPod for drum mute, and a few of my favorite pieces of hand percussion. Also basses, guitars, pedal steel, amplifiers, stompboxes, and a really good cable. I also bring my own headphones (Sony 7506 or Audio-Technica ATH-M50), along with an extension cable.

Sometimes I'll bring my black Pekingese, named Holiday, too. My introduction to her was during a session I was producing.

Do you tailor what you bring according to the session?
I try, because I'm lucky to have access to a large selection of gear that I would love to see as often as possible.

Is your stage rig different from your recording rig?
This depends on what will inspire me to execute a performance or what I have access to at the time. Sometimes I may reach for some piece of gear that does not belong to me, so basically anything that will guide me to feel the music.

What do you like in your headphone mix?
The freedom to dial it in myself. My first preference, though, is no headphones whenever possible. I like to sing with the speakers at low level. If playing live with a band, I'll dial the entire group into the mix. If playing against prerecorded tracks, it's possible that I may not play along with all of the elements on the track. I will try different combinations of elements in the mix until it feels good and I'm the most comfortable.

Do you use a tech? If so, why?
There are many functions that a tech could serve, but this depends on what their capabilities are. I like the ones that can keep me happy by making a proper cup of tea!

What do you think the defining moment for a session player is?
I don't think there is a defining moment for a session player. My disposition is that I never have focused on being, or wanting to be known as, a session player. YUK! A great recorded performance flows through me unconsciously. You make choices to bring life, clarity, and support to the music you are playing. The studio is a stage to me, and I mentally visualize the audience in the room. There is never an end to learning something new about the studio and the session environment. At each opportunity, I find myself sharpening the tool of session playing. You can't have enough tricks up your sleeve.

What do you see that all good session musicians have in common?
A good session player is not necessarily a better musician than a player with no session experience, but a good session player has the advantage of having more tools to choose from and is used to narrowing down the options. Dealing with adversity is key. If your talent is on loan and you're having a shitty day but you've committed yourself to a session, guess what? You've got to show up and play the music! The more I do it, the better I get at it.

What do you know now that you wish you had known when you were first starting out?
That we would come to live in a time when you would not need to have much talent to be successful in the music business. The art of playing music and being commercially successful in the music business are now two entirely different things.

I don't know why humans would bring computers into the recording environment for some of the wrong reasons and deconstruct the craft of creating and making music. I'm not against computers, but I thought music was doing just fine without them. Didn't Milli Vanilli try to hip us to that?

Any advice for someone starting out doing session work?
Don't lose the connection or spirit of playing in a live environment. Spirit is a key ingredient that enables you to shine and make the right decisions in session. And embrace the music with your heart, even if it's not your cup of tea. Be in the moment, and that does not mean play everything you know.

What do you consider your big break?
It hasn't happened yet. I still think there is one to come (I like to daydream).

Do you have any session musician tips?
Be a musician first without any title before the word *musician*. I'll enjoy hearing your playing more. Don't limit yourself. Be in the moment, because in the studio you're making musical decisions that can last a lifetime on a record.

If you were able to go back to those early bands that you played in, what kind of advice would you give yourself?
I wouldn't have joined a few of the bands I was in. I would have practiced more instead.

What's your worst session?
The one when the tape is not rolling when it should be, or the computer crashes.

What kind of sessions are the hardest for you?
When the producer's dreams are unrealized. Sometimes a producer doesn't have the ability to play your instrument, so he or she endlessly suggests the worst musical ideas possible for you to play, or how you should be playing them. Or when the food is bad, which in reality is the same answer.

What kind of session is the most fun?
When it doesn't feel like work and you don't want the session to end.

What's your playing weakness? Strength?
My weakness is my strength. Weakness brings me to discover the unknown much faster.

What do you hate about recording?
Not recording!

Bernie Dresel—Drummer and Percussionist

Like many session drummers in L.A., Bernie Dresel is noted for his ability to not only play any musical style, but also step in and play orchestral percussion or groove hand percussion. Widely recognized for his 15 years with the Brian Setzer Orchestra, Bernie now does various types of studio work that spans everything from television shows such as *The Simpsons* and *Family Guy* to movies like *Speed Racer* to the blues rock of Carl Verheyen to the big band sound of Gordon Goodwin Big Phat Band to R&B icons such as Chaka Khan and Patti LaBelle. You can check out Dresel's credits and more at myspace.com/berniedresel and berniedresel.com.

What are you up to now, Bernie?
I'm currently playing with the Gordon Goodwin Big Phat Band, which is kind of an adventure for me in that I've been playing with this band off and on quite a bit for the

past three years, but I've been known for playing with the Brian Setzer Orchestra for the past 15 years. I stepped down from playing with Brian about a year ago just to [be able to] stay in Los Angeles even more than I had been so I could be more available for session work—and so I could be a little more available for Gordon's band, too. So it's a bit of a change for me since I became known by traveling around with Brian's band. That was really fun to be a part of, since I got to contribute to a band sound where we combined a couple of old styles like '40s big band with '50s rockabilly to create a new thing. It's pretty great when you get to be a part of that process, rather than just going out on the road and covering someone's tunes that you weren't really a part of creating.

Can you take us through your kit? Do you usually use the same kit when recording as when you play live?
When I was touring with Brian Setzer, the kit evolved to be two 24"×14" bass drums with heads on the front and no hole, and an external muffler on the beater side because we were doing a '40s big-band sound, a 9"×13" rack, a 16"×16" floor, and an 18"×16" floor. I even used calfskin heads on the snare drum and the tom batter side. Originally I had the standard DW setup of 10", 12", 14", and 16", with either Remo-coated Ambassadors or coated Emperors, and it was just too modern of a sound. We were trying to get that old tribal '40s Krupa sound, and those were the sizes of the day back then. With the calfskin heads, it gave it less of a pitch and made it much more "thuddy" and tribal. That was the kit seen by a lot of people since 1998. There's a lot of stuff on YouTube from a Christmas show and a show that we did in Japan in 2000, and that's the kit you'll see me playing.

In the studio for doing television shows like *The Simpsons*, *JAG*, *Family Guy*, and *American Dad*, I'd be using my basic studio kit. It's not a double-bass-drum kit, but I do set up a double-bass-drum pedal. I generally have a 22"×16" kick, an 8"×12" high tom, and 14"×14" and 16"×16" floors. I use smaller, tighter drums for the studio, but that's what I would use to go out and play with most bands live, too. The oversize drums that I used with Brian were only for that period sound of the '40s. I can make music with whatever is in front of me, but the idea was to duplicate the sound that they had back then, again with only a 14" depth, and not 16" or 18", as is common now. I experimented with a 26", but the 24" was big enough to be a little tighter and not so boomy. But still, these bass drums were booming. I was playing "four on the floor" and they were easily heard, not like a Buddy Rich or bebop thing where every beat is "feathered" and you feel it instead of hearing it. I tried a calf head on the bass drums, but it would rip too often with a plastic beater.

We would break down to a trio in the middle of the set and just do rockabilly songs, where I would go out front with a cocktail kit that DW made for me with like a big 16"×24" tube where the bass drum beater would come up from the bottom. It's like a huge floor tom with a beater on the bottom, and you can play the top of it like a floor tom, with a sidecar snare and a cymbal attached. It was really bare bones. I could've gone out front and played a full kit, but we were trying for a different sound here, too.

Were you playing standing up?
Yes, exactly.

For basic studio stuff, I have a hole in the front head. I'm definitely a coated guy for the snare and the bass drum. I like the extra attack that the Remo-coated head brings. My thought is that an engineer can always dial out the top end if he wants, but if it's not there to begin with, it's hard to add. Generally I use Emperors on the toms and the bass drum, with Emperor Ambassadors on the snare. Sometimes I'll go to coated Ambassadors on the toms, too, if it's more of a jazzy kind of thing, but session to session you don't know what's going to happen, so most of the time I'll use Emperors on it. Some of that's for durability's sake, too, so you don't have to replace one halfway through the session.

How many snares do you usually bring to a session?
Here's the reality of today, at least with the stuff that I do: there are always budget considerations, so I generally

bring six. I could bring 30 snares, but then the cartage bill goes up and, to be honest, you're usually way covered with the six snares because no one is ever asking "What else you got?" past that. So I bring three different sizes of wood and three different sizes of metal drums. That's not including if I go to do an orchestral date, where I'd bring about eight different orchestral snares.

What's your collection like? Do you have a lot of drums?
Yeah, I guess I do. But it all boils down to, what are you going to send to a session? You have to send something that's pretty versatile, and that's my DW kit. I have Radio King kits from the '40s with 24" and 26" bass drums, a Gretsch kit from 1947, a Leedy from the '40s, four DW kits, and a fifth DW kit that I took the bottom heads off for orchestral toms. If someone asked for a '70s sound, I have it ready to go.

That's not including all the different snares that I have. I even forget all the different snare drums I actually have. I have some Radio Kings, Black Beauties, a lot of cool Rogers stuff, Camco, a little bit of everything. I have six Johnny Craviotto Lake Superior snare drums. I love those snare drums. They found the wood at the bottom of Lake Superior where it was underwater for about a hundred years after the logs sank. The trees were actually old growth from the 1300s, so between the wood and Johnny's construction, they sound special and amazing. That's a newer drum but it's old, old wood.

Generally when I buy vintage drums, I don't buy something that's a collectable item. I try to get something that might have different rims on it, or was messed up cosmetically, or the edges have been redone by Johnny Craviotto, or something like that. These are usually worth less because the vintage market is based on originality or "mint condition." I don't want mint condition. I just want something to sound good. I must say that I have so much stuff now that I feel I don't have to keep collecting at this point.

What did you use before DW?
I've been with DW since 1987. I had a Yamaha Recording Custom birch kit that was all the rage in the '80s, but I got tired of the sound of birch. I like maple shells.

How about tuning your drums? Do you tune to intervals? Do you have a particular method for tuning?
There's a lot of different theories about how a drum should sound, but the one that works best for me is when the top head is not exactly the same pitch as the bottom. The top head I tune about a minor third above the bottom head, when you're just barely tapping it right on the edge near the lug. Now it doesn't always stay right there, because the head might loosen a bit when you're bashing on it or the lugs might slip a little bit, but even if it drops a little to a second or a minor second, it's still tuned above the bottom head.

Do you tune the bottom head to the resonant frequency of the drum?
You mean like when you have both heads off and you hit your fist on the inside of the shell to hear it ring? DW actually writes that pitch in its shells to be sure that all the drums are timbre-matched so that you get a different pitch on each shell and so they're not too close together. I'm not really sure how helpful that is, as I've found that I usually don't tune to that pitch.

Really, the biggest thing is that you don't overtighten and choke the drum or make it too loose, because then it's a rather flat sound. So I just try to get it within the sweet spot of a major third or so where you have some play yet it sounds good. Now if you were going to tune it up high, like for a bebop session, then you'd want it a little choked. So what I try to do between my three toms—the 12", 14", and 16"—is to have them maybe a fourth apart in pitch; that way you don't get an octave between the highest tom and the lowest, and they sound musical together. You could do fifths, but then you'd have a ninth off the top tom, and it just seems too far away in pitch. Now if you have a lot of toms, then maybe tuning them a major third apart could work. But with three toms I think a fourth is good, because all three are tuned within the same octave and a fifth is too much because then they're not.

Again, when you hit the drum it starts to change, so you just try to keep it in check over the course of a song or a gig, realizing that it's never going to be perfect. The old days where you'd spend two days getting drum sounds seems ridiculous now, since after the third hour of getting sounds you'll hear, "Okay, let's change the heads.". *[Laughs.]* Today it might take 15 minutes or a half hour or even 3 minutes to get a drum sound. Before you know it you hear, "Okay, we're ready. Go!" There are some pretty good-sounding drum kits now, and the engineers are hired for their drum sounds and speed because everyone is so budget conscious.

What drum do you start with when you're tuning your kit?
I don't think it matters. You can start at the top, you can start at the bottom, you can start in the middle. I tend to go top down, but just the other day I started with the low one. You just start to get a feeling for how many turns are needed when you're tightening the head. You get a feel for the right tension.

I don't think it's good to tune the snare drum on the snare stand. It's better on a table or floor so it's laying flat. You make sure you get your head on flat if you have to change one, then tighten each lug so that it's barely touching the rim, then just finger-tighten the lugs [crisscrossing as you go] so you make sure that you don't overtighten one. Then you can start using the drum key. If you had eight arms so you could tighten all the lugs at the same time, that would be the best thing. But of course that's not possible.

Do you ever adjust the tuning of your drums to the song?
No, not the toms. Maybe the snare. It's not like you're tuning it to the pitch of the song, because once you start hitting it, it's going to change a little. So being exactly in tune isn't going to happen anyway. I feel that's being pretty anal about things, and the result is really not worth the effort because you're not getting a pitch out of the drum per se. You just want the drum to sound good.

Now I've had engineers and producers say, "I think your snare dropped a little" or "I think your snare is tuned too low. Bring it up in pitch a bit" or "The snare's sitting too tight," so you make those adjustments so it fits the songs. Sometimes you have to change snares from tune to tune, but within an album you don't change toms out. For as much as you're hitting them, it's not that drastic a thing because, after all, they sound like toms. *[Laughs.]* The snare is a little more particular tune to tune, but then again, I've used one snare on every tune on an album and that works fine, too. But it varies from project to project.

Now when I do *Family Guy*, I'll put up a snare drum and they'll say, "Okay, let's go." They figure that I'm going to pick the right thing musically for it. I'll usually use either a 5" or a 4" [depth]. I figure that snare size is something like skirt length. At one point everyone was going for that deep-dish snare sound, and then it changed to piccolo snares. It seems that everyone wants whatever everyone else is using at the time. Musically, I think that a lot of things can work; it just depends upon what the producer is going for or what you happen to pull out of the case that day.

What do you want in the headphone mix when you're recording?
What you really want as a drummer is separate from what other people want. I think that there should be a rule that if there's a wall between you and another player, you need a different headphone mix. Meaning, I hear plenty of drums in the room, but the other players can't hear drums at all. If a bunch of horn guys are in the same room together, they can probably deal with the same mix, but they can't hear the drums on the other side of the wall or the piano that's baffled off. The system where you dial in your own monitor mix [Aviom or Hearback] is the greatest thing, because then you can just mix it on the fly or from tune to tune. If one of your bandmates is having some time problems, you might want to turn him down. Or in the case of the vocalist, you want to hear what's going on, but you don't want it to get in the way of some of the groove things that you're playing.

So these types of things you want in your mix. You want enough click, maybe more than the other players. Since the drums are such a clicky instrument already, you need more click than the other players. I do not want a cowbell or a side stick as a click. I don't want a musical sound, because it affects what I think is happening musically. I want a non-musical sound that's really short.

As far as headphones, I started experimenting with these sound-isolating Shures [SCL5s]. I liked those a lot because I didn't hear as much drums, [and drums are] what usually cover up the click more than anything. Usually I just use whatever phones are available. I just want them to be loud enough, like the Sonys. Generally the studios I'm at all have good headphones, so I'm not particular in that regard.

Are there any particular mics that you like on your drums?
I thought for a while that I liked 421s on the toms because they seemed to make the toms sound fuller. A lot of times AKG 414s sound great, especially if you're playing jazz or brushes, because they have a little more crispness. A lot of times when we're doing television, I see engineers use the Neumann TLM-170s as overheads if they're going for a natural sound. They capture a great drum sound just from the overheads. They have them at Fox and Warner Bros. A lot of the time 414s are used as overheads if they're going for a rock sound. I always see a [Shure SM]57 on the snare. Some guys want a mic underneath the snare, and other guys don't need it and get the snappiness another way. It goes back and forth between an old 57 and [an AKG] 451 on the bottom. I see all sorts of different things on the bass drum. Sometimes I'll see as many as three mics on the bass drum, with something like a Neumann 47-FET way out in front.

The reason I know more about mics now is because I have my own home studio. I only record drums, although I might be able to do bass, too. People from Japan and Europe or even five miles away can get drum tracks from me over the Internet; that way you can save on the cartage and the general expense of booking a studio. The costs are cut quite a bit, because I can schedule it in between my other sessions. People still want me to play sessions because they still want everyone playing at once, whether its an orchestra or just a rhythm section, so that's not going to go away. But now I can do a lot of budget things that I couldn't do before.

What are you using for cymbals?
I've been a Zildjian guy since 1986. I was a Zildjian guy always as a kid, then when I first moved to L.A., I got a gig with the singing group the Lettermen. Zildjian wouldn't give me an endorsement at the time because the Lettermen weren't that big any more, but Sabian did. So I was with Sabian for a second until I got the gig with Maynard Ferguson in 1986. They asked if I had a cymbal endorsement, and I told them I was with Sabian. They said, "Well, you're with Zildjian now." It turns out that Armand Zildjian and Maynard were such great buddies that every drummer in his band had to play Zildjian, so suddenly I was back with who I wanted to be with anyway, and I've been with them ever since.

What sticks do you use?
Generally, I think you need a couple of types of sticks, not just one, in your arsenal. If you're doing a wide range of stuff, you need something that's softer with not as much weight when you need to be daintier, like in a jazz trio. On a live gig where you need to play soft yet strong, you need a thicker, beefier stick. When I played with the Brian Setzer Orchestra, I developed a Regal tip model called the Bernie Dresel model that was kind of a thicker bead with a little more length, a little more weight, and a little more throw, which gets you more power and volume from the stick. So I think a couple of different kinds of sticks are appropriate to have.

Any advice for a young recording drummer?
I teach at UNLV [the University of Nevada, Las Vegas] and give private lessons as well, so I'm really into the teaching process and have tons of advice. I also have three hours of teaching available online at StarsTeachMusic.com: like a three-minute lesson on the jazz ride cymbal, or four minutes on displaced backbeats. For a dollar a minute, you can download the movie or buy the entire block for a lot less money than buying each individually.

I have advice for drummers—whether they're recording or not—since it's not a matter of if the red light is on, because someone is always listening anyway. A lot of drummers miss the boat because they're not concerned with playing time and playing simple basic beats, and being able to clone that beat over and over again like a drum machine, but with soul. A lot of drummers are into the flash and are constantly looking for stuff to play, and they put the kitchen sink into every tune. I heard a story once where Miles Davis told someone, "When you think you want to play something, don't." That story is kinda funny, but it's also true. Don't try to be always playing something. Lay back, play the groove, and wait for your spot. They won't be as often as you think. A lot of times drummers try to play too much, and I'm not talking stylistically, either. Whether you're a fusion drummer or a groove drummer, a lot of young drummers are looking to play too much too often. If you have amazing chops, wait for that right moment to use them. It will mean a lot more.

You want to be playing with a metronome, loops, and sequenced tracks as much as possible, and also playing without them. The last time I went to the NAMM show, I took a picture of one booth there because there were people in every booth but this one. It was the metronome booth, and it was empty. I thought to myself, "Ain't that the truth. Sometimes that's the last thing that people want to think about." It's pretty clichéd, but it's what keeps me working and what people want from a drummer. The drums are a support instrument, and people want time, groove, and musicality from the drums. The rest is gravy.

As far as business, if you're looking to get into session work as a drummer, you can't do it. You just have to play a lot of gigs and wait for the time where you get that opportunity.

What was your favorite gig? Was there one that was particularly magical?

That's kind of like, "What's your favorite color?" for me, because there are so many, but there are moments that stick out. One was getting to play in the U.K. with Ringo on the *Dame Edna Show*, where he sang "Act Naturally." It wasn't an amazing magical musical moment, but for me it really brought my career full circle because I can remember seeing him with The Beatles on the old *Ed Sullivan Show* and going, "Hey, that looks cool." That's why I'm a drummer today, because of that show, so to be able to play with him was a personal magical moment. Playing for 300,000 people at Woodstock '99 with Brian Setzer sticks out, but so many great musical moments come at small gigs, at like The Baked Potato [a small L.A. club] or in Europe with [guitarist] Carl Verheyen. It's all over the board, but I try to have those moments each time I play the drums, and that's no lie.

Frank Fitzpatrick—Composer and Producer

Being in the middle of the Detroit music scene as he grew up helped shape the background that eventually made Frank Fitzpatrick one of Hollywood's most sought-after composers and music supervisors. Frank's credits are many, and he has created the soundtracks for over two dozen feature films (including *Scary Movie 3, Queen of the Damned, Friday,* and *In Too Deep*) and scores and themes for several television shows (including the renowned *Larry Sanders Show*).

Frank has also written and produced songs for Gold and Platinum artists including Jill Scott, Fat Joe, Dave Hollister, K-Ci & JoJo, Brownstone, Lina, Carl Anderson, Ice Cube, Akil (of Jurassic 5), Jazz (of Dru Hill), and The London Symphony. He also contributed the opening song for the *High School Musical* tour and the "Angeli" theme for the Victoria's Secret advertising campaign. Listed in *Variety* magazine as one of the "Top Music Supervisors of the Decade," Frank has contributed to the sale of over 6 million soundtrack albums, including the multi-Platinum original *Friday*.

At the core of Frank's success is his attention to the groove, in which he makes sure that the pocket is so deep that the listener can't help but to dance along. Since both making music [he began his music career by playing guitar] and helping others is at the center of his being, Frank was eager to share his insights on finding the groove and getting the best out of musicians regardless of their skills.

Tell me about some of the early bands that you played in. What kind of music were you doing?
I never played [guitar] as a sideman with any famous bands, and I never created a band that became famous. *[Laughs.]* Because of my Detroit background, everything I play is pretty soulful, so I always played in funk and R&B bands, and sometimes maybe I'd cross over into Southern rock. Then I had a jazz trio when I was in music school, and put together combo dates for parties and events—that kind of stuff.

After I moved to L.A., I only played on records that I was producing, or maybe I'd sit in with a reggae band that I might've been producing or something like that. It was always about rhythm and pocket for me. I've always been very anal about rhythm, great grooves, and paying a lot of attention to pocket.

That's just what I want to hear about.
All that comes from being a player, but a lot of it comes from the producing side. It's about two things: in terms of the band, it's about the energy and the vibe and the feel. You just have to go back and listen to the great rhythm sections that cut countless hit records—the guys in Memphis at Stax, the Funk Brothers at Motown, the Wrecking Crew in L.A.—and you'll find that it's not about a great guitar solo and it's not about anything flashy. It's about solid playing and phenomenal grooves. It's not a head thing—it's a body thing.

The other thing is the truth of the artist, which is the ability to deliver a great song. It's just like what Don Was did with Bonnie Raitt on her big breakthrough album *Nick of Time*. Even with the best of L.A.'s studio players in the studio band, every song still had to carry its own weight just with Bonnie and an acoustic guitar. If it didn't hold up like that, then there's no point in putting production behind it.

Is that what "the truth" means to you?
That and the performance of the artist. You're telling a story that's real to you. Do you believe in what you're singing about? You have to convey it from a place other than your memory of a bunch of words and chord changes.

How do you put a band together to get that great groove? Where do you start?
The groove can start from any element. You can build a groove off something like a rhythm guitar and build around it, but ultimately it comes down to the bass and drums being locked right there with it. It doesn't mean that it's square and machined out—it just means that there's some basic factor in the track that has this irresistible feel to it, and everybody in the band adheres to it.

Quincy [producer Quincy Jones] used to say that some singers have it in the pocket of their voice. Supposedly Michael Jackson has such an amazing pocket that he could sing a line and you could build a groove around it. So it can come from any source, but everyone in the band has to be aware of what it is, and hear it, and feel it.

Can the groove come from the writing?
The groove really comes out of the playing; the writing is more the truth of the song. With a younger band, it's figuring what's not working a lot of times. What I'll usually do is break out elements and see who's not hanging with the rest of the band. You can break it down to what elements feel great by pulling everybody out one at a time. A lot of the time I'll just go back to bass and drums and start adding things from there. As soon as I add something that messes with the groove, I know what's wrong. It could go the other way around, though, in that maybe the bass or drums aren't locked.

How often do you work with a band that isn't a group of session players?
Off and on. Almost any time you work with a band, you come across guys who can get away with stuff on stage that doesn't work in the studio. [Live music] usually [involves] looser playing. You can get away with a lot of stuff in performance, thanks to the excitement of the evening.

What's the one thing that you see from great session players that you don't see from a band?
You don't have to tell great session players what you need—they just automatically go there. When you have

to explain to someone how to make something feel better, it becomes a hard place to have it come from if you have to wrap your head around it first. As soon as you have to think about it, you're going to miss part of it anyway. But you can get there; you just have to listen and practice and always pay attention to it.

For example, if I have Chad Wackerman on drums, I can tell him to lay back one more hair on the beat and he'll know what I mean. Where with younger players, there's only ahead of the beat, behind the beat, and on the beat. For advanced players, there's a hundred variations of all of those places. Most young players hate to do what classical players grow up learning, and that's practicing to a metronome. That's mostly because it sounds so ridged, but you have to develop your internal clock first. You can really learn a lot by just playing to some sort of a clock and recording yourself, because you have to be a pretty advanced player to hear what you're playing while you're playing it.

If you were able to go back to those early bands that you played in, what kind of advice would you give yourself?
Play with a lot more people and practice like a mother as much as possible early on, because you just don't get the opportunity to do it later. It's really hard to play catch-up, because there are too many guys who have done the early work or just naturally have "it" to begin with. If you move to L.A., chances are you'd already be so behind the curve that it [will be even harder] to play catch-up because it's a full-time gig just to stay afloat. The other thing is to try to play with people that are better than you. It's just like tennis. Your game will improve immensely if you play with someone who's twice as good as you.

If you could go back, what advice would you give your old bands to make them better?
The band is only as good as the elements that make it up, so people have to be willing to take responsibility for their part in it. I would have each person in the band make a commitment to raising their level of performance to contribute to the band. I would do the same thing with the

songs: strip them down and make the band perform them with nothing going on, and make sure that everybody still loves them. People get lost in the wall of their own sound sometimes, but if you don't break things down and create space in the arrangements, you never really know what's going on. You're just covering it up with noise.

Onree Gill—Keyboard Player and Drummer

Currently the musical director for superstar Alicia Keys, keyboardist and drummer Onree Gill has worked with a diverse list of artists that includes Missy Elliott, Kelly Price, DMX, Sean "P. Diddy" Combs, Stevie Wonder, Gwen Stefani, Lenny Kravitz, Carlos Santana, Eric B, Anthony Hamilton, Angie Stone, John Mayer, Eve, Big Daddy Kane, Naughty by Nature, Bono, Arturo Sandoval, Paul Simon, Usher, and many more. In addition to producing, playing sessions, and touring, Gill and partner Ralph Rolle will soon launch Imgiggin.com, a networking Website for elite music professionals.

So you started producing records pretty early in your musical career, right?
I started producing records when I was 16 years old working with R&B and urban artists, although I played drums from when I was around 7. When I was 19, I did my first professional gig, playing drums on the *Arsenio Hall Show* with Al B. Sure!

How did you get from drums to keyboards?
At about 17 I realized that if I wanted to write and produce, then I had to know how to play piano, so I started teaching myself. Later on I went to school to find out what the heck I was playing, but in the meantime I was producing and making my own tracks. By the time I was 21, I was playing drums less and less and playing piano more and more because I was producing more. That's how it happened.

I play a little bass, too. I just got off the road with Alicia Keys, where we did 109 arena shows in 16 months all over the world. On the last show we were getting ready to play her hit song "No One," when we all switched instruments and I played bass. So Alicia comes out and looks over at the keys and goes, "Where is he?" Then she saw me playing bass and just laughed. We all thought it was great. So I can play bass on certain things, too.

What do you think helped you get ahead in your career?
My character helped me a lot. Being humble, professional, and punctual helped my career a lot, because I don't profess to be one of the greatest piano players or an incredible force in the music business. But if you need someone who's professional and on time, who does their homework, and does whatever they have to do to get the job done, that's me.

Having that type of mind-set helped me to move to higher and higher levels pretty fast. Like I said, I've been in the music industry since I was 16 years old and I'm 37 now, so it took me a long time to get to this level and accomplish the things that I did. I'm not saying that everyone has to take that long. If you're a good musician that has the skills and you're professional and punctual, you might deserve to get there faster, but you still have to be all of those things.

I also had to network a lot. It's all about networking until you get to the point where your phone just rings. There was a point in time where I had to keep hustling and meeting people.

How did you do that?
What I did was simple. When I was 18 I started going to industry parties, like a birthday party for Bell Biv DeVoe, or something like that. They'd get you for $25 at the door, so the only people there were industry people. I would pay the cover charge or try to get a hookup from someone on the inside, and then I'd ask around to find out who everyone at the party was. It would be like, "The guy over there with the white jacket on is head of A&R for Sony," or "This women in the blue dress works for Columbia." After I found out who everyone was, what I'd do was to walk around and just say "Hello" to everyone. I didn't strike up a

conversation or anything. I'd just walk away as I was making my rounds.

So I kept going to these parties and bashes and kept going around saying hello to the same people over and over. It got to the point that when they saw me coming, I looked familiar to them and they'd think, "He's always at these parties. He's got to be in the music business." At some point months later I'd go, "Hey, you still at Sony?" and they'd go, "Yeah," and I'd pass him my card and he would pass me his and all of sudden I'm setting up meetings. That's how I did it.

Do you find that session musicians share any common traits?
First of all, professionalism and punctuality. But believe it or not, the thing that's common is how unique each musician is, and that's important. When I produce, I call different musicians for different styles. If I'm producing a hip-hop record, I'll call a drummer that I know who plays hard and solid and plays the pocket well, as opposed to a drummer who plays with finesse and sensitivity.

The other thing I look for is uniqueness in the person, because they're giving a part of who they are and no two musicians can do that the same way. I can play piano on a track, read the chart, and play the same chords, but it will sound different from anybody else because I'm giving a part of who I am. It will never be the same.

What do you bring with you to a session?
Lately I'm really spoiled because I don't have to bring much. I like a combination of synths and acoustic instruments, so if I'm doing a session with Alicia, we'll already have an acoustic piano and a Fender Rhodes in the room as well as a Yamaha Motif ES7 or ES8. If I have to bring something I'll bring a Motif, but usually I'll just have them rent some things if they're not already there.

What do you use on the road?
A 1965 chopped Hammond B-3 and a Leslie 122, and a Yamaha Motif ES7 and ES8. From time to time I might take out a Fender Rhodes, too. I do all the drum

programming as well, so I'll do all the recording and editing in Pro Tools, then dump it down to these Roland 2480 machines, and play it back from there.

What's the defining moment of a session player?
I think the moment you step into the studio and realize that it takes a different approach. Some great live players don't do well in sessions because of the precision required. Live, you can play a little looser, enjoy yourself, and have fun. If you hit a flam or misfinger a couple of notes by accident, nobody's going to really care. In the studio you have to be precise, and everything has to be almost perfect. When I step into the studio, I want to play the best that I can yet have it feel like I'm playing from my heart. That's really imperative.

Do you have any tips for guys breaking into session work?
The best way to get work is by word of mouth and establishing relationships. You wouldn't believe the number of calls I still get at 3 a.m. from Sean "P. Diddy" Combs saying, "We need you. How fast can you get down here?" So it's a matter of being professional and networking. That's an important tool.

What's the worst session you ever did?
I've had a couple of sessions where there's a lot of hurry up and wait. Sometimes you'll end up sitting there for hours before you get to work. Some musicians say, "I don't mind if I sit here all day, because I'm getting paid for it." But if you're booked at noon and the artist doesn't come in until 7:30 p.m., you kind of feel sour because now you have to stay and work and you've already been there all day doing nothing. That puts a little damper on the atmosphere.

What kind of sessions are the hardest?
I love a challenge, so it doesn't matter to me. I've had some parts that I had to practice during the session before I could play them, but it's never been a deal breaker on a session. Sometimes people can play it down right away, but sometimes you can't get it cold and have to work it out. It's normal, so don't beat yourself up about it.

What sessions are the most fun?
When you have great writing, first of all. But if you get on a roll with some great musicians, it's a huge amount of fun. I've been on sessions where I didn't know anyone, but then you start to gel and the session takes a whole new form because of the connection. It's the people on the session who make it fun.

Eric Gorfain—Violinist and String Arranger

Combining classical training with rock 'n' roll sensibilities, Eric Gorfain is one of the most in-demand violinists and string arrangers on the scene today. Eric's list of credits are indeed impressive, having played violin with rock gods Jimmy Page and Robert Plant, Eric Clapton, and Rod Stewart; pop divas Christina Aguilera, Kelly Clarkson, and Pink; mainstream artists Bryan Adams, Vanessa Carlton, and Fiona Apple; soul giants Ray Charles and James Brown; and alternative bands Wilco, Live, and A Perfect Circle, to name just a few. And as a string arranger, Eric has added his flair to songs by Christina Aguilera, James Blunt, Grant-Lee Phillips, Sam Phillips, Vanessa Carlton, Sean Lennon, Kelly Clarkson, Sierra Swan, Busta Rhymes, and A Perfect Circle. Eric gives us the benefit of his many hours in the studio in the following interview.

How did you get into session work?
I was living in rural Japan, having spent most of my senior year of college [as a music student at UCLA] as an exchange student over there. After entertaining the idea of joining a professional orchestra, I decided that studio work was more my speed. I traveled to Tokyo to check out the scene and buy an electric violin that I had found advertised in a magazine. Serendipitously, the salesman at the shop turned out to have been a former studio violinist who had quit playing to become an arranger and composer. We became friends, I moved to Tokyo, and he got me my first session in town a few weeks later.

What do you bring with you to a session?
Typically, I bring my violin, my own headphones, and a pencil. Often I bring the sheet music for the string arrangement I may have written for the session.

Do you tailor what you bring according to the session?
Yes. When I'm playing a solo session (rather than with my string quartet, The Section Quartet, for example) and, depending on the genre of music to be played, I'll sometimes bring an extra violin that has more of a "fiddle" sound.

Is your stage rig different from your recording rig?
On stage with The Section Quartet I use a violin that has a pickup inside the bridge, and I run it through a few effects pedals.

What do you like in your headphone mix?
I like to have plenty of rhythm [kick and snare are crucial], a good amount of bass, enough of the chordal instruments for pitch, and just a little bit of vocals. If I'm playing solo, then I like having myself in the mix, but if I'm playing along with other string players, then I prefer to leave the live strings out of the headphone mix.

What kind of headphones do you like?
AKG K-240s are great. I use a Sony mono earphone when playing in ensembles.

What do you think the defining moment for a session player is?
The defining moment for a session player is when that player is recognized and hired for their own unique musical voice.

What was your defining moment?
My defining moment probably came on the road when I toured with Jimmy Page and Robert Plant on their Unledded tour as the concertmaster of their orchestra. That tour was the ultimate blend of rock and classical genres (not to mention Arabic music). I learned from Jimmy and Robert that while technical prowess is paramount, playing "in the moment" makes a musical performance something to remember.

Who are your biggest influences?
For violin, Mark O'Connor. As a fellow multi-instrumentalist, Mark's stylistic versatility, as well as his multi-instrumental talents, is inspiring.

What do you see that all good session musicians have in common?
Every session musician that I know has calm, confidence, creativity, quick thinking, affability, politeness, and punctuality.

Any advice for someone starting out doing session work?
Even if you know your instrument inside and out, learn as much as you can about the recording process [microphones, mic preamps, and so on] in order to know as much as possible about what's going on on the other side of the glass.

Do you have tips for aspiring session musicians?
Always be on time [translated: always show up 20 to 30 minutes ahead of the session downbeat]. Be interested in the music you're being asked to perform, and be flexible, helpful, creative, respectful, and musical. In other words, be easy to work with as well as a great musician.

If you were able to go back to those early bands that you played in, what kind of advice would you give yourself?
I didn't grow up playing in bands, but I will say that I was happiest when I was the least talented or experienced person in a band, because I was able to learn a lot and improve my own playing.

What was your worst session?
When I was new in town [Los Angeles], I showed up to a session for string quartet and found out that the string arranger had scored the arrangement in a key one step below the actual key of the song. This was in the days before advanced notation software and the prevalence of laptops, so transposing and reprinting the scores on the spot wasn't a quick option. So the producer asked us to tune our instruments up one step and play the arrangement as written. Well, acoustic nonfretted string

instruments don't especially like being tuned up a full step, and string players aren't accustomed to fingering a B, for example, and hearing a C instead. Ten frustrating hours later, the producer couldn't understand why four nonfretted instrumentalists couldn't play in tune with instruments tuned up one full step, and the session ended mercifully.

What's your playing weakness?
Classically trained musicians tend to be hard on themselves, especially when recorded. I've come a long way from those early days, and now really enjoy the recording and music-making process. Mistakes can be the magic a track needs.

Jerry Hey—Trumpet Player

There may be no other trumpet player as respected and widely recorded as Jerry Hey. He's been the first call for most Hollywood recording horn dates for more than 25 years and has played on thousands of recordings with just about every major artist as well as on movie soundtracks too numerous to mention here.

I understand that you have strong feelings about how people mike your horn.
I guess I have strong feelings because over the course of my experience, being in great situations and being in awful situations, I've learned a lot.

You carry your own mics, don't you?
I have for about 10 or 12 years. When you go into studios like Capitol or Oceanway, they have a good microphone collection, so you don't have to worry. But with home studios being such a big part of recording now, a lot of times they don't have any good mics. It forced me to take one part of the equation and make it the same every time, so that I always know that it's not the microphone's fault if something doesn't sound right. I carry three Royers [model R-121] with me now.

Why three Royers?
Usually, in my horn section there are two trumpets, one trombone, and one sax. The trumpets play on one mic, and trombone and sax play on a mic each. The Royer has become sort of a standard for horns now. Most of the studios now have bought them, so I don't have to even take them into a lot of places.

So do you just have someone use your mics right away, or do you wait to see what it sounds like?
It depends on the engineer. For instance, Bruce Swedien has a great mic collection that he bought new that no one else has ever touched, and he's put a whole host of microphones in front of us. We did a very high-intensity tune for Michael Jackson once, where Bruce put his RCA 44 on the trumpets, and I told him, "Bruce, you're the only guy that I'd ever let put that microphone in front of us." He said, "Wait until you hear it." It just sounded amazing, because it was in such pristine condition. In a situation like that, where a guy has world-class microphones, there's usually not a problem. But in situations where I'm in somebody's home and they have little or no microphone selection and they put up something that I know doesn't sound good, I'll tell them I have the Royers available.

Do you have a favorite placement?
Because the Royers have a figure-8 pattern, the room is an issue in the placement. If you're in a smaller room with four horns, you can't have the mics too far away from the trumpets at the level we play because the room becomes a factor on the back side of the mic. So the placement can be anywhere from a foot and a half to four feet or so away. We've done some Earth, Wind, and Fire stuff where it's been six feet away. That was kind of roomy because the room was small, but that was the sound that we were going for: a "live" kind of sound. So it does depend on the size of the room and how far away you are from the wall that you're playing toward and how much slap off the wall you're going to get. But generally, I'd say about two feet from the end of the trumpet bell takes most of the room away from it.

How do you determine where in the room you're going to play?
That depends on the acoustics of the room. In a moderate-size room like Oceanway, Conway, or Capitol, when you play soft it sounds like you're playing soft, and when you play loud it sounds like you're playing loud, and you can hear yourself all the time. Almost anywhere in those rooms sounds great. If you go into another room that has carpeting on the floor or has soft walls or ceilings, the quality of sound doesn't change that much [from soft to loud] and you feel like you have to work harder. In a deader room it helps to be closer to a wall so you can get a little feedback from what you're playing; otherwise, it's easy to overblow and work harder than you need to work.

Do you mean play into the wall?
Not into the wall, but move a step or two closer [to it] to get a little bit of feedback. When you're playing trumpet, your effort is a factor on how much you can hear yourself; so in a deader studio, it makes it a lot more difficult to play and to hear everybody. So if you move up a little closer to the glass or the wall, it can make you not work so hard.

Does that still matter if you're wearing headphones?
We always us one-sided headphones, because it's very difficult to expect the engineer to get your balance good enough with the rhythm section and also balance the horn section the way it should be in order to play in tune with double-sided phones. That puts another cog in the link of recording when you have to make the engineer work that hard. Also, with one headphone we can hear everyone in the room, which helps keep the time and phrasing the same.

Do you always play with the same guys?
If I can. The other trumpet player is Gary Grant, and we've played together for over 30 years. I know what he's going to do and he knows what I'm going to do, so it's just like a clone standing right next to you. The saxophones have changed a bit over the years, with Dan Higgins or Larry Williams or a few others that I've used. Bill Reichenbach

on trombone has been the guy for a very long time. It's understood that we go in there as a team, with everyone going at it at the same level. It makes life easier and we have a good time.

Rami Jaffee—Keyboard Player

One of L.A.'s most prolific session figures, Rami Jaffee received his break in the business playing keyboards for the Platinum-selling Wallflowers. Rapidly expanding into session work, Rami's played on recordings by diverse acts such as Fall Out Boy, LeAnn Rimes, Pearl Jam, Melissa Etheridge, Keith Urban, and Ziggy Marley, among many others. He's also now an unofficial member of The Foo Fighters.

Give me some background on how you got into session work.
When I first started working with The Wallflowers in the early '90s, I met Benmont Tench [the keyboardist from Tom Petty & the Heartbreakers] through Jakob [Jakob Dylan, singer for The Wallflowers]. Benmont took a liking to me and asked if it was okay to hand off my number when he passed on a session. Let's just say now I owe him a little something!

What do you bring with you to a session?
It really depends on what they [the producer, band, artist, and so on] want. I'm mainly asked to do my Hammond B-3 organ stuff, but sometimes they just say, "I need accordion on one song." Bringing clients into my studio is usually the smarter idea. That way, all the toys are at our disposal when I first hear the songs.

Do you tailor what you bring according to the session?
Of course. Hopefully I'm told what direction the session is to go in. That way I can pack accordingly. I hate showing up to the Caribbean with snow boots! *[Laughs.]*

Is your stage rig different from your recording rig?
Most of the time. When I was in The Wallflowers, I really stayed with a select few staples: the B-3, an upright piano,

and a Mellotron. Now, in the Foos, I use that setup but add an accordion, a Casio SK1, a Wurli [Wurlitzer electric piano], and a bunch of Memory Mans [Electro-Harmonix delay pedals]. My recording rig for a studio session might consist of that gear, but I might reach further into the toy box, too.

What do you like in your headphone mix?
You know those fancy headphone mix stations? Yeah, they're scary. I'd like to start with where the mix is at because most of the time, it's toward the end of tracking so the mix can be rather full already. I want to hear where the song is at so I can add to it in proper proportion. Having said that, sometimes I need some more drums so I can lock in better.

What kind of headphones do you like?
I'm all about the M-Audio Studiophile Q40. [They're] the best reference for me, and isn't that important?

Do you use a tech? If so, why?
Yes! You ask why? Have you seen the size of Hammond B-3 organs and grand upright pianos? Oy vey!

What do you think the defining moment for a session player is?
When you realize you're making a song better. I'm not going to say, "When you stop jerking off," because sometimes that's just what the song needs. You just have to know; otherwise, the producer throws tomatoes at you!

When does the light come on?
The light comes on when you drop all your personal problems; read the minds of the producer, the artist, the engineer, and the A&R dude; and make shit happen. That's easier said than done! Checking an artist's Web site or MySpace page and googling the producer sounds silly for prep, but not *that* stupid if you want to do what's right.

What was your defining moment?
I've had so many defining moments! Really, that's what's kept me wanting to do this. At first, it was playing for the

song; then it was the challenge to play in all genres. So the defining moment always changes.

Who are your biggest influences?
Wow, I have so many. As a recording keyboard player, I'd say Benmont Tench. He taught me how to use control and the possibility for genius by playing simple parts. He's a huge inspiration to me!

What do you see that all good session musicians have in common?
What I see is that look of "How the hell did we get so totally blessed to be part of all this?" *[Laughs.]* Really, I think we're all different, but what may link us all together is our ability to put the ego in the back pocket and play for the song in a way that heads it in the right direction . . . No. 1 on the charts!

What do you know now that you wish you knew when you were first starting out?
That's tough to say. Maybe I'd say to stop playing so busy and to simplify parts; but recently I've found that sometimes you can add excitement by getting into the busy playing world. Hey, if a song has a bunch of boring playing out of respect to pop genre, it needs some wackiness. You just gotta rip some character!

Any advice for someone starting out doing session work?
Yes. Please make music better. Listen to the music. Try your hardest to read the artist and the producer. Do your best to get your point across to the engineer. Use all dialogue possible with each and every one involved. These things can make or break the charts. Don't think, "Oh, whatever," even if the studio atmosphere is chill. This is music that, at best, will live on way after us. Show some soul, mama!

What do you consider your big break?
My big break in session work was mainly from Benmont Tench passing my number along to the biggest producers

around. Being a player after Benmont's style, being a Grammy winner, and selling millions of albums didn't hurt either.

If you were able to go back to those early bands that you played in, what kind of advice would you give yourself?
Oh gosh. Let's start with "What the hell is wrong with your hair?! " *[Laughs.]* Seriously, I'd probably say, "Please listen to the band!" I swear, when you're young, your ego is so swollen that you probably barely listen to anyone.

What was your worst session?
Probably one of those where the producer is arguing with the artist about where the song should go, and the argument concerns what I'm playing. And all while I'm sitting there trying to play and ignore calls from my ex-wife's lawyer! (Well, you asked!)

What was your best?
I think where I genuinely feel that I played the right thing for the song, and the artist and producer feel I took it to a place they never knew existed.

What kind of sessions are the hardest for you?
Believe it or not, the kind where the singer or producer has an idea and shows me on the keyboard. Even if it's an easy part, I have a weird mental block on other people's style and not just flowing with my own instincts. It's funny because that's completely opposite from most players.

What kind of sessions are the most fun?
The same as what I told you for best sessions, because the best ones are usually the most fun. Also, I really love playing in a room with a whole band, which very seldom happens.

What's your playing weakness? Strength?
My weakness is playing busy right off the bat, but my strength is that I tidy up and play simply by the second take.

What do you hate about recording?
When a producer or artist is letting their life difficulties take over while they work. It's totally understandable and I can relate because the lives of musicians and producers do have drama, but when it reflects on the attitude of the session and you're asked to go circling around different keyboards and styles, you're going through useless motions sometimes. When I'm producing and those scary moments in someone's personal or professional life come up, I make the call right away and say, "Can we try this tomorrow?" It's a simple call, really.

Ricky Lawson—Drummer and Composer

It just might be easier to say who Ricky Lawson hasn't played with rather than list all of his credits. Having performed with the likes of Quincy Jones, the Brothers Johnson, Phil Collins, Steely Dan, Eric Clapton, Babyface, Lionel Ritchie, Anita Baker (*Rapture*), Whitney Houston (*I Will Always Love You*), and not to mention working as musical director for Michael Jackson, Ricky was also the original drummer for The Yellowjackets, where he won best R&B Instrumental Grammy in 1986 (*And You Know That*). There's obviously a reason why these musical superstars have Ricky on a first-call basis, and that's not only because he is so massively talented and guaranteed to give a record a giant grove, but he's so exceedingly humble and helpful to others as well. More about Ricky, as well as his enormous credit list, can be found on either rickylawson.com or myspace.com/rickylawson.

Can you describe your kit? Do you take a different kit on the road than the one you use in the studio?
I've been with the Pearl company for about three and a half years now, and use a Pearl Studio Master kit with maple shells. I use a different kit on the road from in the studio because the studio is such a detailed environment and everything has to be precise since it's always under a microscope.

On the road things don't need to be so precise, so I do take a different kit. With the economy being what it is these days, we can't always afford to take equipment with us on the road, so we get backline companies to supply us with equipment. I just order what I have at home, and they supply it for me.

How do the kits differ?
They differ only because of the wear and tear on the road. You set it up, tear it down. Set it up, tear it down. Now that I'm blessed enough to have my own facility, I can set my gear up and leave it, and it's always ready to go.

What size are your drums?
I generally use five toms in the studio: 8"×8", 10"×10", 12"×12", 14"×14", and a 16" over on my hi-hat side. The bass drum is usually 22"×16". I'll use a host of different snare drums depending upon what you're going for. For a hip-hop or R&B kind of vibe, I'll use a snare that's 14"×6" or 6½". Something that's reasonably deep.

Sometimes for something that's a little on the pop side, I may use a 14"×4½" piccolo snare or maybe even a 13" snare, which has become very popular because it has the weight to it but still has the snap because of the smaller diameter. I've used snare drums as small as 10" in diameter and maybe 5½" deep for jazz projects and hip-hop projects. Usually I enjoy the wood snares better because they have a tendency to sound a little warmer than the metal snare drums, but it's all a combination of drumheads and microphones and processing and the engineer to make things sound good. You can have a $10,000 drum kit, and the engineer can make things sound like cracker boxes—and you can have cracker boxes, and he can make them sound like a $10,000 kit. There are a lot of little factors that make a difference, and what we try to do is cut down as many as possible or turn them to our advantage.

So I have my own kit tuned the way I like it, with the heads that I like and with the kind of microphones and the kind of engineer that I know can capture it. Because a lot of engineers cannot capture what a real acoustic drum set sounds like.

What heads are you using?
I use Remo heads. I like a Control Sound–coated snare head with the dot up under the bottom, because it's coated so that I can use brushes on it if I have to. Then on the toms I use Emperor heads on the tops and Ambassadors on the bottom. Sometimes I go with the clear head because it's a bit more metallic and cracking, but if I'm doing something that's more jazzy, I'll use a coated Emperor head. I just kind of move the combination of drum heads around to get different things. If I want a heavier sound, I'll use a thicker head. If I want it brighter with more attack, I'll use a thinner head. I usually don't go any thinner than an Ambassador, and I usually don't go any thicker than an Emperor. I go with Remo because they make more combinations than anybody out there, and their stuff is more consistent.

For the bass drum I use a Power Stroke, which is not as thick as a Pinstripe but not as thin as an Ambassador. I try to use a 16" bass drum because that'll give me a little more weight and body to the kick drum.

It's so funny—when I played with Phil Collins, he used a 20" bass drum but it's 16" deep. He has to use a smaller bass drum in order to get the toms physically in there, because he has those big giant toms. Yet if you listen to *In the Air Tonight*, that 20" bass drum sounds a lot bigger because it's all in the engineering.

What do you like to use for mics on your kit?
I always use Shure mics because they're consistent and they always work. When I toured with Steely Dan, those were the mics that we used. We used the KSMs, the VP-88, and the Beta 52. If a guy pulls these mics out, I know it's usually going to be great. Ninety-five percent of the time they use an SM57 on the snare drum. I've seen some teeny, tiny mics where the guy got a killer sound, and I've had a session where the guy used $30,000 worth of mics on the drums and it sounded like $500's worth. I'm telling you that the sound is in the engineering and the studio environment. It's not really what I like to see on the drums; it's who I see engineering. Because you can get a cat that

doesn't know what he's doing and it can be a nightmare. Back in the day, they might have only used three or four mics tops, but if a guy knew what he was doing, he got a killer drum sound. It's the engineering factor that plays such a big part in the situation.

Do you tune your drums to intervals?
What I try to do is to tune to where the drum sounds good. You can take a drum and you can tune it out of the range of what it likes to be in, so I just try to find the sweet spot for that drum with the combination of heads that I'm using. I like the top head a little bit tighter, and then I use the bottom head just to bring in some tone. For more of a big tom kind of vibe, I've been using some open-bottom toms that don't have a bottom head, and that's pretty interesting too. On some of the George Duke projects that I've done, I didn't use a bottom head on my first four toms. It's a little bit more of a caveman kind of tom sound. I kind of jump back and forth depending upon what is needed.

How many snare drums do you bring to a session?
Usually anywhere from five to six. At my studio I have about eight that I'll regularly choose from. You'd be surprised. Different drums bring out different spirit in the music. I used some snare drums that were as big as coffee cans, and they sounded huge just by backing the mic away and capturing more of the sound with the overhead mics. If you play a fatter drum, you have to get in a little bit closer so it can capture that meat, that body of the drum. I went through four snares on the last session that I did—not because they sounded bad, but because the client wanted to blend my snare along with the electronic snare drum they had going on. We changed them until we found the right one, because my job is to give them what they're looking for and in this case, that's what they wanted.

Sometimes people think that a snare drum is going to sound a particular way because of the size of it, but it all depends on the tuning of the drum. So I always tell them, "Hey, let me know what you need, and I'll get you there." Because that's our job, to get them exactly what they need.

Do you tailor the kit that you bring to the session to the type of music?
Yes, sir. If we're doing pop stuff I'll make sure that I have some big toms, and if we're doing jazz stuff the toms will be a little bit smaller so the sound isn't as bombastic. A lot of times I choose a kit that's pretty general that I can use on just about anything. With the 8", 10", and 12" with 14" and 16" floor toms, I can do pretty much anything that's going down. I can play jazz, I can play funk, I can play pop, I can play gospel with that kit. Whatever is necessary.

At my studio I use four toms, and I have the ability to add two more to that configuration. But I bring five toms to an outside session.

Do you tune your toms to intervals?
No, what I do is find the range of the drum and get the drum sounding good. If you get the drum sounding like what it's supposed to sound like, then I'm done. Maybe a little duct tape to take out some of the overtones, but other than that, I'm through.

Do you have a hole in your kick drum, or do you take the front head off?
Sometimes I have to take the front head off, but generally I have a hole in it. That hole is usually anywhere from 8 inches to maybe 12 inches.

What kind of cymbals do you use?
Right now I use the Paiste Signature line. I used them on the Steely Dan tour, the Phil Collins tour, all over the place. The hats are 13" heavies. You can play pretty much any style of music with those. I use a 17" crash, a 16" crash, a 20" dry ride, and a 20" China that I can use on straight-ahead, Latin, jazz, or funk. The nice thing is that they stay brighter and clearer longer. I use a wood-tipped stick so [that] they sound cleaner and make it easy for me to do what I do.

What do you like to hear in the mix?
I like to hear the piano, a little bit of the bass, and ambience on myself and whatever the lead instrument is so I can

get a feel for the melody to know how to approach my particular part. Gotta have the click, too.

Do you like a musical click, or something mechanical?
Preferably a musical one, but I'm one of those kinds of cats that can work with whatever. Give it to me more on the musical side, but if not, I'll use whatever you got. It can be an old lady clapping her hands, I'll take that and work with it. I'll get used to anything. I've done sessions where the guys have had it together, which is great, and I've done sessions where the guys didn't have it together. The key is to get in and make it happen in the least amount of time.

I actually prefer to work at my place because it's already set up, it sounds really good, and we can work a lot more efficiently in that we can do more tracks in not a lot of time. On one session recently, we cut nine tracks in seven hours because of the efficiency of the studio. The artist was losing his mind, because he was used to getting maybe two tracks on a good day.

Is there a set of headphones that you like to use?
I like the Sony professional headphones. I like the way that they fit on my head. There's an AKG that I really like that sounds fantastic.

Any advice for someone just starting to record?
Yeah, come over to the Ricky Lawson studio and take a quick lesson. *[Laughs.]* I enjoy teaching and I wish I had had someone do this with me when I was a young kid, so if someone wants to come over to my place to watch a session, great. Come on over, because a lot of it is not only the playing but the fellowship and how you talk to people and get along with people and comprehend what someone is saying.

As far as advice, the first thing is to play good time. Secondly, you have to make it feel good. If you don't, you're going to get beat up from having to play it over and over again. I usually try to get stuff done in one or two takes. Hopefully I can get it done in one *[laughs]*, but if not, two or three is not bad. But job 1 is to play good time.

Do you have any tricks for making things feel good?
No, man. I just listen to the music, and I try to play it as if I wrote it. When you think like that, you have a tendency to play it a lot differently than if you just got it cold. A lot of the time we haven't heard the music or seen the artist before. That's the biggest drag. It's hard to get the music cold, figure it out, and then play it as if you've been playing it for years. Then you have to make it happen in the least amount of time on top of that. Usually a session is three and half hours, and you've got to get it done in that time—and that's if you're by yourself [overdubbing drums].

Sometimes the other drag can be if you have other musicians involved, because you may have to pull them into it as well, which adds another factor to what's going on. But if you have good guys, it's almost like a good basketball team. Once the music is counted off, they know exactly where they're supposed to go and how to get there. They just come in and take everything to the next level, and that's a hit when you can do that.

What's the most magical gig you've ever done?
Michael Jackson's gig was the ultimate just because of the quality of the musicians and the dimension of the show. That was one of my best. Also, working for Walter Becker and Donald Fagen [Steely Dan]. Working with those guys you can't help but kick booty. And of course, The Yellowjackets, where writing your own music and then having it win a Grammy and be recognized at that level felt so good. The thing is, the Yellowjackets were just a band playing music that we liked. It wasn't like, "Let's go out and change the world." We were just having fun and it really worked out. Now I hear that music somewhere every day.

Brian MacLeod—Drummer and Songwriter

Brian MacLeod has been one of the most in-demand session drummers in L.A. for quite some time now, and with good reason. Brian has the ability to make tracks feel not just pretty good, but awesomely great. Although he has plenty of chops, just listen to the groove in Sheryl Crow's breakthrough hit "All I Want to Do," and you'll hear exactly what Brian is known for. And if you're a fan of the television shows *The Office* or *Dirty Sexy Money*, that's him playing on the theme songs. Add to this credits like Christina Aguilera, Madonna, Chris Isaac, John Hiatt, Tears for Fears, Jewel, and many, many more, and you get the picture of just why the Brian MacLeod touch is so sought after.

But there's more to Brian than just drumming. As a member of the band on Sheryl Crow's debut album, *The Tuesday Night Music Club*, which shot her to fame, he's been Crow's frequent songwriting collaborator in the years hence, helping pen (among many other songs) the ever-popular "Every Day Is a Winding Road," which every year takes on a new life with a cover (most recently by Prince) or as the soundtrack for a television commercial. You can read more about Brian at www.myspace.com/brianmacleod.

What's your kit like?

I switched from using my vintage gear to a custom Ddrum kit. The company's been around for a long time making drum triggers, but this is kind of a new thing from them. I still love my old Gretsch and Ludwig kits, but Ddrum made me a beautiful custom kit with a lot of pieces, like different-size kick drums. They made me a 20", a 22", and a 26" because they each have specific sounds: the 20" is punchy for R&B, the 22" is good for modern rock and commercial stuff, and then the 26" is for that John Bonham thing with both heads on.

These are all 16" deep?

The 26" is 14" deep. The other two are 16" deep. This Ddrum kit is all maple and really sounds warm. It has wood hoops on all the toms and is kind of modeled after the old marching kits that Levon Helm [of The Band] used to play. I've been using it a lot as my starting place, but I'll use different gear for different projects. Sometimes I won't bring everything, but I generally like to have a lot of options, so I'll bring a big arsenal. And then I like to have a lot of odd toys, like toy snare drums that I've picked up along the way, which are great for making drum loops. I have a bunch of lo-fi trashy cymbals that I use sometimes when I don't want to go for a hi-tech sound. But I like to have a big array of available sounds to choose from that go from hi-tech to lo-tech.

I have this other drum that's really interesting, called the Trash Cat, which is like a timpani but it's made out of a trash can. I can use it like a floor tom or like a timpani. A lot of producers have really fallen in love with it.

So it's nice to have odd, different things. I interject them when the producer is looking for something special. It really takes a lot of teamwork with the producer as a session drummer. You have to go with the flow and not interrupt things, but at the same time have something to bring to the table if needed.

How many toms do you bring?
I generally play a 12"×8" and a 16"×14", but I also bring a 14"×14" floor tom if I need another one.

What kind of heads do you use?
I generally use Ambassador coated heads. I'm not afraid to tape up my kit if I need to get it to fit better with the song, though, because you have to tune your drums for the microphones. Sometimes the drum kit might not sound good in the room after you tune it, but it might sound amazing when you hear a playback. This can be very deceiving, for young drummers especially. A young drummer might have his kit tuned so it sounds just wonderful live, but you tune it differently for recording. Sometimes I'll use tons of duct tape. I'm not afraid to tape up drums or pad them down to get a nice tight sound if that's what the producer is looking for.

How do you tune your drums? Do you tune to an interval?
I'm not one of those guys who gets into interval tuning. I think that most drums have a sweet spot, and that's what I try to find. It might not necessarily be an interval with another drum, although sometimes I will do that with the snare drum,

especially if it's wide open for a real loud and cracking sound. Then I'll either tune it to the pitch of the song so it sits in there nicely, or just the opposite, where it's out of pitch with the song so it clanks a bit. Sometimes that means just detuning one lug of the snare to get a nice loud crack out of it.

When you say the "sweet spot," do you mean the resonant frequency of the drum?
Yeah, that's what it is. I learned a lot about tuning from working with the Drum Doctor [Ross Garfield] for so many years, and John Good from DW taught me a lot about the sound that each shell has. Just naturally when you're playing with the drum, you'll hit a spot where it feels really good. Some of the older drums that have rounded bearing edges have kind of a deader sound, so it's harder to find the sweet spot. This Ddrum kit that I have doesn't have the standard 45-degree edge like most new drums. It has a 30-degree edge, so it sounds more like older drums because that's the sound I really like. I'm having them build a mahogany kit for me, because it's a warmer sound than maple. Some of my old Slingerland Radio King kits are mahogany, and they just sound so warm. But the sweet spot you seem to instinctually find.

Like I was saying before, sometimes I'll hit a drum and it just doesn't sound good. But before I'll go and tune it, I'll wait until the engineer tells me what he's hearing in the control room, because the sound that you hear sitting behind the kit is so different from what the mics hear. Sometimes I'll think that the drum sound is amazing, and the engineer or producer will go, "Man, that tom is a little ringy and high. Can you tune it down a bit?" And I'll tune it down a bit and it will sound floppy to me and might not even physically feel right hitting it, but when I go back into the control room and listen to it, it just sounds huge and wonderful.

So tuning can be a bit of a mystery. It's very instinctual. There's no real math to it, as far as I know.

Do you use the Drum Doctor on sessions?
When the session budget is big, I like to use him. When the budget isn't big, I have to do it myself. I've learned a lot

by working with Ross for so many years so I can make it sound pretty good, but it's really nice to walk into a session and know that he's tuned it up and I can just show up and play. I don't like to get bogged down in the studio tuning drums. It can really slow down the session, and I like to keep the pace of the session up and moving forward.

You mentioned the fact that you bring different drums to different types of sessions. How do you determine what to bring for something like, say, a Chris Isaac session as compared to a movie or television gig?

Generally, I try to get a heads-up from the producer or the producer's assistant as to what kind of song we're doing and what he wants it to sound like. Like if he says they're doing something that's a retro-'70s Led Zeppelin type of thing, then I know to bring my 26" kick and an old Radio King snare. If he says that it's a midtempo R&B kind of thing, then I'll know to bring my 20" or 22" kick. So I try to get as much information as I can from the producer before the session and find out as much as possible about the artist, the specific band, and the direction of the music.

It sounds like you have a big drum collection.
Oh yeah. *[Laughs.]* I've got a huge collection parked at the Drum Doctor's, and my garage is completely full, with just a very small isle down the middle. I'm constantly scouring eBay for new, weird things like plastic snare drums and odds and ends. I like to have a lot of toys just to make sure that the recording is interesting. That's something I got from Jim Keltner [another well-known session drummer]. He taught me a lot about that. Sometimes if he's in a session in the studio next to mine, we go hang out together and we're like little kids, comparing our new odd toys and instruments. He's always been a big help on that kind of stuff.

How many snares do you bring to a session?
I have two trunks that I generally bring that contain ten snare drums, plus I have an old vintage '70s Black Beauty that I hand-carry with me. That always stays at home with me, and I bring it to work just like it was my briefcase. *[Laughs.]* I've got some old '20s chrome-over-brass drums,

and some big old mahogany drums that are great for that '70s sound. They have six lugs and round bearing edges, so they tune down really low; and if you tape it up, it gets a really fat sound that's great for ballads. I generally don't use a piccolo, but I have one in my arsenal. You have to make sure that you have everything, because whatever it is that you don't bring to the session, that's what the producer will ask for. So I like to be prepared and have plenty of options.

But once again, that has to fit with the budget. If it's a full record, I try to bring as much stuff as I can, and almost every day that I come in I'll bring even more stuff. If I hear something for a specific song, I'll dig around and maybe find something that I think will work if I bring it. So it varies, but I generally have ten snare drums that represent a good spectrum, from piccolos to big, fat '70s sounds.

What do you use for cymbals?
I've been using Paiste Giant Beat cymbals, but I have so many old vintage Zildjians from the '50s and '60s, which I collect. I like to have a pair of 13", 14", and 15" hi-hats available at a session. The 13s are really tight, and the 15s are really dark and warm. I've noticed over the years that recording hi-hat can be really tricky. You might put a mic on it and never even use it because the hi-hat is so loud, so I like to have some quiet hats around. I have these 15s that are quiet and nice sounding.

Then I generally use 17", 18", and 20" crashes and a couple of 20" and a couple of 22" rides. Then I have one sizzle cymbal that I bring, although some engineers are allergic to them. *[Laughs.]* The sizzle cymbal opens a whole floodgate of people who either love them or hate them, but I make sure that I have some with me at all times.

How about sticks?
I usually play 5As because they're such an all-around good stick, but sometimes I'll use different types. I'll use the Fatar Recording drumsticks that have a small bead on them, which I like because then you can get a really good cymbal sound. It's amazing how a different bead can make the cymbal sound completely different when you're riding

on a cymbal. If you use a round head, you'll get a lot of attack. If you use a plastic head, you'll get more attack. If you use a larger wood, you can get more of a wash from the cymbal. So I definitely have a lot of different sticks and brushes, and mallets, too, because someone will always ask, "Can you do a cymbal swell?" If you look in your stick bag and you don't have something necessary, that's the part of being a session drummer where you have the most anxiety. It gets embarrassing if you have to tell them, "I can make some mallets with some tissues and duct tape." *[Laughs hard.]* I like to make sure that my stick bag is loaded with hot-rods, brushes, different-size sticks, and mallets.

You don't do too much live work these days, do you?
No, I don't do much at all. It's so funny, because since I've moved to L.A. I've played live maybe ten times in 15 years. I don't really tour too much, because I like to be available for sessions. The last big tour that I did was with Tears for Fears, but I had to come back and reestablish myself with all the producers because I was gone for such a long period of time. Out of site, out of mind, as they say. Now if Nick Mason decides he doesn't want to play with Pink Floyd anymore, then that would be something I'd have to think about. *[Laughs.]*

That begs the question, would your road kit be different from what you'd use in the studio?
Probably. I probably wouldn't use wood hoops, and it would be tuned more open and live. I'd work with the front-of-house guy to dial in the kit. Then visually I'd probably do something a bit different, too. When I did the *Jay Leno Show* with Seal, I used my clear acrylic DW kit because it just looks so good on TV. The lighting people just love it. So yeah, I'd use a different kit live, because I'd go for the fashion. *[Laughs.]* It's like wearing different ties with your suit. And that's what's so funny about the studio, because sometimes I'll just have such a mismatched kit with like my red sparkle 14" Ludwig floor tom with my DW 26" kick and an old Gretsch 13" rack tom. They look like a disaster together, but sound great.

What are you looking for in the phones when you record?
That's a great question. Generally it depends on how we're tracking. If I'm tracking with a bass player and we're doing overdubs to an existing track, I'll try to get a nice, even level so it sounds like a record, with the vocals and the bass player just above the music. I want to hear the bass player so I can be sure to lock my kick drum with him. Then if I'm tracking live, I want whoever is the leader of the song to be above the track. Like if the guitar player has written the song, he might be doing some important inflections that I need to hear. If it's a vocalist who has written the song and they're evoking some emotion that they really want, I'll make sure that is above everything else. So I latch on to whatever the main instrument of the tracking date is, or whatever the biggest concern seems to be when laying down the basics.

I'll also have the click at an ungodly level, which can drive producers and engineers crazy, so I like to use closed headphones for that. I'm still looking for the perfect set of headphones, because you don't want the click track leaking into the song. On Christina Aguilera's "Beautiful," you can hear a bit of the drum machine on her vocal track, but the vocal was so amazing that they just went with it. You have to be careful especially on endings of songs. I try to get the engineer to cut the click off so that the cymbal sustain doesn't have any click bleed. I'll even punch-in the ending of a song if they can't catch it at the right time.

What kind of click sound do you like?
In the old days, I used to be very specific about it. I used to like a cowbell or some sort of side-stick sound, with a shaker doing 16ths or 8ths depending on the feel of the song. I have to say that's still my favorite click track, but I'm getting used to just the Pro Tools click. I've adjusted over the years, but my preference still is the cowbell and shaker.

Do you have any mic preferences?
Depending on the engineer and the producer, if they have a preference I'll go with what they want, but I gotta say I really love an FET-47 on the outside of the kick drum. That's

one of my favorite mics. I like ribbon mics a lot for room and overheads. I like the Beyer M-160 ribbon on the hat. That warmed it up a lot. I did a session the other day where we used Sony C-37s [which haven't been made since the late '60s] on the toms and they sounded amazing. The producer said, "If you weren't the drummer, I wouldn't put them up," because they're so fragile that you have to be afraid of hitting them. That was really quite a compliment. Then again, some people get great results from Sennheiser 421s.

I don't generally do top and bottom mics on the toms. I don't like too many mics on the drum kit unless the producer and engineer are really paying attention to the phase cancellation, but I have had good results with people who have done it that way. I walked into a session with a metal producer who shall remain nameless, and he had the kit miked up with what looked like 40 microphones. I thought, "This is ridiculous," but I played the track and it sounded amazing. Then sometimes I'll work with just three mics on the kit, and it will sound great, too. Everybody has their own technique, and I try to be flexible because most of the people that I work with are so high end that I trust them to get my drums sounding the way they want them to sound.

There's a defining moment for every player when they finally "get it." What was yours?

That's an interesting moment for me. I think it was on my first trip to L.A., on my first kind of big session. It was with Patrick Leonard [producer for Madonna, Rod Stewart, Jewel, Bon Jovi, Elton John, and Pink Floyd, among others]. He flew me down from San Francisco, where I was teaching drums and playing live. I had toured a bit and done a few albums in England at that point. Pat was starting a band and was auditioning me to be the drummer. I played on a couple of tracks that were already finished with a click. After the second song he said, "Hey Brian, can you come in here [the control room] for a minute?" I thought to myself, "That's my audition. I guess I'm outta here," so I actually grabbed my stick bag and zipped it up so I wouldn't have the embarrassment of having to walk back out into the studio to get it. I figured that the door out of the studio was in the control room, and if he was firing me, I just wanted to leave as fast as I could.

So I zip up my stick bag and walk into the control room, and he looks at it with a confused look on his face like "What are you doing?" So I go, "What's up?" and he says, "I love the way you play to the song with the click track. You know how to lock into the click track and not make it sound mechanical. I love your feel, and I want to hire you to do this record." Then he says, "Oh, by the way. Listen to a track I just finished," and he cranks up Madonna's "Like A Prayer" at full volume. That was the moment I felt like, "Wow, I think I get this. This guy has done all this amazing work and he's telling me that my feel with the click is nice." I realized at that moment that I really could play to a click and make it breathe at the same time. And that really is an important thing for drummers to learn. If you play to a click, don't be so focused on it that you lose sight of the fact that you're actually playing a song.

Do you have any other advice for a young drummer just starting out?
Yeah, I'd say try to play to a click as much as you can so you can learn to play with it yet lose sight of it at the same time. You want the feel of the click track to become like intuition, so it doesn't make you feel shackled to it.

Also, when you work with a producer, be as flexible as you can. Don't be stubborn, and trust the people you work with. If the engineer or producer has a suggestion, trust their advice. I was talking to a producer the other day about how he'll sometimes have a drummer come in that will insist on playing his own kit. If I work with a producer who wants me to play his old vintage kit, of course I'll play it; it's important to be flexible. Even if you show up with your gear, if he has his kit miked up and he knows what it sounds like, I'll generally do that. Then, if they're not satisfied, then I'll use my drums.

Another thing: if you have any ideas, make the suggestion if the time is right, because it's all about teamwork and you're on the team.

Do you have any advice for the guy who's playing in clubs about how he can bring his level of playing up?
I think one thing is to realize that you are a drummer, but you are also are a musician. You're not a drum machine just there to keep time; you have to play everything with a great feel. Listen to your favorite albums and check out the feel of the drummers and how they make the music breath and how their dynamics go along with the music. It's all about being a musician, to me. A lot of the best drummers I know also play another instrument besides drums, even if not well. That way you start to understand music more. Playing piano is a great thing for a drummer to learn at some point. I'm still working on it myself. But be able to be in touch with the music and the songs, and really understand what's going on besides just the time aspect of the music.

So work on your feel, your time, and your fills. A lot of drummers have great time except for when they do fills. I've heard from producers, "So and so has such a great feel, but his fills are always out of time." So just trying to be musical is important. Rushing the fill is a really common thing for a lot of drummers. The way to cure that is just practicing to a click track a lot.

You mentioned before about Patrick Leonard inviting you to L.A. to record. Would you consider that your big break?
I think so, because after we finished that I record I was pretty much planning on moving back to the Bay Area. But Patrick said, "Hey Brian, if you lived in L.A., I would use you on the records I work on." Ironically, the engineer/coproducer on that record was Bill Bottrell [who eventually went on to produce Sheryl Crow, Michael Jackson, and Shelby Lynn], and he said the same thing to me. So I had two top-of-the-line producers tell me that if I lived in L.A., they'd use me on their records. It became a no-brainer for me to run up to the Bay Area, pack my things in a U-Haul, and get my butt to L.A. Then it kind of expanded from there.

I had no delusions of moving to L.A. before those sessions. I was too content up in the Bay Area, where I had a nice life teaching drums and playing live almost every night; it was wonderful. So I really didn't want to move to

L.A. unless there was a good reason, because I didn't just want to try to break in the way everyone seems to do it. It would have been too frustrating for me.

But this is actually some good advice for a young drummer. If you're in a band and working with a producer, really pay attention and work with him to help him make that record sound better. You're more likely to be called for another project afterwards. He might have had so much fun working with you in your band that he'll think of you for a solo artist he's working with. That's how I developed myself. I worked with Tim Palmer in London with my own band, and that's how I got the job playing with Tears for Fears. So I've developed relationships with all the producers I've worked with over the years in my own band.

What's your favorite type of music to play?
It's an interesting spectrum. I love retro-funk, and I love old hard rock. I think that stems from my older brothers blasting The Beatles to Led Zeppelin in their bedrooms while my mom was out vacuuming the living room listening to R&B. With my mom listening to Aretha Franklin and The Supremes and my brothers teaching me about rock 'n' roll, that's really how I got started. My brothers were guitar players and they needed a drummer, so they got me a drum kit. They were trying to make me the first human drum machine at eight years old. *[Laughs.]* But I just fell in love with it and became obsessed. I knew even at that age that that's what I wanted to do. I used to stare at pictures of The Who and Led Zeppelin playing in the studio and go, "That's what I want to do. I want to work in studios."

What's the best gig you've ever had?
I would have to say being part of the Tuesday Night Music Club. As you know, we wrote and conceived what became Sheryl Crow's first album. It was awesome. We were all working in the studio, and (producer) Bill Bottrell made sure that everybody participated to the point where sometimes I wasn't even playing drums. He'd make me play bass or something. It was kind of frightening, but fun at the same time. It was one of the most incredible experiences

in my life to participate in, not just as a drummer but as a musician and a lyricist. He really opened the door to all of us to push the envelope. That whole period of time was really wonderful, but continuing on writing songs with Sheryl Crow after that was really great, too. She's always been open to my ideas. It's great to have someone believe and trust in you like she has. I just wrote a song for and played on her new record as well.

And I have to say that touring with Tears for Fears was really wonderful, too, because they had such great songs. Just playing those songs live was pretty awesome.

What's the worse gig you've ever had?
The artist shall remain nameless, but this artist lost his drummer in the middle of a tour and desperately needed me to come out and play with him. He called me on the phone and said, "I'll make this really easy on you. Just learn these 12 songs, and if you can be out here by tomorrow that would be great." So on my flight out to the East Coast, I just crammed all night long learning those songs, making charts and mental notes. I got to the gig and out of those 12 songs we only played 3 of them. He threw all these other songs at me and kept turning to me during the show and yelling, "That's not right!" "Play faster!" "Play slower!" "You're blowin' it!" He ended up firing me after about three gigs, and it was just the most miserable experience of my life. [Laughs.] It scared me enough not to play live for a while, which actually improved my studio work, so my hat's off to him in a strange way.

Was there a particularly bad session?
There was one session where I can't even remember the producer's name. We set up all the gear and played maybe half a song, when the producer came into the studio and went, "I'm just not feeling this. There's something wrong. You guys are all getting paid, but this is just not right. I can't do this." And he walked out. We all just looked at each other like, "Okay, what just happened here?" That might be one of the worst sessions because we all left with a question mark over our heads. Did he not like our playing? Was he

having a personal problem? Didn't the artist like us? We never found out, but we got paid. Everyone involved still laughs about it to this day.

What kind of gig is the hardest for you?

The hardest gig is when the artist or the producer doesn't know what they want and they're not open to suggestions. That can be really difficult, because even though they don't know what they want, they won't accept any help to find out what they may want. I've done a couple of records like that, where I pull my hair out because they just keep experimenting. "Let's try it reggae style." "No, let's try it as a waltz." They just keep going around in circles, but at the same time don't want to hear your opinion or suggestion. "We just want to keep going around chopping the legs off the chair until there's no vibe left."

I've had the same thing with songwriters who keep rewriting the song over and over. They don't make it better; they just make it different.

Exactly. It's like, is this getting better, or is it just different? I actually avoided a session with another very famous female singer because I was given the heads-up that she never knows what she wants and is always going around in circles. They asked me to do the record, but I had to decline because I just wasn't prepared to be that patient, even though it was good money. I realized that mental and physical health is more important than flying out of town and working with an artist who doesn't know what they want. And I was not the only drummer. There was a line of drummers who either quit or got fired from the gig. I don't really need that in my life.

What are the most fun gigs?

Working on this Chris Isaac record that I just did was really fun because we tracked it live. Tracking live is so much fun when I play with musicians that I really connect with. That's the most fun for me, because I get a little of that live feel and edge; but it's in the studio, so it sounds good. It's musical communication and connection. I like that feeling. I guess it goes back to looking at those records when I was a kid. To see The Beatles all set up in the studio with George Martin in the middle talking to them, I pine for those days. *[Laughs.]*

Is there an aspect to recording that you don't like?
Yes, when they "drive past the money." If there's an amazing take that was done live and they say something like, "We don't like the ending to the song. Can we do another take?" When you feel like you've done something really wonderful and either the producer or the artist kinda just drives right past it, and then beats the song into the ground and sucks the life out of it. Sometimes there's magic in takes that end up never getting used. That can be really frustrating. That's happened a lot, unfortunately.

I think that it's one of those things where you almost have to be playing to know when you've really nailed it. It's really hard to be on the other side of the glass and know when you've caught the magic. That's the trick of being a producer.

Exactly, and I've had to swallow my pride and play something faster or slower and it doesn't sound as good. But if they want that way, you've just got to do it. This isn't my record, after all—it's theirs.

Is there an aspect of drumming that you don't like?
Hauling my gear around. *[Laughs.]* The day when I bought my convertible and could drive it to a session, I felt like success. I thought, "I don't have to drive a van around anymore. I can just come in my Alfa Romero to this wonderful studio with these wonderful musicians with my drums already tuned to where I just walk in and play." I know that sounds spoiled, but at some point in any musician's life, that's a reward.

Denny Seiwell—Drummer

Having establishing himself as one of the premier session drummers in New York, Denny Seiwell's career took a side trip into rock 'n' roll, beginning with an invitation from Paul McCartney to move to London and become a founding member of the post-Beatles group Wings. While in London, he played on songs that have gone on to be radio staples, including Wings' "My Love" and the Oscar-nominated "Live and Let Die," and worked with hit makers Joe Cocker, Donovan, and The Who with the London Symphony Orchestra in their groundbreaking version of the rock opera *Tommy*.

Adept at any musical style, Denny has a signature drumming style that can be heard on records by Art Garfunkel, James Brown, Astrud Gilberto, Deniece Williams, Janis Joplin, Billy Joel, and, of course, Paul McCartney. Denny is now a part of the Los Angeles studio scene and always in demand for many of the most prestigious television and film dates available.

Give us some background on how you got into session work.
My first sessions came from a live gig I was doing at the Mount Airy Lodge resort in the Pocono Mountains. We were sight-reading big books of material for singers, dancers, comedians, just about anything. On the weekends they would bring musicians up from New York City to augment the band. They brought in a bassist named Russ Savakas, who happened to be a contractor for the studios in New York. He heard me play and said, "I gotta bring you into the city!" He got me my first sessions in New York. He took me to hear Gary Kester play on Burt Bacharach and Dionne Warwick's "Do You Know the Way to San Jose?" I got to sit next to Gary on a 40-piece orchestra date. That was my introduction to the studios.

What do you usually bring to a session?
Either Russ or Joe Beck gave me one of the best tips on recording: "Come in with your ass through the door!" which means come in with a lot of positive energy, optimism, power, and feeling like you belong there, then slam through the job. It was a great tip.

As far as gear goes, in the peak years back in New York, the drums were always there in the studio, so I brought a trap case with my snare, cymbals, and footpedal. We had a guy that would deliver my trap case for five bucks! Around late '68 most of the drum sounds were terrible, so I started bringing my own tom-toms. I asked Remo to make heads without the white coating, and they may have been the first clear heads. Instead of going *duenk*, my drums went *boom*! At first the engineers hated it, but they grew to really like it.

Is your stage rig different from your recording rig?
Yes. My stage rig has always been really simple, with a 20" or 22" bass drum, a 12" and 13" rack tom, a 16" floor tom, three cymbals, and a hi-hat. It took nearly 20 years to put that second rack tom up! I was with Gretsch for years, but now I'm with DW.

What do you like in your headphone mix?
Everything but drums, but I especially need the vocals or lead instruments. Drums make enough noise. You don't need them in the cans.

Do you use a tech?
No, never. I'm the tech. A lot of my success in the studio was due to the way I tuned, muffled, or demuffled the drums, and no one ever has done that for me. That's where the expertise comes from playing so many different kinds of live gigs and recording in so many different studios.

What was your defining moment as a session player?
Within six months of moving to New York, I was doing three to five dates a day. Within my first year I fell in with the "first-call cats." When you're with those guys, everything goes up—the music, the level of musicianship, the pay. That era was my defining moment, because I was way up on that list of "cats to call." This was mid-1968. In fact, I was on a date a year or two into it, and Will Lee was on his first date.

Who are your biggest influences?
Mel Lewis, Elvin Jones, and Ringo. Mel Lewis I love for his whole concept of making it tasty. Elvin Jones for his animal

energy and just killin' it. The guy I always listened to for rock 'n' roll is Ringo, and that's probably how I got the gig with McCartney. I just made believe I was Ringo when I was playing with Paul.

What do you see that all good session musicians have in common?
They get to the heart of the music, and they play for the song. They play the proper thing for that piece of music, whether it be a polka, a rock ballad, or a jazz piece. You've got to leave your ego out and put the music in.

What do you know now that you wish you'd known when you were first starting out?
I wish I'd known a lot more about the business side of being a musician when I first started out. You can really affect the rest of your life with your business decisions, especially in the beginning. Know what you can be compensated for, and stand up for it. There's a lot more to the business side of music than meets the eye. There was a lack of good advice in this area when I was young, but it's not that way now. Know your business. It goes hand in hand with playing your instrument.

Any advice for someone starting out doing session work?
Leave your ego and your chops at home. One day you might build a shelf, and one day you might build a house. Just do the job that's required.

Do you have any session-musician tips?
Don't try to impress a producer with what you can do. You'll never get called back.

What was your worst session?
I can't remember a bad recording session. We had a saying, "You're only as good as your last take." I was always grateful I had something to throw in the kitty—it's all about attitude!

What kind of sessions are the hardest for you?
Orchestral dates with James Newton Howard and other film composers. It was part of my background, but not at that level, because they're the most demanding. Those dates require every bit of musical knowledge and intuition you've got.

What kind of sessions are the most fun?
The most fun I've ever had were the *Ram* sessions with Paul and either Hugh McCracken or David Spinozza on guitar. It was just the three of us, and Paul was just on fire. He'd just left The Beatles, and he had all this music that just had to come out. For six weeks we worked from nine in the morning to six at night. Show up, have a cup of tea, and start playing at 10 a.m. He'd play us the song we were doing that day, and your jaw would just hit the floor. We'd spend a few hours rehearsing the song, and nobody was told what to play. He relied on our musicality and trusted us to come up with our own parts. At the end of the day we'd listen and choose a take, and it was just ridiculous! That is the most rewarding studio experience I've ever had.

With Wings, I was still learning about rock 'n' roll. Coming from being a studio musician to being a band player was interesting. You can't approach a band gig like you approach sessions. I went from playing with the best studio players in the business for that time to playing with Paul McCartney, who is absolutely one of the best players on the planet. But the other guys in Wings were different from the guys I had been playing with in New York. I had to put on a different head and set of ears to hear how they were playing the music. I never had to play up or down to anyone's level, but it was a different mind-set. We always played from the heart, and in Wings, I had to listen to everybody and not just the song to come up with the right part.

What's your playing weakness and your playing strength?
I always aspired to be a "jack of all trades" and a "master of all trades," whether it's jazz, funk, or rock. That's what I consider to be a complete musician. Studio musicians are expected to be able to do it all with conviction, authority, and expertise.

Is there anything you hate about recording?
I hate the political nature of the recording business in California. When I first relocated out here, you had to be on certain lists to work. Those lists were not based on your playing or musicality; they were based on who you knew. It is my belief that at times this was to the detriment of the music.

What do you love most about recording?
I love the task of having a clean palette, hearing a song for the first time, deciding on a part that's best for the song, and then performing it.

Leland Sklar—Bass Player

Known for his distinctive long flowing beard, Leland Sklar is one of the most respected and in-demand bass players on the scene today. Lee has contributed his skills to literally thousands of albums, soundtracks, films, and television shows with such diverse artists as Clint Black; Jackson Browne; Jimmy Buffet; Crosby, Stills, and Nash; The Doors; Vince Gill; Ricky Martin; Diana Ross; and, of course, James Taylor.

Give us some background on how you got into session work?
I never really thought about being a studio musician, since I was always a band guy who liked to play live. When I met James Taylor in 1969 and "Fire and Rain" [Taylor's first single] went through the ceiling, I started getting calls to do records. [Drummer] Russ Kunkel and I were paired as a rhythm section and started working together. That's turned into a long career for me without really having had to think about it. I feel very blessed by this. I was at the right time and in the right place, as they (whoever "they" are) say!

What do you bring with you to a session?
I bring several basses, a few effects, a DI box, an amp (no rack!), and a lot of enthusiasm!

Do you tailor what you bring according to the session?
Not really. If I know in advance of any special needs, I'll take care of that. But in general, I'm prepared for almost anything that might be asked of me.

Is your stage rig different from your recording rig?
Yes, but not by a lot. I probably have less with me on the road than I would in the studio. I generally bring two basses on tour. One is a backup for that "just-in-case" moment. I use the same amp I use in the studio, but would probably add a second cab depending on the venue. I've been using Euphonic Audio amps and speakers for several years now. In the studio, I use a [Euphonic Audio] iAmp 800 Combo. On tour I would use an iAmp 800 head with a 2×10 cab and a 1×12 cab. I was using a GrooveTube Brick or my Tube Works DI, which is what I normally use in the studio, and a Yamaha Sub-Kick in front of the 12" cabinet as a mic. It's an amazing sound. That piece of gear is normally used by drummers on their bass drums, but I tried it once on my setup, and it's killer. I don't use any pedals live, except perhaps a Boss OC2 Octave pedal. I try to keep the bass as pointed and clean as possible so that the house mixer has something to build the rest of the instruments around.

What do you like to hear in your headphone mix?
It depends on the session. If we're playing to a click, then that's what I want the most of. I always prefer something like an old Urei click generator. I really hate when they try to make the click musical and it just disappears in the track. The click is there for a reason, and it doesn't help you if you can't hear it. After that, it depends on what other instruments are being recorded in regards to where they would be in the mix level-wise. Most of the time these days I go to guys' houses and overdub bass on preproduced tracks and it's just me playing, so I grab whatever I can that will be useful to me and go for it. But it really depends on the individual circumstances of the session.

What kind of headphones do you like?
I am not particular at all as long as they're not too tight, but not loose enough to fall off when I get into it.

Do you use a tech? If so, why?
On the road, I would use the guitar tech if there was anything really necessary. Other than that, I just need someone to set up the bass rig. I like to change my own strings and batteries so I can stay in touch with my gear. In the studio, I've never had a tech. It's not necessary for that gig.

What do you think the defining moment for a session player is?
When he gets his or her first work call, does the session, and the producer/artist/players go "Yeah!" You are now part of the community.

When does the light come on?
When you sit down with the chart or whatever it is that's put in front of you, you see the red light come on in the studio, and you say, "This is so cool!" Now it's for *real*!

What was your defining moment?
It's hard to say at this point, because it was a long time ago. Probably when I started getting calls that were unrelated to James Taylor and realized there was a world away from him. I remember one of my first calls was for a Brian Hyland session with Del Shannon as the producer. I was in a room with guys I didn't know and still had to get into it. It was such a great adventure, and it still is to this day.

Who are your biggest influences?
That's really hard to say because there are so many. McCartney was a major influence that took me from my classical background to rock 'n' roll. I was a huge Hendrix fan along with all the bands of that era. In L.A., music was everywhere. I would go and see Canned Heat, Sons of Champlin, and Sly and the Family Stone in one show, and then Cream would be playing at my college gym. I was

drawn in by it all and loved every minute. I think I can take away something from everyone I see playing music. It's so subjective, from the most primitive to the most mind-blowing. There's something different around each corner.

In what ways were you influenced?
I was in a band called Group Therapy in 1967, and Mike Post, who is one of the greatest TV composers, was our producer. When we went into the studio, we were not allowed to play on our record; we only sang. The "real" players did the music. I sat and looked through the window at them and it was amazing. But the most amazing thing for me was that a couple of years later, I was with those guys and I was *one of them*. Hal Blaine, Larry Knechtal, Jim Gordon, and so on. These were the cats, and now I got to hang with them every day. I still pinch myself over that.

What do you see that all good session musicians have in common?
There are many qualities: great ears, focus, dedication, ideas. It's a special breed of player. You have to bring a lot more than just your facility on your instrument to the date.

What do you know now that you wish you'd known when you were first starting out?
How much more money the composers make than the players (sort of just kidding!). I really don't think I needed to know more because few of us really knew anything, and that's why so much great stuff got recorded. We were writing the book as we went along.

Do you have any advice for someone starting out doing session work?
Be focused. Have ideas that go beyond the required playing. Be involved. When the song is done and it is time for playback, don't go the other way and start making phone calls or playing around on your laptop. Stay involved. Listen back to the performance, and if you have any ideas, throw them out there and try to make the performance the best you can. And if the session starts at 10 a.m., don't be pulling into

the driveway at 10 a.m. Be tuned up and have your sound together and be ready to start recording at 10 a.m. Not all dates are like this, but it's good to be professional and not treat this lightly. If you get to do this, it's one of the great blessings in life. Treat it with respect.

What do you consider your big break?
Hooking up with James Taylor.

If you were able to go back to those early bands that you played in, what kind of advice would you give yourself?
Embrace every moment, because it goes by so fast. My only regret, as far as my career is concerned, is that I didn't have a camera with me at every session. A shot with all the artists, musicians, producers, engineers, seconds, and everybody would've made for a great memory book.

What was your worst session?
The worst for me is when you work your ass off, and then the check is bad and you never get paid. It leaves a really bad taste in your mouth for what might have been a fun time. That doesn't happen very often, so it really stands out when it does.

What was your best session?
That's really hard to answer because I've been blessed to have done so many different kinds of projects that were all great experiences. I'm still excited every day I get to go to work and make music.

What kinds of sessions are the hardest for you?
If I get called to do a pop/slap-funk date I'm not happy, because I do not slap. I can fake it, but don't really do it well. When I get that kind of call, I tell them that's not my style, and I give them some names of friends who can play the shit out of that stuff.

What kinds of sessions are the most fun?
The ones that have great songs, great players, a great engineer, and free food.

What's your playing weakness? Strength?
As I just said, my weakness would be my inability to pop and slap. It doesn't bother me, but it is my weakness. My strength would be that I listen to a song and try to find the best possible part to help weave it together. I can usually do it in 1 or 2 takes. I'm an off-the-seat-of-my-pants kind of player and don't spend a lot of time trying to figure out parts. I go with my guts, and they seem to be a friend to me.

What do you hate about recording?
Very little. I love about 90 percent of it. The only thing I don't like is the new technology of the digital world that's allowed a lot of people into the business that should never be here. No time, no pitch, no . . . "Oh well, we'll fix it later." Bullshit! Do it right, or go away! And the new world of Pro Tools and digital workstations means that everyone has a studio at home, so now I don't see the other cats I like to play with as much. It's not nearly as much fun or as creative to just sit in a guy's garage and overdub bass with no input or other players. When we used to do dates together, there were always four to eight players on the live date and ideas flew around the room. Now when I get called for a date with a full band in a real studio, it's like a gift.

Gary Solt—Guitar Player

While some might think of session musicians playing on mostly contemporary music with high-flying rock and pop stars and their producers, there's another segment of the business that is frequently overlooked and largely unheralded, yet is heard by a far larger audience—that is, music for television and film. Gary Solt is one of the few guitar players adept enough to play orchestral dates for television shows like the *Star Trek* series (*Next Generation, Deep Space Nine, Voyager,* and *Enterprise*), *Knots Landing,* and *Becker* as well as numerous shows for National

Geographic and Showtime. A master of many styles, Gary also plays in the pit bands of many Broadway shows, and was kind enough to provide some insight into a side of the business that few seldom see.

What do you usually bring with you to a session?
It depends. Since I usually have the luxury of knowing the composer, he calls me and tells me what he wants. If it's someone that I don't know, I try to get some indication up front of what they'll need. If it sounds like the guy doesn't have a clue, then I'll get a cartage guy to take everything I own to the studio. If it's a session that I do for Jay [composer Jay Chattaway], it's usually some sort of electric guitar with effects, steel-string acoustic guitar, and nylon-string guitar. I've also played a lot of Dobro and banjo for him, as well as a little mandolin and baritone guitar.

Are these all instruments you own?
Yeah, you've got to own the tools, or you can't go build the house. *[Laughs.]* So he'll call me up with specific requests, like "Bring your Telecaster this time," "Bring your 335 this time," or "Bring your Les Paul this time, because we're going to do a bunch of heavy, distorted stuff." So I'm fortunate in that he usually knows what he's looking for, so I can bring the things that I need with me instead of having everything I own schlepped over there for me.

What amp do you usually bring?
If I don't know what the session is, I usually bring a '65 [Fender] Bandmaster head with a couple of different Thiel-style cabinets. One's loaded with a 12-inch E/V, and the other's loaded with a 12-inch JBL, so one is a little darker and heavier, while the other is a little brighter and edgier. When I get to the studio, I figure out which one makes the most sense for the sound that they want. If it's a funk or '70s-music type gig, I bring an old Yamaha G100-12 that has a great poppin' sound with the Tele. The other amp head that I use a lot is an Acoustic Image Claris, which

I use for jazz gigs because the sound is clear and uncolored. If I have to play either a steel-string or nylon-string acoustic amplified, I have a little boutique amp from AR Acoustic [that is no longer made], which is biased perfectly for acoustic instruments and sounds killer. You can either come directly out of it or hang an SM57 nine or ten inches from the 10-inch speaker and it sounds great.

You don't mic the acoustic guitar directly?
It depends on the situation. If I have to play in some sort of ensemble where the sound itself isn't going to be sufficient, then I'll use the amp. It's not a loud amp, but the sound is brilliant. When I record, sometimes I'll use two tracks: one is the mic on the guitar and the other is the amp sound, and then they're blended together.

What kind of pedals do you usually bring?
I have a bunch of boutique pedals that I can bring—Line 6, Fulltone, etc. If it's a gig that calls for distortion, I bring an Xotic AC Plus. For a single pedal, it covers a lot of sounds. When I do something like a theater gig, I bring a Digitech Genesis 3 that I've tweaked all the presets on so they'll work well with my instruments and amps. If I have to go direct, I have other banks just for that, as well. I don't get a lot of calls to just turn up a Marshall all the way and bang out a bunch of power chords. When I do get a call for that, the AC Plus pedal sounds great, and I have a Mesa/Boogie preamp with a whole rack built around it that I can take. Those calls are getting few and far between any more.

Most of the gigs I get called for are for older, vintage sounds. I did a show for Alan Menken [a top Broadway and film composer] that was all '70s disco, so I had a rig for that. I did a show for Barry Mann and Cynthia Weil [hit songwriters of Brill Building fame] that was all '80s pop, so I had another rig for that. I did another show called *Vanities* that was mostly '60s Motown, and I had a rig for that. So most of the calls that I get are not for cutting edge "today's sound." They call me because they know I can sound like different periods.

How does your studio rig differ from your live rig?
If I bring my Digitech, I have a separate bank of sounds to go direct out of that. They're EQ'd differently, and the settings on the distortion and delays are different. If I'm using that setup, which is the easiest to take with me, I have banks that are dedicated just for my amps and banks that are dedicated to go direct.

Can you describe what happens at something like a Star Trek *session, where you're playing with an orchestra?*
The orchestra is usually 50 or 60 of the A-list string and horn players in town. I'm usually there as a separate voice that represents a character or represents a mood. In a typical session, I would have a booth to myself where I'd have an electric setup with a Les Paul and Telecaster into my Bandmaster rig. If I knew there wouldn't be a call for a lot of distortion, I'd just use the amp; and if there was a call for a lot of distortion I'd bring a boutique pedal. A lot of sessions are acoustic, so I'd have a Martin OM-21 that's a great instrument that records really well. It's really even up and down the neck. I also have a handmade nylon-string guitar built by a guy named Holtier that records really well. The sound and intonation are on the money. I'll also have a Dobro and banjo ready.

How long does it take to record all the cues for a typical show?
For a *Star Trek* session, we would record probably anywhere between 19 to 26 minutes of music in two different three-hour sessions, so it was slammin'. The sessions would usually run from 10 a.m. to 1 p.m., and again from 2 to 5 p.m. The producers never wanted to run over, because there's a minimum of 50 people in the orchestra that have to get paid overtime, as well as the engineer and the studio, so there'd always be a big time and money constraint so you couldn't go in there and screw up.

The 10 a.m. to 1 p.m. session would always be the longest cues; the ones that were from four to five minutes long. Jay was always smart in that he'd find a place in the middle of the cue where he could stop, so we could record just the first half a couple of times, then go on to the second half. This could be seamlessly pasted together so you'd end up with four to five minutes of consecutive music where you're not necessarily playing four to five minutes at once. Normally on long cues like that, the show was blowing a bunch of stuff up on the screen, so there'd be spaces for explosions and everybody would be playing their brains out. There would be a lot of intense playing, especially for the brass players, so it made more sense to break it up into two components and join them later.

If I was playing on the cue, I'd usually be doubling the low strings or I would have my own line that was coupled with a different group of instruments.

How many takes would you usually do on a cue?
A lot of times we'd get it on the first take. After we'd get into the groove of the session to where the hardest and longest ones were out of the way, the cues after that were usually thematically related to cues we'd already seen, so we could just get it down on one take. Granted, there was an amazing level of musicianship in the room. There was a lot of pressure, but there was a lot of excitement to sit there and say, "Wow, we turned all this stuff out in one hit."

You did cues that didn't involve the orchestra as well, right?
Yeah, on *Deep Space Nine* there was a recurring character who always showed up in a Holosuite Las Vegas program as a lounge singer, so we did six or seven shows where it was just the rhythm section of piano, guitar, bass, and drums (although sometimes it was Hammond B-3 instead of piano). Occasionally it was guitar, bass, drums, and tenor sax. A lot of those cues were more lead-sheet oriented, where we'd play an idea for a tune and then everyone would solo over it and they'd cut it up later to use as underscoring. Sometimes we'd have specific tunes that the character would sing, and we'd back him up.

The final episode of DS9 was written like a Henry Mancini scoring session, where it was a full big band, full string section and rhythm section, where we played all standard tunes and it sounded killer. For that I took my L-5 and just played Freddie Green style [Freddie was a master of the rhythm guitar in the big-band era]. I thought to myself, "I never had a chance to do a session with Mancini, and this is going to be the closest I'll ever come to that experience." It was absolutely brilliant.

When you record just the rhythm section, would you still record in the large studio?
No—in a smaller room, because it makes no sense to have this big cavern with only four guys.

There aren't a lot of players that have the experience of playing with an orchestra.
There's not a lot of call for it. I have to say, though, the thing I like the most about recording with an orchestra is that the sound is timeless. That was the reason that they always used an orchestra in *Star Trek*. You don't know what music will be like in the future, and you can't use some band that sounds like the Eurythmics, because it's completely out of the time period. So the orchestra thing was always cool because it was timeless, and then they were able to weave in other specific things as well. I did one session where all I played was banjo, because there was a character that was an old banjo player. I had to play to picture to where he was doing some weird little things on the neck, and I had to try to come up with something that matched what he was doing.

Did you learn to play the banjo before or after you began to play sessions?
Before. I learned to play banjo when I was young, and the reason why was when I played some Broadway shows early in my career, there were four or five tunes that called for banjo. The same thing with mandolin. I got calls to play shows, and mandolin and banjo were doubles; if you couldn't play the doubles, you couldn't play the show and you didn't work. I'm not sure that too many guys have that together now because it's a different time, but when I came up as a working musician, you had to do that to work.

When you play with an orchestra, how is that different than just playing with a rhythm section? Is your approach different? Do you think differently?
Yeah, you're sitting there scared to death because all these guys in the orchestra grew up learning how to play their instrument by only being able to read music. No improvising, no stretching out, just "Here's the note, see the note, play the note, get the check, go home." Maybe only 5 percent of guitar players grew up learning how to play via reading music. Reading music to me, even though it's my strong suit that gets me work, is still scary when you go sit with a bunch of guys who can sight-read Shostakovich and Stravinsky. Of course, if you put an A♭ blues in front of them and say "Blow," then there's silence.

Playing with an orchestra's different than playing with anything else, because you have to be totally precise. You have to play exactly what's on the page, and it has to match phrasing-wise, balance-wise, and intonation-wise with what everybody else is doing. When you play with a rhythm section, the parameters are looser, because you have to create your own part on the spot. Here's a lead sheet, here's a set of chord changes, here's the form of the tune, here's the style, here's the tempo, play your instrument.

You just mentioned precision and intonation with the orchestra. How difficult is that? Is that something you had to learn? Obviously you already have a good sense of it before you get there, but do you have to take it to another level?
You have to be very aware of it all the time. You can't just sorta slap your fingers down on some frets and hope that it works. You have to, first of all, own quality instruments that you can trust will rise to the same level as these guys playing $75,000 to $100,000 violins. Even though they're nonfixed pitched instruments, those guys really know how to play the pitches well. Number two, you've got to be aware that you have to match your pitch with theirs, but if you're a good musician and you're constantly listening to what's going on around you, that's just part of the process. You can't put on blinders and put in earplugs to play your part. You have to make your part fit, and that's why they call it *music*.

What was your big break?
My biggest break in life was when I was 21 years old and in college in Ohio. On weekends, I went back to the town where I grew up to teach guitar lessons to make some money. One night I got a call saying [jazz singer] Nancy Wilson was in town doing a show in the biggest theater in town and they needed a guitar player, and could I do the gig? I owned all her records already and thought, "This is incredible." But the more I thought about it, I went "Wait a minute. I'm some 21-year-old kid, and there's a bunch of really great guitar players in town. Why are they calling me?" The reason was because I was the only guy who could read music, although at the time I wasn't really a very good reader at all. I could read just enough to kind of sweet-talk my way through the gig. It was my first time to have to sit down with a bunch of professionals, have a book in front of me that I'd never seen with all kinds of stuff in five flats, and not screw up! My performance certainly was not stellar, but that was the gig that really lit the fire under me to think, "Wait a minute. Here's a whole area of music I never even knew existed." It was more fun, challenging, and rewarding than anything I had ever done in life, so I decided, "I gotta go chase this." After the gig was over, I literally didn't sleep for three days thinking about the whole experience. That's how it started.

As time progressed, I saw the value in reading and playing different styles of music. I think today the best advice I could give to any young guitar player is that if you want to be a success, first of all learn how to read. And second, learn how to play styles convincingly. Don't make yourself a one-trick pony unless you've got something that is so magical that it will go out and take over the world. If you don't have that, learn to play styles, because then you can always function.

How about when you got to Hollywood? What was your break into session work?
I was playing on a little "jazzual" [a jazz casual] with a piano player who was wired in to the TV show *Knots Landing* because he was the piano player for one of the

main actors on the show who was a singer. The piano player got us on a couple of episodes to be the backup band for the singer. The production people loved it, and that developed into the piano player being able to score a bunch of sessions. That was my break.

After that I met a few other guys and got called to play on their stuff, and finally Jay [Chattaway] left New York and moved out here [Los Angeles]. I knew him on the East Coast, so when he started working, I started working.

Sad but true, I think the best thing I could tell anyone trying to do this is to meet people. Once you arrive here or in New York, the town is full of guys who play great, so that's not even on the table. You have to find people who are doing what you want to do and connect with them, and when your shot comes, *don't screw up!* It's as simple and as cold as that.

To me New York and Hollywood are the only two places that you're going to make it to the top rung of the ladder. Each town has gotten along for decades without you, so you're not going to have one of those moments where you pull up in a limo and everyone breathes a sigh of relief that you're here. They were doing just fine without you. What can you do that will make you valuable? That's the best thing that a new person on the scene can figure out. What can you bring to the table that not too many other guys are bringing?

Everybody has a defining moment in the business when they think, "Now I get it." What was yours?
I did a two-guitar session, and the other guitar player, George Doering, was probably the most recorded guy in town at the time. He's a phenomenal player, can play anything, and has ice water in his veins. In my opinion, he's the studio guy you'd want sitting in the chair when there's the most pressure. I did this session with him, and I was really pretty nervous because it was one of the earlier sessions in my career. He was already a well-respected and established guy who had like 20 refrigerator-type racks with blinking lights and lots of knobs, and cases and cases filled with every instrument you could think of. I came in with just

my little rig. We played together, everything fit, and he was very nice to me. I felt like, "Okay, I'm able to do this sitting next to the best guy in town. This might work out." After that, every other session that I went into I would always think about that moment and it would cool me out.

There are very few guys in this town like that any more who are able to do five, six, seven dates a week. In the old days, everybody was running their brains out doing three dates a day, but that was when the magic of L.A. was happening. Now, with the way the music business has gone, if a guy does a couple of dates a week he's very fortunate. The thing that's also very fortunate is that they are doing it every day, because it's a skill, and to keep your skill honed, you've got to keep doing it. It's harder for a guy like me, who does a few dates a month, to stay at that level and still sound like you're doing it every day, so you've really got to practice. The great thing about playing Broadway shows is that you are able to keep your skills strong. I practice every day. I don't have a clue why I'm practicing sometimes, but the next gig somehow shows up. You have to stay sharp so you don't stumble and make a fool of yourself, because the one time you do, it's pretty much your last time, then you're back playing bad bar mitzvahs.

Do you prep for a session?

Absolutely. I try to find out as much as I can out front. If I know they'll want specific instruments, all the strings are changed and everything is ready by the time I get there. If it's a certain style they'll want, I try to work on that style to get it together. I did a movie that I had to play all Dobro on, and the composer didn't have a lot of understanding of what the Dobro could do, so he didn't really write a lot for it. He said to me, "Come up with some stuff that gives this mood, and we'll go with that." If you have some clue before you go in, you can have it together. I had an idea beforehand of what the guy wanted, so I had worked out four or five thematic ideas, and it all ended up working out great.

So to me, preparation is the most important thing. Every Broadway show that I do at the Pasadena Playhouse,

I always ask for the music as far in advance as I can [get it]. That way, when I go in there the very first day of the rehearsal, I've already got my part together and have all the sounds dialed in. I don't have to worry about anything. The reason why that's important, especially for what I do, is all these productions are coming together and being refined for the last time before they go to Broadway. That means the composer is there, the orchestrator is there, and the producer is there. All the music gets totally changed around from the first rehearsal until when the curtain goes up for the first performance. That means you're going to see different stuff as it evolves, but the upside is that you already have the concept and understanding of what they're looking for. Then it's just refining and doing variations, so it's not all new and weird stuff.

Tell me about these shows.
Pasadena Playhouse is a theater that brings in shows that premier [running the show for the first time with full orchestra and name cast in preparation for Broadway]. Since [the shows have] never been performed before, the director, producer, choreographer, and composer are at all the rehearsals. When I did *Sister Act*, Alan Menken [the composer] and Doug Besterman [the orchestrator] would sit a couple of feet from me and zero in on my part, so there was a lot of pressure there. But it's a different kind of pressure from sitting in a studio for a session. Different because this guy wrote all this music and he's never heard it fleshed out before, so you've got to figure out real fast if you're playing what he wants to hear.

I also did *Mask*, which was written by Barry Mann and Cynthia Weil, who were two of the composers from the Brill Building era [they wrote "Just Once," "On Broadway," and "We Gotta Get out of This Place," among many others]. Barry was a great guy to work for because he really understands how to write tunes. The hardest thing about this was that he wanted the live theatrical presentation to sound just like a CD, so we had to figure out how to get the music to jell so it didn't sound like it was a concert but so it sounded like someone just put a CD on. He was very particular and knew exactly what he wanted.

I did another show called *Vanities* that was more of a traditional Broadway show, with the music written by David Kirschenbaum. That show was demanding because I had to play a lot of music that was Motown based, so I had to sound like the Motown guys. I had to come up with the voicings and the right place to play them on the instrument that was reflective of that time, as well as what kind of processing to use (and what kind *not* to use) so it would be historically accurate. In addition, there were a lot of acoustic and nylon-string guitar parts that were exposed [primarily by themselves], as well as some banjo. It was also the first time in my life that I had a double playing triangle *[laughs]*, which was brilliant.

But that's the way these shows work. If you're in on the ground floor, the luxury is that you kind of get to make the part that the guy in New York is going to have to play to sound like you. So it's not me trying to sound like some other guy; ultimately that guy is going to have to sound like me, which I love. There are magic moments like when you play something, and the next day you come in and on the music stand is a copy with that part on it that you created.

Coming back to sessions for a moment, what's the best one you ever did?
I don't have a good answer for that. Most of them have been great, although I can think of some of the worse ones I've done.

That was my next question.
I got a call to do a record date for a really big Latin pop star that was for big band [four trumpets, four trombones, five saxophones, and a rhythm section]. It was for a Christmas album, but we recorded it in the last week of July so it was about 90 degrees out at 9 a.m., which does not exactly put you in the spirit. I thought this was going to be great, because I was hired by a contractor that I hadn't worked with before, and the piano player was probably

one of the most recorded players in L.A. that I had never worked with, so I thought, "This is going to open some doors for me."

So I get there and look around and see that all the A-list guys are on the date, so I'm thinking, "This is going to be killer." The artist arrives with a big entourage and comes into the studio, introduces himself, and we all start to feel really good about the session. Then his assistant passes out all the music, and we literally have maybe 30 seconds to look it over before we have to run it down. So we play the chart down and get finished with it, and there's just dead silence in the room. We all look at each other and nobody knows what to say. The chart looked like it was written by a sixth or seventh grader; it was just awful, with all kind of clams [wrong notes] and phrasing problems. We were all just kind of stunned, sitting there thinking, "Oh, no!" So what do we do, because we have another seven charts to play, and if it's anything like this it's going to be unbelievable! Of course, every chart we play after that was pretty much the exact same way—just filled with all kinds of mistakes. So what should have been two three-hour sessions to record seven tunes turned into a lot of overtime in the third session, since we had to correct and almost rewrite all the charts on the fly. We only got to play five or six of them. Everyone left just shaking their heads going, "What was that? How did that happen?" Later on I come to find out that they completely replaced the orchestrator as well as everything we played with a whole new band. We didn't actually make it onto the CD, although we still get got credit and I still get checks for it. I've seen the piano player a couple of times since, and he doesn't even talk to me. *[Laughs.]* He's just erased that day from his mind.

Back to doing orchestral sessions. You use headphones, right?
Oh yeah. Even in the theater things that I do, we all use headphones and usually Avioms to give us our own mix. In the studio, they come up with a separate rhythm-section mix, but when you have 50 or 60 people playing

their instruments as loud as they can, the mix is never any good. It is what it is, so you have to trust that everyone else is playing their part and that what you're playing will line up with it. A lot of the time I'll use just a single Sony recording headphone that I bought in Japan, so I'm able to hear the orchestra mix out of one ear and then hear my sound out of the other, so now I know I can lock in what I'm playing with everyone else. That makes it a lot easier. A lot of guys are now going the single-headphone direction because with two, your ears are sealed up and you'll never hear enough of yourself.

What do you find that all the A players you work with have in common?
When the red light comes on, they're all perfectionists. Everyone is there to play their part as perfectly as possible. When the red light is off, the personalities are as diverse as you would see anywhere, but when it's time to make music, everyone's focus is 100 percent locked on the music. That's the one trait I see, always.

So that's different from other musicians that you play with? They can take their focus to another level?
Absolutely. I wouldn't say their focus is better, but their focus is aligned specifically for what that moment demands. With an ensemble of 50-plus people, you can't have a bunch of ragged edges. Obviously, this is something that anyone who wants to play at the highest level possible will have to do, but in an orchestral situation, that's the main thread that holds it together. You can't waste any time when you have 50 other people sitting there waiting for you to play your part.

The thing I always especially liked on the *Star Trek* sessions would be that the very first take would sound perfect. It's not like, "I can't hear enough of this," or anything. The first take was just, "Wow! This is unbelievable." That, to me, is still the most astonishing part about it. The fact that there are so many people at that level who can just sit down and make it happen the first time it's scary.

Have you ever done jingles?
Yeah, and they're totally different. I worked for a long time with a composer that did a lot of national TV spots. That was always fun, because it was always different instruments and I'd always have to create a part in 30 minutes. Those sessions are always 30 to 45 minutes and then you're gone, and you hope that it gets picked up because then you get checks every 13 weeks. It's looser in the sense that you could go in and create your part, unless it was a lead line or an acoustic-guitar part that was written out that you had to play. But if it was a comping part or something, it'd be, "Make it up."

If you had the ability to go back to when you were just starting and tell yourself to concentrate on something, what would it be?
Law school. *[Laughs.]* Probably be more aggressive in promoting myself. To me, it's really hard to work on your craft as a musician and get it to where you're even halfway pleased with what you're doing. Then having to go out and tell people that your stuff is so great that they're hurting themselves if they don't have you is not an easy thing. There are a lot of people who have that ability, but a lot of the energy they use to do that is taken away from their ability to play their instrument, and that's just the way it works. But if I could do one thing differently, it would be being more aggressive in letting people know that I can actually do this stuff.

What do you think is your strength as a player?
Being able to play different styles.

And what's your weakest?
Never asking for enough money. *[Laughs.]*

What's the thing you hate most about doing session work?
Sometimes it's a very sterile kind of an atmosphere. You're there to create noises off of a piece of paper. To me that's the least rewarding part, but unfortunately, that's mostly what I do. It's not like going in to do a record, where it's,

"Let's come up with an idea for a tune, turn the lights off, burn for a couple of hours, and see if it goes anywhere." That's fun. But the sterility of banging out whatever's on a piece of paper hasn't always been rewarding. I like it for the challenge and because it's something I'm able to do well.

What's the hardest thing or type of music that you have to do at a session?
Classical guitar, because it's very difficult music to go in and sight-read. If you think of most classical-guitar players, they have a repertoire that they've worked on for 5, 10, even 20 years. When you do a date with a composer who wants to hear that kind of style and they're not a guitar player, they don't write it out "guitaristically." You have to sit there on the fly and dissect what they're trying to achieve and kind of sound like what they wrote, and not screw up. That to me is the hardest thing. And those parts are always exposed. It's not like you're hiding behind 20 people. So it's not only getting the right sound out of the instrument and all the technical things right, but trying to interpret it before you find that you're three measures behind. That's the hardest thing, and usually when I think, "My career is over." *[Laughs.]*

Peter Thorn—Guitar Player and Vocalist

Peter Thorn is the perfect example of someone who proves that if you are willing to take the giant step of leaving home for the big city and working hard at your craft, a lot of really good things can happen along the way. Peter left his native Canada for Hollywood, soaked up as much information has he could, worked constantly on his chops and sound, and eventually became a much-in-demand session and touring guitarist and artist in his own right. Peter is a shining example of a professional musician—excellent chops and excellent sounds (he's a great singer, as well), yet easy-going, humble, and approachable. Below he outlines his keys to success.

How about some of your background?

I grew up in Edmonton, Canada, and started playing guitar when I was 14. When I was 19, I moved to Los Angeles to go to the Musician's Institute and attended that for a year. When I got out of school, I joined a band with a couple of older musicians [Frank Simes and Jennifer Condos] who were pretty well known in L.A., and who were touring with Don Henley at the time. Frank had a bunch of songs and was trying to get a record deal when he wasn't playing with Don. It was cool because they were much older than me—they were in their mid-30s and I was like 19—so I learned a lot from those people. I spent about five years in the band, and we did a record for Japan and Southeast Asia. When that ended around 1995, I started doing a lot of sessions and touring.

Right now I'm playing with Chris Cornell, but before this I played with a bunch of other artists like Jewel, Daniel Powter, Alicia Keys, and Courtney Love. I was also in the group Five for Fighting for a while, and toured with them.

What's your live setup like?

With Chris I'm using a "wet-dry-wet" rig, which uses a typical head-and-speaker-cabinet combination, but takes a tap taken off the signal that's going to the cabinet. That's fed at line level out to some effects that are fed into a stereo power amp that's connected to a couple of cabinets that sit on either side of the main one in the center. So the center cabinet is the dry, direct guitar sound, and the outside cabs have a stereo delay or a bit of reverb in them. That allows both me and the soundman to have independent control over the dry signal and a blend of the stereo effects, so if I've got a stereo Leslie thing going on, or stereo delays bouncing back and forth on those outside cabs, he can control it if he thinks he's got too much in the house. The other thing is, I can mix the dry signal into the wet cabinets to get louder if I need to for a solo boost or something. It's just a very flexible way to do it.

What kind of amps do you use?

Right now I'm using a few different things. In the studio I'll use all manner of different amps, from vintage amps like Fenders and Marshalls to weird things like Supros. But on the road I use a combination of different heads. I'm using one built by a guy named John Suhr [suhrguitars.com] that's a custom-made head based on his OD-100 amp; it's called a PT-100, for my name. It has two channels—one that's Fender clean, and one that's a Marshall-like distortion channel. I also use a Divided By Thirteen [dividedby13 .com] RSA-31 head, which is another boutique amp. At times I'll also use an amp by Comet [electrosonicamplifiers .com], so I'm sort of a boutique-amp guy. I like the hand-wired small-company stuff.

What guitars do you take with you?

With Chris I'm using five different Les Pauls, as well as a Darco model, which is like a 335. Then I have a Tele and two Strat-like guitars built by John Suhr.

What are your effects?

Right now I've got the TC [Electronic] G-System, which is my MIDI controller as well as a loop switcher, that I can [also use to] integrate various pedals like a Trinity overdrive, a Boss Fuzz, a Line 6 rotary simulator, and a Peterson tuner that are on the pedalboard. Back in the rack for the wet-dry-wet system, I use a unit called the Axe-Fx [fractalaudio.com], which is a 2-rackspace processor that's like a big superpowerful Pod; it has amp simulators and everything in it, but I'm only using it for effects. So I have the TC and all the pedals in front of the amp [signal-wise], and then postamp I have the Axe-Fx for long delays and reverbs and stuff like that.

What do you usually bring with you to the studio?

I don't bring much any more, because if I'm working at [producer/writer] Linda Perry's, she has so much stuff there that it's sort of fun to go and just pick through the stuff that's there. [Author's note: Linda's studio has the most fantastic collection of vintage gear I've ever seen in a studio, and I've been in hundreds of studios all over the world.] If I am going to do a session on my own and I need to bring something, I'll bring the TC pedalboard and either a 1×12 or a 2×12 speaker cabinet with these little heads built by Suhr called Badgers; there's one that's 18 watts and another that's 30 watts. I really like them because they're versatile and sound great with pedals. For guitars, I'll try to bring a Les Paul, a Strat, a Tele, and maybe one acoustic.

Do you have any tips as a session musician?
I would say an important thing for me is to serve the song at all times. Try to keep an open mind, and if someone has an idea in the room, then always let that idea be heard. If it involves you trying something different in the part that you're playing, you can't get defensive about it. You have to just let it happen, because that really goes a long way toward creating a good atmosphere in the room. When everybody drops their ego and just tries to serve the song, I find that the best idea will rise to the surface, and everybody will recognize it. It's human nature to want our ideas to be the best ones, but if you can be open to others' suggestions, you can learn something and maybe do something that you wouldn't have thought of doing.

Now that you've worked your way up through the ranks to where you are now, what kind of advice would you give to someone who's just working in a club or cover band?
If you're in a bar band and playing covers, it really depends upon your goals and aspirations. A lot of people don't want to write songs and go any further than that, because they're happy just playing on the weekends. So then it comes down to honing your songs and your chops and maybe taking singing lessons to make sure that your background vocals are really tight.

If what you're trying to do is break out to have a career as an artist, I'd be playing in the clubs on the weekends but be constantly writing songs and recording as much as possible. When I first moved to L.A. in that band I was telling you about, we'd go play cover gigs two or three nights a week for fun and to make some money, but during the week we'd always be writing and recording. We cranked out about 50 songs over a couple-year period, and that eventually got us a record deal [which is what everyone wanted back then]. When you do that, you just get better and better at writing and honing the sound of your band. I've got a lot of friends who played in cover bands, particularly where I came from in Canada because there was a really strong cover band scene there. But they never were really able to bust out of that, because all they did was play covers and never tried to write anything. But like I said, it all depends on your goals. Some people don't want the work that comes along with developing your own music because they only want to do it for fun.

One of the things that will really help if you're in a cover band is to work individually on your parts before you get to rehearsal, because you can get so much more done. You can get through a lot of songs if everyone has done their homework, because it's just fine-tuning the song in rehearsal at that point.

What was the defining moment for you as a guitar player . . . the moment when the light when on and you went, "Now I get it"?

I had a couple. One was at GIT [the Guitar Institute of Technology in Hollywood]. Everyone thinks of GIT as strictly academic and that you can't learn about the real world there, but I had a couple of moments. They had these live-playing workshops where everyone would learn a song by AC/DC or something like that. There would be a bunch of drummers and bass players and guitar players that the teacher would randomly assign, so you never knew who you were going to play with, but there was a set song for everybody to play. Then, the teachers would critique you afterwards. I remember that I went in and really played this song perfectly (I can't remember what it was now). A guy got up after me and played the song about 70 percent of what I did, but he had a lot of feel and attitude. The teacher pointed it out afterwards that sometimes that goes a long way, especially in rock 'n' roll. It's not all just about the notes; it's about performing and having a stage presence. So that was an important lesson for me. At the end of the day, you're entertaining people and you have to be free and expressive and having fun with it.

Another defining moment was when I realized that the thing that's going to set you apart from people is your attention to detail, like really having your gear and your sounds together and knowing how it all works. It's going into a rehearsal or audition and really having your parts down and your scene together so you stand out.

I started getting a lot of gigs that I was auditioning for in the late '90s, and after a while I tried to formulate why it was happening because I seemed to be pretty good at auditioning and scoring these gigs. I may not be the greatest guitar player in the world, but I seem to know how to get work. *[Laughs.]* It kind of came down to the fact of knowing your stuff and being prepared. Like if you're auditioning for an artist that's about to go on tour and they just spent a year working on an album, they know it inside and out and they're passionate about it. A lot of people will just learn the chords and blow their own solo over the section, and maybe plug into the rental amp that's at the audition. But if you're the guy that goes in with your amp dialed in with all the right sounds off the record and you've learned the parts really well, you're really putting your best foot forward and also stroking their ego in a way that leaves them thinking, "Wow, this guy really cares about my music. He's really put the time in." That's when I went, "Oh, I get it." Be it in a session or an audition, having your gear together and being able to play the parts is it for me. There are a lot of guitar players, but you have to go one step beyond the other guy to get the work.

GLOSSARY

advance: A portion of expected royalties or fees paid before the royalties or fees are due. Usually paid upon signing a contract or after the completion of a session.

bed: A finished track with no vocal or melody instruments. The basic rhythm-section tracks (drums, bass, guitar, keys) to a song.

big ears: The ability to be aware of everything going on within the session and with the music. The ability to rapidly dissect a track in terms of key and arrangement.

Brill Building: Located at 1619 Broadway in New York City, the Brill building was the home of many music publishers and songwriters.

buyout: You get paid only for your initial work and nothing thereafter.

callback: A brief "quick fix" session that involves little or no logistical hassle and usually only takes a few minutes.

cartage: A service that moves your equipment to and from your recording session or gig.

casual: A category of musical performance sometimes known as a "club date" that includes jazz, standards, pop tunes, Top 40 rock, country, R&B, and funk combined in a way that is palatable to the broadest possible audience for that moment. Weddings, private parties, and some corporate affairs are considered to be casuals.

contractor: The person in charge of hiring musicians for a union session. Occasionally nonunion dates use nonunion contractors.

conversion fee: A conversion is where a person takes an existing bed of music and creates a new commercial in a different medium. For example, if a producer wishes to take an existing bed of music from a television commercial and place that music in a radio commercial, the producer will pay a conversion fee (which is 75 to 100 percent of the original session fee). A conversion can also be done from radio to TV.

cue: A short piece of music composed specially for a certain section of a film or television show.

DAW: Digital Audio Workstation.

demo: The abbreviation for "demonstration recording"; represents an example of what the final version can sound like.

DI, or direct inject: A box that allows you to directly connect an electronic instrument such as a guitar, bass, or keyboard directly to a recording console without using an amplifier and microphone.

direct box: Another name for a DI.

DIY: Do It Yourself.

downbeat: A session's official start time.

dub fee: A dub is where a person takes an existing bed of music and creates an additional commercial within the same medium. The producer pays a dub fee that is 75 to 100 percent of the original session fee.

feel: The sense of groove or swing in musical performance.

FOH, or front-of-house: The soundperson who mixes the sound that the audience (the front-of-house) hears.

folk style: Chords played in the open first position (E, A, D, C).

jingle: Any form of music used for an advertising spot on any media.

library music: Non-exclusive music licensed to producers for use in a film, television show, or jingle.

mailbox money: Residuals or royalty checks for previous work that come in the mail or via prearranged direct deposit.

master: A final version of a recording that is destined for distribution.

pad: A chord with long, sustaining notes (sometimes called "footballs").

pitch: A presentation. Not to be confused with the pitch of an instrument or voice.

points: A percentage of sales or other revenues.

possible 20: Twenty minutes of overtime that may be added to a session.

preproduction: A process of familiarizing a session player or ensemble with the material before recording it.

residual: A royalty paid to a performer for the repeat broadcast of a performance such as on a commercial.

spec: No money paid up front, but with the promise to be paid later if the track is used.

spec date: A session done "on spec."

sweetening: The process of overdubbing an additional part or parts so that a recording becomes more musical.

track: A term sometimes used to mean a song; in recording, a separate musical performance that is recorded.

union: The American Federation of Musicians, or AFM. The musicians union.

union date: A session governed by the bylaws of the union, including the pay scale.

up-front deposit: Money paid to you before the session to make sure you're available for the date.

wolf tone: A note that plays quietly compared to others on the instrument, or a note that lacks the *fundamental* (lowest frequency in a harmonic series).

INDEX

12-string 70-71, 100
acoustic 34, 57, 66–67, 71, 80, 91, 100, 126, 237, 242, 246, 255, 285–287, 295, 298, 302
American Dad 184, 227
Ampeg 72, 110, 134-135, 139
amplifier 57, 69, 78, 122, 130, 136, 141, 165, 223, 306
amps 69, 110, 118–122, 125–126, 134, 139, 280, 286–287, 301
analog-to-digital converter 170
Arp 166
arrangements 240, 245–246, 305
artist managers 28–29
artists xiv, xvi, 5–8, 17, 23–24, 27, 32, 40, 48, 59, 76, 85–86, 101, 108–110, 219, 220, 236, 240, 244, 279, 283, 300
Ashford, Jack 4, 206
A-Team 6, 26
Atkins, Chet 70
Audio-Technica 223
background vocals 33, 39, 184, 302
bands ix, xiii, xiv, xv, 3–9, 17–18, 23–24, 29, 38, 43–44, 46–47, 59–60, 67, 89, 106, 112–113, 121–123, 143, 147, 154, 163, 217, 220, 222, 224–227, 234, 237–240, 244, 246, 250, 253, 260–261, 264, 268, 271, 275, 278–279, 281–285, 288–289, 292, 295–296, 300, 302–303
banjo 66, 285, 287, 289, 295
Beatles ix, xv, 85, 134, 236, 271, 274–275, 278
big ears 87, 220, 305
blues xiii, 16, 24, 90, 145, 226, 290
Boss 72, 126, 280, 301
Bowie, David ix, 26
Bozio, Terry 148
Brill Building 286, 294, 305
Brown, James ix, xiv, xv, 89, 244, 275
cables 65, 128, 131, 138–139, 141, 158, 167–168, 170, 172
capo 100, 123, 132
casual 45, 305
cello 27, 57
charts 16, 33, 35, 90–92, 110, 113.129–130, 140, 159, 171, 187, 193, 203, 210, 242, 252, 272, 281, 296
Ciago, Ronnie xiii, 68, 206–208, 215
Clapton, Eric xiv, xv, 8, 15, 123, 244, 254
click 16, 113, 146–147, 158, 160, 199, 206, 219, 221, 232–233, 259, 267, 268–270, 280
Coldplay 164, 166
composers xiv, 9, 10, 23, 26, 34–37, 197, 200, 236, 278, 282, 294
compressor 104–105, 170
contractors 22, 24, 26, 44, 59, 62, 101, 198, 306
Cream 281
Crow, Sheryl xv, 45, 148, 261, 270–272
cue 37, 76, 86, 168, 192, 200, 287–288, 306
cymbals 154–155, 157, 223–234, 258, 262, 265, 275–276
Danelectro 72
Davis, Miles 144, 235
DAW 10, 31, 104, 124, 306

Deep Purple 16
demo 10, 23, 31–33, 54–55, 59, 64, 76, 90, 113, 130, 140, 159, 171, 187, 193, 210, 306
Derek and the Dominos 123
DI 78, 104–105, 132, 139, 142, 279–280, 306
DigiTech 126
direct box 105, 173, 306
DJs xvii, 4, 18, 28–29, 34, 200
Drayton, Charlie xiii, 85, 148, 222
Dresel, Bernie xiii, 44, 68, 144, 151–152, 154, 156, 226, 234
Drum Doctor 148, 263–264
drummers xiii, xiv, xv, 4, 7–8, 10, 27–28, 33, 44, 60, 63–64, 80, 106, 113, 124–125, 136, 143–148, 150, 157, 206, 217–219, 222, 226, 232, 234–236, 240, 242, 254, 260, 262, 264, 266, 268, 269, 270–274, 280, 303
drums xiii, 4–10, 15, 17, 28, 33, 39, 57, 63–64, 67–68, 73–74, 78, 80, 88–89, 106, 110, 112, 121, 124–125, 134, 136, 143–153, 155–158, 160, 178, 199, 207, 209, 215–218, 222–223, 227–233, 235–236, 238–240, 242, 251, 255–258, 260–265, 267–271, 274–276, 280, 288, 305
dub fee 55, 306
Dunbar, Sly 7
Dylan, Bob ix, 178
dynamics 147, 205–206, 219, 270
Eagles 124
ears 17, 18, 83–87, 90, 200, 220, 278, 282, 297, 305
Echoplex 73
effects 66, 69, 73–74, 118, 120, 125, 134, 170, 245, 279, 285, 300–301
Electro-Harmonix 72, 73, 251
engineer xvii, 14–15, 27–28, 33, 43, 45, 50, 75, 85, 96–98, 101, 104–105, 107, 110, 120–122, 125, 129, 137, 140, 154, 158, 170, 183–184, 186, 190–191, 193, 198, 203, 208, 210, 228, 248, 249, 251–252, 255, 263, 267–270, 283, 287
Epiphone 70
episodic television 37
EQ 287
Erskine, Peter 148
feel 15–16, 26, 32, 34–35, 37, 43, 45, 50, 53, 81, 83, 85–86, 88–89, 93, 98, 108, 129, 136, 140, 144–147, 158, 177, 193, 203, 206, 210, 223, 228, 237–239, 243, 259–260, 267, 269, 270, 273, 303, 306
Fender 68, 70–73, 110, 111, 118, 122, 126, 134–135, 138–139, 164, 242, 285, 301
Fender Precision 72, 134, 138–139
fiddle 6, 245
fills 146–147, 166, 270
film and TV work x, 16, 26, 32, 34, 36–38, 45, 56–58, 87, 108, 198, 266, 282, 306
film date 37, 275
Fitzpatrick, Frank xiv, 89, 178–179, 236
FOH. *See* front-of-house
folk style 123, 307
Foo Fighters xv, 148, 250
Four Tops 4, 89
front-of-house 28, 266, 307
Funk Brothers 4, 17, 98, 123, 237
Gadd, Steve 8, 9, 15
getting paid 24, 243, 272
ghost 23
Gibson 70–72, 125
gig 14–16, 18, 27–29, 44, 54, 63–64, 68, 81, 84, 101, 128, 138, 157, 170, 179, 181, 189, 230, 234–235, 239–240, 260, 264, 271–273, 275, 277–278, 281, 285–286, 291, 293, 305
Gill, Onree xiv, 46, 86, 240
Gorfain, Eric xiv, 200, 244
groove xiii, xv, 86, 88–89, 133, 144–146, 177–178, 206, 216–219, 226, 232, 235–236, 238, 261, 288, 306
guitar xvi, 4–10, 26, 32–33, 47, 64–67, 70–71,

76, 80, 88–89, 90–91, 100, 110, 111, 117–128, 130–134, 141–142, 147, 163, 177, 199, 223, 236–238, 267, 271, 278, 281, 284–292, 295, 298–299, 300–306
Guitar Player's Utility Kit 130–132
Hamilton, Jeff 148
Hammond 16, 68, 73, 111, 164–165, 242, 250–251, 288
harmony 183–184
harp 57
headphone mix 105–107, 186, 200, 224, 232, 245, 251, 276, 280
Hey, Jerry xiv, 247
hi-hat 145, 255, 265, 276
Hiwatt 71
Höfner 72
Hohner 73
home studio 40, 81, 105, 233
horn 10, 38, 65, 105, 189–191, 194, 198, 232, 247–249, 287
Horn Player's Utility Kit 194–195
humbucker 70, 120
Ill, Paul i, ii, x, xi, xvii, 27, 125
instruments xiii, 14, 22, 48, 57, 60, 65–66, 68–70, 74, 86, 91, 104, 120–122, 125, 134, 136–137, 163, 170, 192, 200–201, 207–208, 211, 215–219, 221, 241–242, 245–247, 264, 276, 280, 285–286, 288, 290, 293, 297–298, 305
internal time 145–146
Iovine, Jimmy 91
Jackson, Michael xv, 45, 148, 178, 238, 248, 254, 260, 270
Jaffee, Rami xv, 24, 94, 250
Jamerson, James 4, 89
jingle xiii, 22–23, 27, 31, 33–36, 47, 55, 86–87, 108, 215, 222, 298, 307
John, Elton ix, 268
Jones, John Paul 6, 18, 135
Jones, Quincy xv, 178, 220, 238, 254
keyboard xv, 5–10, 39, 57, 65, 74, 78, 110, 163, 164–170, 172, 240, 250, 252–254, 306
Keyboard Player's Utility Kit 172–173
Kravitz, Lenny xiv, 123, 148, 240
Led Zeppelin ix, 6, 17, 27, 67, 135, 264, 271
Lee, Will 8–9, 24, 276
Leslie 70, 73, 111, 165, 242, 300
Les Paul 67–68, 70, 80, 110–111, 120, 125–126, 285, 287, 302
lessons 181–182, 234, 259, 291, 302, 304
library music 37, 307
limiter 170
lone wolf 18
loop 33, 146, 301
Ludwig 68, 73–74, 261, 266
Lynyrd Skynyrd 7, 123
MacLeod, Brian 27, 39, 44–45, 50, 67, 97, 147, 157, 260–261
mandolin 66, 100, 285, 289
Marilyn Manson 148
Marshall 68, 71, 80, 121–122, 126, 286, 301
Martin 71, 118, 287
M-Audio 251
McCartney, Paul xv, 126, 275, 278
Memphis Horns 5, 189
Metallica 124
metronome 157, 235, 239
microphone 78, 104–106, 110–112, 132, 142, 149, 155, 168, 173, 183, 190, 194, 198–200, 202, 209, 223, 233, 246–248, 255–257, 262–263, 265, 267–268, 280, 286, 306
mic technique 183, 190
Miller, Steve 166
Minimoog 73, 166
mix 23, 28, 32, 34, 40, 97, 105–107, 113, 120–121, 154, 177, 181, 186, 199–200, 221, 224, 232, 245, 251, 258, 276, 280, 296–297, 300, 307
motion 56, 205–206

Motown ix, 4, 17, 89, 123, 135, 206, 218, 237, 286, 295
musicians ix, x, xi, xii, xiii, xiv, xvii, 3–7, 9–11, 14–18, 21–26, 28, 31–32, 34–41, 43–44, 46–50, 53–55, 58–64, 74–76, 81, 83–91, 93–94, 97–101, 104–113, 117, 120, 129, 130, 139, 144, 158, 164, 175, 179, 187, 189, 193, 199, 210–211, 215, 224–225, 236, 241–244, 246–247, 252, 254, 260, 270, 272–275, 277–279, 282–284, 289–290, 297–300, 302, 306, 308
Music Man StingRay 72, 134
Musitronics 72
MXR 72–73
Nashville style 91
Neve 112
Octavia 72
orchestral rate 56
organ 5, 16, 111–112, 163–165, 173, 250
pad 164, 166, 262, 307
Page, Jimmy xiv, 6, 18, 27–28, 244–245
Paiste 258, 265
passion 175–176, 178
pay scale 35, 40, 308
Peart, Neil 144
pedals 33, 64, 67, 74, 80, 118–120, 126, 132, 134, 136, 141–142, 160, 168, 170, 172, 223, 227, 245, 251, 280, 286–287, 301–302
pedal steel 223
percussion xiii, 8–9, 121, 205–208, 212, 215, 217–218, 223, 226
Percussionist's Utility Kit viii–ix, 211–212
Perry, Linda xiii, xvii, 28, 39, 66, 91, 215, 301
piano 5–8, 28, 45–46, 73, 76, 91, 110–111, 135, 163–165, 170, 173, 177, 199, 221, 232, 240–242, 250–251, 258, 270, 288, 291–292, 295–296
pickups 70, 120, 245
pitch 121, 135, 150–151, 154, 176–178, 182, 186, 199–200, 227, 230–231, 245, 263, 284, 290, 307
plug-ins 165, 170
pocket 57, 88, 94, 175–178, 221, 236–238, 242, 252
Porcaro, Jeff 148
possible 20 34, 307
preparation 16, 90–92
preproduction 91, 307
producers xiii, 10–11, 22–25, 32, 34–36, 43–45, 48, 59, 77–78, 85–86, 90, 97, 101, 109, 118, 128, 147, 190, 197, 205, 207–208, 231, 252, 254, 262, 266–267, 270–271, 283–284, 287, 307
Pro Tools 85, 243, 267, 284
reading (music) 35, 38, 47, 86–87, 90, 275, 290–291
record dates 23, 31, 39–40, 47, 86–87, 110, 198
recording 3, 6–8, 14–17, 21–22, 25, 31–38, 40–41, 43–45, 48–49, 53–55, 57–64, 68, 74–75, 77–79, 84–85, 87–88, 90–91, 95, 97–99, 101, 104–105, 109–111, 113, 119, 122, 124–125, 127–128, 130, 134–141, 146–148, 154–157, 159, 163–165, 169–72, 175, 184–185, 187, 190–191, 193, 197–199, 201, 203, 207–210, 216, 217–218, 221–223, 225–227, 232–234, 239, 243, 245–247, 249–252, 254, 262, 264–265, 274–277, 279–280, 283–284, 289, 297, 302–303, 305–308
recording studio staff 23, 27–28, 101, 109, 168
rehearsals 14, 16, 125, 179, 294, 303, 304
Remo 149, 227–228, 256, 276
residual 35, 307
Reverb 71, 170
Rhodes 73, 164, 242
rhythm guitar 33, 80, 88–89, 177, 238–289
rhythm section xiii, 7–8, 14, 26, 28, 37, 38, 63, 89, 112, 124, 133–134, 222, 233, 237, 249, 279, 288–290, 295

Rich, Buddy 220, 228
Rickenbacker 70, 72, 134, 138
Seger, Bob 7, 26
Sennheiser 268
setting up 46, 167, 142
Shure 200, 233, 256
signal chain 15, 104–105
singers xvii, 8, 14, 18, 22, 24, 28, 32, 35–36, 40, 45–47, 59, 84, 87, 93, 101, 106, 177–182, 184, 187, 189, 238, 250, 253, 273, 275, 288, 291–292, 299
Singer's Utility Kit 187–188
singing 15–16, 25, 35, 98, 112, 175–186, 234, 237, 302
single-coil 70, 120
Sklar, Leland xv, 8, 83, 279
snare drum 17, 67, 73–74, 124, 145, 151–152, 156–157, 178, 199, 227, 229, 231–232, 255–257, 262, 264–265
solos 8, 14, 16,–18, 23, 44, 59, 80, 93, 106, 120, 124, 166, 197, 200, 216, 222, 237, 245, 271, 288, 300, 304
Solt, Gary xvi, 46, 48, 51, 66, 84, 90–91, 284
songs xiv, xv, 4, 7, 10, 14–16, 23,–25, 28, 32–33, 38–39, 46, 49, 50, 59–60, 62, 64, 67, 76, 79, 85, 86, 88–91, 93–94, 97–98, 100, 110, 112–113, 121–125, 130, 133, 136, 138, 140, 143, 146, 149, 151, 153, 156, 159, 164, 170–171, 176–178, 183–184, 187, 190, 192–193, 202, 206, 208, 210, 218–219, 221, 223, 228, 230–231, 236–238, 240–241, 244, 246, 250–253, 261–270, 272–275, 277–279, 282–284, 300, 302–303, 305, 308
Sony 46, 216, 223, 241–242, 245, 259, 268, 297
sound xi, xiii, xvi, 5, 6, 8, 11, 14, 16–17, 22–23, 26, 32, 35, 37, 44–45, 48–50, 64–72, 74, 80–81, 85–86, 91, 93, 96, 98, 100, 105, 107, 110–112, 118–126, 128, 132–136, 138–139, 147–151, 154, 156–157, 163–166, 169–170, 184, 192, 198–199, 206, 207–208, 216–217, 219, 226–233, 240, 242, 245, 247–249, 255–258, 261, 262–269, 271, 274, 280, 283, 285–287, 289, 293–295, 297, 299–300, 302–303, 306–307
speaker cabinet 66, 126, 302
Springsteen, Bruce 148
standard session procedure 127, 137, 155, 169, 184, 191, 201, 208
Stratocaster 70
string player 9, 27, 65, 106, 197–198, 200–201, 203, 245, 247
String Player's Utility Kit 203–204
strings 9, 200, 245
string section 197, 288
studio xi, xii, xiii, xiv, xvii, 3–11, 13–19, 21, 23–24, 27–28, 31–33, 35, 37–40, 43–44, 47–48, 50, 53, 57–61, 63–64, 66, 68, 72, 78, 80–81, 83–91, 93–94, 96, 98–99, 103–105, 107–108, 110–111, 113, 118–122, 124–125, 127–130, 133–134, 136–140, 144, 147, 155–156, 158–159, 165–172, 175–176, 178–179, 181–183, 185, 187, 189–193, 197–201, 203, 207–211, 216, 222, 224–228, 233, 237–238, 243–244, 247–252, 254–259, 264, 266, 269, 271–276, 278–282, 284–285, 287, 289, 292, 294, 296, 301–302
studio bands 3–5, 9, 17–18, 23, 47, 237
studio etiquette 7, 47, 50, 95–101
studio musician xi, xii, xiii, xiv, 3, 5, 9–11, 17–18, 23, 31–32, 35, 38–39, 43, 47, 50, 53, 59, 61, 63, 81, 83, 85, 87, 89, 93, 94, 98–99, 104–105, 107–108, 111, 120, 129–130, 139, 158, 193, 210, 278–279
Suhr, John 301
Supraphonic 73
sustain 119, 165, 172, 267
sweetening 32, 35, 308

tambourine 4, 39, 206, 218–219
Telecaster 34, 70, 80, 285, 287
tempo 28, 144–145, 206, 290
Temptations 4, 89
texture 122, 205–206, 217–219
toms 147–148, 152–154, 227–233, 255–258, 261–263, 266, 268, 276
tone controls 120–122
track xi, 16–17, 27, 32, 34, 36, 38–39, 50, 54, 61, 69, 74, 81, 87, 89, 97, 106, 113, 118, 119, 121–122, 124, 133–135, 138–139, 147, 157–158, 163, 165, 190, 192, 197, 199, 202, 206–207, 220–222, 224, 238, 242, 247, 267–270, 280, 305, 307, 308
tracking 23, 91, 106–107, 111, 113, 138, 167, 192, 198, 202, 223, 251, 267
tubes 119, 128, 130, 138, 141, 170, 228
tuner 65, 126, 131, 138, 142, 194, 204, 301
tuning 28, 64, 100, 129, 138–139, 148–149, 154, 156, 160, 166, 192–193, 202, 211, 230–231, 257, 262–264, 303
Underwood, Carrie 32
union 22, 37, 54,–58, 60, 81, 306, 308
Uni-Vibe 73
Univox 73
vibrato 120, 126, 199
vintage gear 66, 68–69, 261, 302
vinyl 38
vocalist 105–106, 175, 177–179, 182, 184, 190, 232, 267
vocals 24, 32–35, 39, 84, 106, 112–113, 124, 175–177, 179–185, 199–200, 245, 267, 276, 302, 305
voicings 123, 295
Vox 71, 73, 110, 122, 165
warm(ing) up 128, 139, 158, 171, 180, 185, 192, 202, 209
Winter, Johnny 70
wolf tone 308
Wrecking Crew 5, 47, 108, 237
Wurlitzer 73, 164, 251
Yamaha 118, 229, 242, 280, 285
Zildjian 154, 234